The Bretons

The Peoples of Europe

General Editors
James Campbell and Barry Cunliffe

This series is about the European tribes and people from their origins in prehistory to the present day. Drawing upon a wide range of archaeological and historical evidence, each volume presents a fresh and absorbing account of a group's culture, society and sometimes turbulent history.

Accessible and scholarly, the volumes of 'The Peoples of Europe' will together provide a comprehensive and vivid picture of European society and the peoples who formed it.

Already published

The Mongols
David Morgan

The Basques
Roger Collins

The Franks
Edward James

The Bretons
Patrick Galliou and Michael Jones

In preparation

The Thracians
Alexander Fol

The Picts
Charles Thomas

The Illyrians
John Wilkes

The Armenians
Elizabeth Redgate

The Celts
David Dumville

The Gypsies
Sir Angus Fraser

The Huns
E. A. Thompson

The Spanish
Roger Collins

The Turks
C. J. Heywood

The Sicilians
David Abulafia

The Goths
Peter Heather

The Early Germans
Malcolm Todd

The Early English
Sonia Chadwick Hawkes

The Irish
Francis John Byrne and Michael Herity

The Etruscans
Graeme Barker

The English
Geoffrey Elton

The Lombards
Neil Christie

The Bretons

Patrick Galliou and Michael Jones

BLACKWELL
Oxford UK & Cambridge USA

First published 1991
First published in USA 1991

Basil Blackwell Ltd
108 Cowley Road, Oxford, OX4 1JF, UK

Basil Blackwell Inc.
3 Cambridge Center
Cambridge, Massachusetts 02142, USA

Library of Congress Cataloging in Publication Data
Galliou, Patrick.
The Bretons / Patrick Galliou and Michael Jones.
p. cm.—(The Peoples of Europe)
Includes bibliographical references.
ISBN 0–631–16406–5
1. Brittany (France) – History. 2. Bretons – History. I. Jones,
Michael (Michael C. E.) II. Title. III. Series.
DC611.B854G35   1991
944′.1–dc20   90–24758
CIP

British Library Cataloguing in Publication Data

A CIP catalogue record for this book is available from the British Library

Typeset in 10½ on 12½pt Sabon
by Hope Services (Abingdon) Ltd
Printed in Great Britain by Butler & Tanner Ltd., Frome, Somerset

This book is printed on acid-free paper.

Contents

Plates

Figures and Genealogies

Genealogies

Preface

The Bretons presents a synthesis by an archaeologist (chapters 1–5) and a medieval historian (6–13) of the history of the Armorican peninsula and its inhabitants from remote times to the end of the Middle Ages, with a brief epilogue (14) on the modern period. In this sense it follows more obviously the pattern set by *The Basques* rather than *The Franks* or *The Mongols* amongst early volumes in this series devoted to 'The Peoples of Europe'. Like the Basques, the Bretons still today preserve their own language and exhibit ethnic and cultural distinctiveness. Both have for millennia inhabited a particular region. At the same time they have both been subject to strong external forces as well as the dynamic of their own domestic evolution. Both enjoyed periods of political autonomy and developed their own institutions, though they are both now subsumed within greater political entities. This relationship is not without contemporary importance, especially for those wishing to maintain a specific Basque or Breton identity. Conquest by Rome, rivalry with the Franks and the subsequent rise of the French national state with its powerful centralizing tendencies, among other factors, have shaped both peoples' histories.

More particularly, immigration from Britain in the post-Roman period had a profound and long-lasting effect on an already ancient Celtic civilization in Armorica. Most obviously it provided us with the Bretons, *sensu stricto*, a racial amalgam of the earlier Gaulish and Gallo-Roman inhabitants of the peninsula with close neighbours from across the Channel to form a succession of new polities: the early medieval Breton principalities or chiefdoms, then the kingdom and its successor, the duchy of Brittany. It is this longer perspective of 'Breton' experience that we wish particularly to emphasize: to demonstrate that the Armorican peninsula, situated at one of the Atlantic ends of Europe, has always been open to outside influence whilst developing its own characteristics and rhythms of existence. Many enduring features of the peninsula – like its human settlement pattern, agricultural regime and social practices, even beliefs, during the medieval and the modern period – should be traced back into this remote Celtic past if we are to obtain a proper understanding of the Bretons and their history.

Inevitably choices have had to be made in our account. These reflect both the interests and competence of the authors. We are conscious of omissions and imbalances. The nature of surviving evidence means a certain unevenness in treatment of those topics we have chosen to include – a full chronological or narrative treatment up to the present, for example, would have produced an entirely different kind of book. Before the central Middle Ages, in the absence of written records, it is archaeology which provides the most important guide not only to material culture, but also to political organization, religious and social ideas. Then the balance tips the other way and 'The Bretons' can be traced more easily in literary sources – chronicles, charters, administrative documents, law codes and so forth. The beginnings of a specific Breton political ideology can be discerned along with the rudiments of a medieval Breton state. At the same time the careers, sometimes even the personalities, of relatively minor figures can be described in some detail and the lives of ordinary people as well as of princes can be examined. The wealth of this type of evidence for the later Middle Ages, combined with the fact that this was the period when the dukes of Brittany enjoyed for practical purposes an almost unfettered freedom of action in their duchy and also maintained an independent position in western European affairs, has led to a concentration on politics and society at that period. However, because of the long period covered in this book, often in general terms, no attempt has been made here to document every statement. Those wishing to pursue matters in more depth are invited to consult the extensive bibliography.

This also provides some acknowledgement of our heavy debt to the work of other scholars: Breton historiography is currently enjoying a golden age. Recent archaeological investigation has placed that discipline on a new and secure footing, whilst a series of remarkable theses, editions of texts and detailed monographs has likewise brought a wealth of new material into focus for the whole Breton Middle Ages. In bringing some fruits of this work before an English readership, we would particularly like to mention our indebtedness to the following friends and colleagues whose work and conversation have especially enriched our own understanding: Patrick André, Annie and Jean-Pierre Bardel, Jacques Briard, André Chédeville, Wendy Davies, François Fichet de Clairefontaine, the late Léon Fleuriot, Pierre-Roland Giot, Pierre Gouletquer, François Goupil, Hubert Guillotel, Katherine Keats-Rohan, Jean Kerhervé, Loïc Langouët, Donatien Laurent, Jean-Paul Le Bihan, Jean-Pierre Leguay, Charles-Tanguy Le Roux, Hervé Martin, Gwyn Meirion-Jones, J-L. Monnier, Alain Provost, Julia Smith, Bernard Tanguy and Noel-Yves Tonnerre. M. J. owes a special debt to James Campbell for early guidance in late medieval history. Hilary Turner and Ann Mason, an eagle-eyed copy-editor, made valuable stylistic suggestions which we have gratefully adopted. The illustrations were prepared by Andrew Ellis, Gareth Owen and Don Shewan from City Cartographic and DTP Unit, City of London Polytechnic, to whom we are deeply indebted for their kind cooperation. We are also grateful to the Director of the Institute of Historical Research, London, for permission to re-use material in chapters 9 and 10 that first appeared in *Historical Research* lxiii (1990), 1–16. To our respective institutions, the Centre de recherche bretonne et celtique, Université de Bretagne Occidentale (UA 374 du CNRS) and the University of Nottingham, we offer thanks for material and other support over many years.

Abbreviations

AB	*Annales de Bretagne*
BEC	*Bibliothèque de l'école des chartes*
BG	Caesar, *De Bello Gallico*
BN	Bibliothèque Nationale, Paris
BP	Before Present
BSAF	*Bulletin de la société archéologique du Finistère*
C-d'A	Côtes-d'Armor (formerly Côtes-du-Nord)
CCM	*Cahiers de civilisation médiévale*
CIL	*Corpus Inscriptionum Latinorum*
DCRAA	Dossiers du Centre Régional Archéologique d'Alet
F	Finistère
I-et-V	Ille-et-Vilaine
l.	*livre*
L-A	Loire-Atlantique
l.t	*livre tournois*
M	Morbihan
MSHAB	*Mémoires de la société d'histoire et d'archéologie de Bretagne*
Questions	*Actes du 107e Congrès national des sociétés savantes, Brest 1982, Section de philologie et d'histoire jusqu'à 1610, ii. Questions d'histoire de Bretagne* (Paris, 1984)
RHDFE	*Revue historique du droit français et étranger*
s.	*sou*

Acknowledgements

The authors and publishers are grateful to the following for permission to reproduce photographs used for illustrations in this book: Archevêché de Rennes (p. 162); Bibliothèque municipale, Bordeaux (p. 189); Bibliothèque municipale, Boulogne-sur-Mer (p. 160); Collection Roger-Viollet (Paris), pp. 281, 283; Editions Jos le Doaré (cover, pp. 275, 276, 278); G. I. Meirion-Jones (p. 258); J. Briard (p. 24); J-P. Bardel (p. 97); J-P. Le Bihan (p. 38); Julia Smith (p. 174); Musée historique des Tissus, Lyon (p. 228); Musée de Bretagne, Rennes (pp. 65–9, 90, 109, 119); Musée de Morlaix (p. 48); Patrick André (pp. 16, 34, 245); R. Coutant (p. 49); SAVUBO (p. 126); The Hulton–Deutsch Collection, pp. 286, 287. All other photographs have been supplied from originals by the authors.

For Anne-Marie and Elizabeth
with love and gratitude

Introduction

Brittany is today recognized both by its modern inhabitants, by people living in other French provinces and by foreigners, as possessing particular characteristics which differentiate it from other regions of metropolitan France. In particular its Celtic inheritance has given it a separate language, Breton, and cultural traditions that distinguish it from other constituent parts of the modern French state. It occupies a position in France very much like that of Wales within the United Kingdom; the Bretons, like the Welsh, are at the same time both familiar and yet alien to their fellow countrymen in the larger political unions of which they now form part. A popular mythology compounding such diverse elements as the enigmatic early stone monuments, which exist in great abundance and diversity of form, supposed druidical or Arthurian connections, magical fountains and enchanted forests, has created in many minds a fairy-tale view of a Celtic twilight zone existing on the periphery of an otherwise rational and dynamic late twentieth-century state.

This book seeks to examine a reality: the development of specific Breton characteristics, institutions and material culture over a long time-span, including the changing relationships of the inhabitants of the peninsula and their neighbours in response to evolving political, social and economic circumstances. Currently, it must be admitted at the outset, many of these specifically local characteristics, engendered by long and complex historical developments, are in danger of disappearing as communications improve and modern life brings an increasing material and cultural uniformity. The Breton language, for example, is today spoken by less than a third of the 3.5 million inhabitants of the region. At the same time popular misconceptions abound: there are still many French people who think that Breton (in fact one of a group of closely cognate Celtic languages, including Welsh and Cornish) is simply a dialect or patois and not a separate language from French itself.

At a superficial level the casual visitor to modern Brittany is less likely to be aware of the distortions of Celtic history and myth than of the increasing disfigurement of the outskirts of every Breton town and *bourg* by garish commercial centres built by and for national supermarket chains. The infinitely varied coastline, one of the natural glories of the province and from which it took its former name, *Armor*, the land facing the sea, is likewise under threat from the ubiquitous and relentless spread of campsites, marinas, seaside villas, chalets and all the other facilities required to cater for the huge seasonal influx of tourists that provides one of the province's major 'industries'. There are long stretches which offer vistas of rather dismal suburban-style ribbon development where once there were picturesque bays, deserted creeks and inlets. The Rance estuary has been dammed to create a remarkable tide-driven electricity generating station, but this has deprived some upstream reaches of their natural vitality. At the mouth of the Loire, smoke stacks and vast storage tanks are the most prominent features of a giant oil-refining complex at Donges, whilst just down stream, beyond the bold, sinuous elegance of the Pont de Mindin, at Saint-Nazaire the supertankers which transport that oil are built and serviced. The motorist, who will eventually use the refined product, applauds the way in which most urban centres have been provided with modern by-passes, but many of these have been carved ruthlessly through a long-cultivated countryside with little apparent respect or sympathy for scenic considerations. Like a gigantic puffball, the *radome* at Pleumeur-Bodou sprouts in-congruously amongst the gorse bushes and bracken of a typical Breton heath (*landes*). More generally, the reorganization of agriculture encouraged by EEC subsidies, most notably in the consolidation or *remembrement* of many small farms to form more economic units, has in many areas literally erased the peninsula's traditional landscape of small fields, woods, heaths and enclosures by creating much larger open prairies.

Since the end of the Second World War the province, recently shorn of one of its five historic *départements* (Loire-Atlantique, now attached to the newly created administrative region of the *pays de la Loire* in the interests of central planning), has thus experienced more extensive and rapid change than ever before. A slow-moving and largely agrarian society, farming its land by means that were certainly centuries if not millennia old, has been dramatically replaced in the course of a few years, often at the cost of much personal anguish and painful readjustment. As late as the mid 1960s one of the authors remembers his astonishment at seeing old ladies in traditional costume harvesting corn by hand with sickles in some of the poorer parts of the province; now combine harvesters and every other kind of mechanical aid are in universal use. Peasant families which a generation ago were still literally sharing their single-storey homes with their animals and using the adjacent farmyard or fields for calls of nature, now live in modern houses with full sanitation.

These are, of course, some of the many advantages and benefits accruing from recent improvements in the general standard of living experienced by most inhabitants of the province. The changing pattern of modern industrial life, much of it now involving advanced technology, has altered settlement patterns and struck a fairer economic balance between town and countryside. Better communications both within Brittany and with the rest of France have likewise transformed the region's prospects. The *train à grande vitesse* (TGV-Atlantique) now departs from Nantes and Brest; there is a huge and continuing investment programme in the road network; airports are rapidly expanding their business; Brittany Ferries carry an increasing volume of freight as well as tourists each year to and from the British Isles and Spain. In 1989 they had 2.2 million passengers. Central government, now much more conscious of provincial feeling than it was only a generation ago, has consciously encouraged economic and cultural initiatives in the province. This is particularly seen in social welfare and educational provision – new universities, colleges and schools, libraries, *médiathèques*, *salles polyvalentes*, *palais de culture*, hospitals and so on. Radio, television and telecommunications ensure that the inhabitants of Brittany are kept abreast of the most recent developments in every field and share the French national enthusiasm for technological and material progress.

As the province experiences a dynamic period of change that is so clearly altering its character, it is appropriate to reflect on

Brittany's rich and varied history so far and on the factors which have shaped its inhabitants' perception of themselves and their neighbours. We have tried to do so by steering a course which we hope will not prove too austere in a field where legend, nostalgia and romantic yearnings have often had an unfortunate distorting tendency on what may more impartially be discerned as historical reality. Nor do we hold a brief for any modern Breton independence movement; indeed the book's treatment of recent centuries and the political issues which arose from Brittany's incorporation into the French state is perfunctory where a manifesto would find much essential material. Nowhere better could be found for examining the complex questions of relations between central authority in an increasingly authoritarian state and local ambitions and aspirations than in the case of Brittany in modern times. That, however, would have entailed a different kind of book and required different competence from that possessed by the authors of this one.

What we offer is a longer perspective: an explanation of the origins and development of a distinct people and society with their own achievements, political and cultural identity. And if a more particular excuse is needed for a book of this kind which deals with 'The Bretons' for much of their recorded history but stops short of providing a detailed account of modern times, it is conveniently provided by the five-hundredth anniversary this year of the province's effectual attachment to France following the marriage of Anne, its last duchess, to King Charles VIII of France on 6 December 1491. This resulted in what has nostalgically appeared as the last Breton golden age to many in later generations. In keeping with the book's aim of tracing Breton development over a long period, the authors' account begins in remote, indeed, geological times with a brief description of the physical development of the Armorican peninsula, within which in the fullness of time 'The Bretons' emerged.

1

Early Armorica

The physical setting

Brittany, like Cornwall and Wales, is a land of old rocks. It is also one of several peninsulas forming the Atlantic ends of Europe. Its fundamental physical characteristics were principally formed more than seven hundred million years ago when sea-bed sediments were deposited. Shaping much of the Breton landscape, the oldest of these – soft Brioverian rocks – were subsequently folded into a mountain chain into which the first Armorican granites were intruded. Gradually eroded and flooded by the sea in the Paleozoic period, these rocks were partly overlain by more recent sediments (shales, sands, etc.), which were also folded some three hundred million years ago and turned into harder slates and quartzites. Into these younger sedimentary rocks granites again intruded. A further sequence of carboniferous sediments, especially along the northern and southern coasts of the peninsula, was similarly folded and toughened into shales and slates.

These repeated foldings have fashioned the Breton relief into roughly parallel low lines of granite and slightly higher ridges of slate and *grès armoricain*, separated by depressions floored by softer schists. The whole system is orientated along west-east alignments, which often impede circulation across the peninsula. Erosion has abraded much of the former uplands. Brittany is now a land of broad, gently rolling plateaux sloping to the sea, but with a coastline frequently deeply indented by river valleys. Long ridges of harder rocks run from west to east, though never rising above 391 m (Montagne Saint-Michel in the Monts d'Arrée), the highest

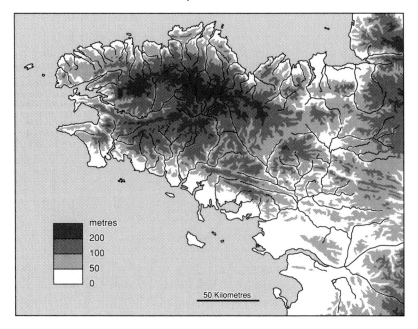

Figure 1   General relief map of Brittany

land being concentrated in Finistère and western Côtes-d'Armor (formerly Côtes-du-Nord). The shallow valley of the Loire, on the southern flank of the Armorican massif, though connecting Brittany with central France, has always formed a major cultural divide with Poitou and south-western France. Whereas, to the east, the Rennes basin, in some sense a western extension to the Paris basin, is more open to continental influences.

This complex geology has given Brittany a wide variety of soils, ranging from the thin dry soils and humus-iron podsols of the ridges to the deeper, fairly well-drained, brown earths which overlie softer rocks. These latter soils, though acid and therefore requiring constant enrichment, are today quite fertile and intensely cultivated – as they certainly were in the past – whereas the rockier, drier areas support either woodland or *landes*, vast stretches of waste or commons. These, though largely deserted now, were quite commonly cultivated in the past and in addition provided rural communities with fuel, bedding and fodder.

Though firmly rooted in the European mainland, Brittany is first and foremost a 'country of the sea' – hence its Gaulish name *Aremorica*, the land facing the sea.[1] The ocean is both an awesome presence, with its dreadful gales, menacing rocks and treacherous currents, and a generous provider of food and fertilizer, as well as a crucial link with other maritime areas. Here again, geology has given the peninsula a particularly distinctive coastline. Its hard rocks (granites and gneiss) form dramatically jagged headlands and capes, often fringed with half-submerged reefs and rocky islets like Cap Fréhel and the Pointes Saint-Mathieu, Raz and Penmarc'h. These alternate with sandy coves and wider bays – Mont Saint-Michel, Saint-Brieuc, Douarnenez and the Rade de Brest. Strong tides, exposing huge expanses of rock and sand at low ebb, offer seaside communities ancillary food resources in the form of various kinds of shellfish, as well as large quantities of seaweed, used as fertilizer on neighbouring fields. This intimate bond between land and sea is further strengthened by tidal rivers – rias – which penetrate inland often for many miles and bring the hinterland into close contact with the coast. The interpenetration of land and ocean influences the climate. This is prevailingly moist, especially on the western uplands. Winds are quite strong, often blowing to gale force, but the climate is, on the whole, moderate. Summers are rather cool and winters fairly mild; days of frost per annum are few and snow unusual. This temperate, oceanic climate, together with a general availability of food and minerals – tin, lead and iron in particular – favoured human settlement and population growth after the end of the last glaciation (around 10,000 BC).

Early man in Brittany: the Paleolithic hunter-gatherers (700,000–10,000 BP)

Brittany has neither limestone nor much flint. The peninsula was thus long believed to be almost entirely devoid of Paleolithic remains. Recently, however, archaeology has firmly established the presence of hominids (*Homo erectus*) in western France as early as 700,000 B[efore] P[resent], for example, at Saint-Malo-de-Phily

---

[1] Though the term, shortened to *Armorica*, is in common usage among Breton archaeologists and historians, Ancient writers actually applied it to the whole of north-western Gaul between the Seine and the Loire.

(I-et-V). The crude sandstone and quartzite pebble-tools (choppers) they used gradually evolved into the finer bifacials of the Middle and Late Acheulian found at Quimper, Tréguennec and L'Hôpital-Camfrout (F), and elsewhere. Many of these were hewn on major production sites like Kervouster, Guengat (F), and Le Bois du Rocher, Saint-Hélen (C-d'A). The early encampment site at Saint-Colomban, Carnac (M), a cliff-cave used as a temporary shelter *c.* 300,000 BP, has shown few traces of social organization, whereas the Late Acheulian settlement at Grainfollet, Saint-Suliac (I-et-V), had huts and hearths, near which horses, deer and mammoths were butchered, flayed and eaten.

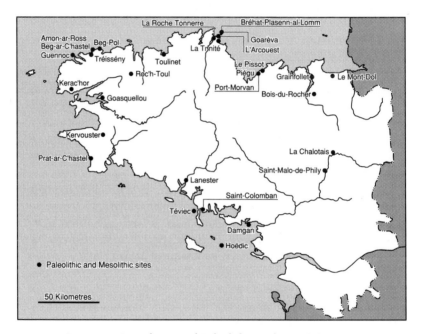

Figure 2   Distribution of Paleolithic and Mesolithic sites

The Middle Paleolithic (80,000–40,000 BP) is characterized by important changes in human morphology. *Homo erectus* developed into *Homo sapiens neanderthalensis*, Neanderthal man. At the same time a new tool technology, the Mousterian, produced finer and more effective stone implements. Though a few Mousterian tools do occasionally turn up in western France at the end of the Riss glaciation, *c.* 90,000 BP, most of the evidence concerning the period belongs to the early phases of the Würm glaciation (Würm I and II), from 80,000 to 70,000 BP, a time of extremely cold conditions when the whole of Brittany became tundra or frozen steppe, grazed by herds of woolly rhinoceros, mammoths, reindeer and musk-oxen. This abundance of food meant that the few small groups of hunters and gatherers, scattered over the peninsula, could grow in size and number in spite of a hostile environment. In addition, vast expanses of low-lying coastal areas were laid bare by the Würm glaciation which froze sea-water into ice-sheets, thus allowing the inhabitants to cross to islands, for example those now lying off the Morbihan coast which were then attached to the mainland. Much of the evidence concerning the presence of Neanderthalers in these areas disappeared when the sea-level rose *c.* 10,000 BP in warmer conditions. Settlement sites of the Mousterian period are therefore thin on the ground and tend to be concentrated at the base of former cliffs – then standing far inland – where caves and overhangs provided shelter from the elements. The best evidence comes from Goaréva, Bréhat (C-d'A); La Cotte de Saint-Brelade, Jersey; and Mont-Dol (I-et-V). At this last site a rocky outcrop overlooks a marshy area in which mammoths, rhinoceros, reindeer, wolves and lions were trapped and killed by Mousterian hunters.

In the very cold conditions of the Upper Paleolithic (Würm III and IV, 40,000–10,000 BP), *Homo sapiens sapiens* gradually replaced and perhaps even eliminated the Mousterian Neanderthal stock. The old stone industries developed finer and more elaborate flint tools, perhaps under Perigordian influences. Settlement sites did not, however, change much. Cliff-bases and spreads of massive erratic boulders were favoured positions for living as at Amon-ar-Ross, Beg-ar-C'hastel, Kerlouan (F, *c.* 20,000 BP), sometimes sheltering huts or skin tents (Plasenn-al-Lomm, Bréhat, C-d'A, *c.* 15,000 BP?).

Towards sedenterization: Mesolithic hunters and gatherers (10,000–5000 BC)

As the last glaciation came to an end in the last millennia of the Pleistocene, climatic and ecological conditions changed dramatically. The gradual warming of land and sea entailed the progressive replacement of the frozen steppe by forests of pine and beech (*c.* 10,000 BC) and eventually by a typically temperate vegetation of oak, elm, alder and lime (*c.* 7500 BC). As the ice-sheets melted, the sea-level rose once more, severing islands from the mainland, filling bays and estuaries. These radical changes meant that post-Pleistocene human groups had to adapt themselves to a new environment in which the larger Paleolithic mammals, already much depleted by hunting, disappeared altogether, to be replaced by deer, boars, foxes, beavers, hares and goats. Hunting was supplemented by the gathering of shellfish; this is demonstrated by the large Mesolithic shell-middens (*kjökkenmöddings*) of Téviec, Beg-ar-Vil (Quiberon, M), and Beg-ar-Dorchenn, Plomeur (F). At Téviec there were attempts at domestication of goats. New subsistence strategies created major changes in tool type and size. Though Late Paleolithic (Epipaleolithic) industries continued well into the Mesolithic (Roc'h-Toul, Guiclan; Guennoc, Landéda, F), new implements appeared of microlithic type using tiny flint blades which were mounted on bone or wooden handles for a variety of uses. Stone-working areas, where flint nodules collected from the sea-shore were struck into tools, were often located on cliff-tops.[2]

The close study of such small groups of hunters and gatherers has offered some fascinating insights into the life and structure of Breton Mesolithic communities, above all in relation to funerary practices. At Téviec, not yet an island, a Mesolithic group buried its dead – one individual had been killed by an arrow – in pits dug into the kitchen middens of the settlement and carefully sealed by layers of stones. The position of the bodies, adorned with shell-beads and sprinkled with ochre, a remarkable beehive of large antlers placed over two bodies, the lighting of fires and deposition of grave-goods on the tombs all suggest collective rituals and social cohesion, together with some degree of social specialization. The emergence of chieftains, 'artists' and shamans among hitherto undifferentiated communities may indeed be substantiated by the presence of 'richer' graves among the Téviec and Hoëdic (M) groups and the appearance of incised decoration – possibly connected with a 'calendar' computation – on shell and bone artefacts (Téviec, Beg-ar-Vil).

---

[2] Cap Fréhel (C-d'A); Bertheaume, Plougonvelin (F); Kerouyen, Plovan (F), etc.

A new subsistence economy: Neolithic farmers (5000–2000 BC)

It is widely accepted today that the economic conditions of European communities improved largely during the Neolithic period, as farming techniques spread from Anatolia and Greece towards the west along the main waterways and major land routes. The gradual adoption of the cultivation of cereals (emmer wheat, einkorn wheat, six-row barley, etc.), together with the domestication of sheep and goats, pigs and cattle, meant that human groups could now rely on fairly regular food resources and therefore grow in size and complexity. The Armorican evidence fits, on the whole, this simple pattern. Increased lithic production reflects the need for a more extensive tool-kit designed for agricultural work and land clearance. Widespread funerary and ritual structures suggest population growth and an intensification of social exchange.

The regional culture known as the Breton Primary Neolithic is first recorded in the early fifth millennium BC, with evidence largely provided by funerary monuments such as Dissignac (L-A, 5100–4600 BC), Barnenez I (C-d'A, 4600 BC), Geignog III (id.) and Kercado, Carnac (M, 4670 BC). Most of these sites had fairly archaic flint industries, showing some degree of Mesolithic continuity among the early Neolithic communities. Major social and economic changes are however clearly perceptible through the pottery evidence, in traces of land-clearance and agricultural activities and, above all, in very large and elaborate communal graves. Distributed along the coast and extending some way into the interior, impressive structures of stone and earth, often sited on high ground, overlie multiple-passage graves with burial chambers made of dry-stone walling and/or large orthostats (upright stones), roofed with slabs or corbelled domes and provided with a low entrance passage. Most of these early monuments include orthostats roughly shaped to human form or engraved with a variety of symbolic patterns ('U' signs, axes, snakes, etc.), though the astonishing wealth of designs to be seen on the twenty-three orthostats of Gavrinis, Larmor-Baden (M), is unmatched elsewhere.

Since the grave chambers were of insufficient size to accommodate the remains of an entire community, it is quite likely that such monuments were the resting places of local leaders and their families. Frequently sited on high ground, they must have served as

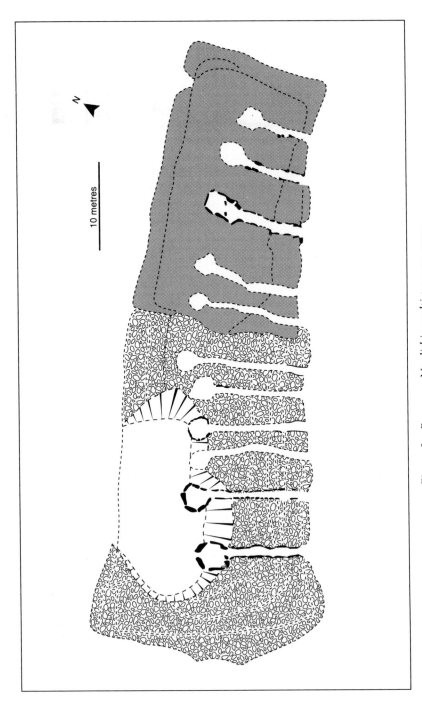

10 metres

Figure 3   Barnenez Neolithic multi-passage grave

Plate 1   Gallery grave, Mougau-Vihan, Commana (F)

territorial markers. They were certainly associated with communal ritual activities, in the course of which fires were lit in front of the passages and pottery containers placed nearby. Too little is known of related settlements, however, to allow any precise knowledge of social and economic structures or of major cultural changes. But the artefacts found on both burial and settlement sites do indicate significant developments in tool technology in the early fourth millennium BC. Thus polished axes appear, made of a variety of regional hardstones, including Plussulien (C-d'A) dolerite A. The impact of Continental cultures (Cerny, Chassey) on local pottery styles can be detected.

In the first half of the fourth millennium BC, though large passage graves of the fairly uniform model described above were still being built in the west, a whole range of new burial types appears along the coast of southern Brittany. This suggests an increase of social and cultural differentiation. Most remarkable among the new kinds of burial sites are the very large barrows of the Carnac group, scattered on both sides of the Golfe du Morbihan. These, though generally including a central or peripheral passage grave, basically seal a series of small cists. These were sometimes provided with rich grave-goods, such as the fine stone axes and thousands of variscite beads found in the central cist of the mound at Saint-Michel, Carnac. Simpler passage graves, built in a variety of regional plan-types – with a single compartmented chamber, with transepted chambers, or with lateral cells – probably received the remains of lesser dignitaries.[3] In the course of the third millennium BC they evolved into angled structures with longer burial chambers displaying a remarkable range of finely decorated slabs and anthropomorphic engravings. Such typological evolution as this in southern Brittany clearly results from changing fashions within fairly stable, hierarchical communities.

By contrast the Late Neolithic funerary architecture of northern and central Brittany reflects radical social changes, so far unexplained. The gallery- and lateral-entry graves, built in large numbers in the third millennium, were no longer reserved for a mere fraction of the population but served as communal ossuaries. Most are 10–20 m long, with parallel-sided chambers and orthostatic walls supporting large covering slabs, an antechamber and, often, a terminal cell. The whole structure is buried in a long, low mound. Because of acute soil acidity, few or no bones survive from most Breton examples, but the contents of similar monuments, common in Normandy, make it clear that these burial chambers were designed for whole communities. They contain up to two hundred inhumations and show indisputable evidence that bones or bodies were pushed aside to allow for new burials. The grave-goods are, on the whole, few and poor. But engravings of axes, blades and pairs of breasts, to be seen on the orthostats of some gallery-graves, point to the continuation of ritual activities, offered up, in this case, to some unnamed female deity, also figured in the round in the form of free-standing 'statues' at Kermené, Guidel (M), and Le Trévoux (F).

The most ubiquitous megalithic monuments of Brittany, however, are not the large funerary structures just described, but the standing stones popularly called menhirs. These, though quite common throughout western Europe, are found in particularly large numbers in western France. Generally isolated, sometimes found in groups of two or more, they vary greatly in height from a mere metre to 10 m (Kerloas, Plouarzel, F) or more. They are

---

[3] Single chambers: Kerleven, La Forêt-Fouesnant (F); transepted: Les Mousseaux, Pornic (L-A); lateral cells: Larcuste II, Colpo (M).

Plate 2   Neolithic statue, Le Trévoux (F)

usually irregular blocks roughly hewn out of the locally available bedrock or outcrops, though some large menhirs of western Brittany were clearly given more careful treatment. Other menhirs, weighing up to 150 tons, have been brought from a considerable distance (up to four kilometres). This certainly involved pushing

Plate 3   Alignments, Carnac (M)

and pulling on log rollers by large numbers of helpers before the menhir was tipped upright into a foundation pit.

The precise significance of such megaliths is much disputed but there can be little doubt that some, at least, were not mere functional markers but were related to collective ritual activities, for votive offerings such as pots and stone axes are found in most foundation pits and, very occasionally, menhirs bear engravings. This is also certainly the case of the many megalithic alignments and enclosures scattered over the whole peninsula. The former, including varying numbers of menhirs ranged in a single line or distributed in several parallel rows, differ greatly in size and complexity from the simple line of three stones at Tri-Men, Saint-Goazec (F), to the extensive alignment of 500–600 stones in four rows at La Madeleine-Lestriguiou, Penmarc'h-Plomeur (F), and the enormous megalithic systems, comprising several thousand uprights, stretching between the rivers Etel and Crach in the vicinity of Carnac. They are sometimes associated with various types of more or less elaborate enclosures – also common as free-standing structures – which were certainly used for astronomical sightings, predicting eclipses and 'calendar' computation, and for related community rituals and ceremonies.

The considerable body of evidence provided by both megalithic tombs and monuments suggests, in the light of various ethnological parallels, that Breton Middle and Late Neolithic communities were fairly large units, in the main strongly stratified and hierarchical, in which the collective rituals involved in the making and using of such monumental structures played a cohesive role. Environmental data and finds of agricultural implements (stone axes and grindstones in particular) show that most of these communities had come to practise a farming economy based on livestock and the growing of cereals, with techniques reliable enough to support

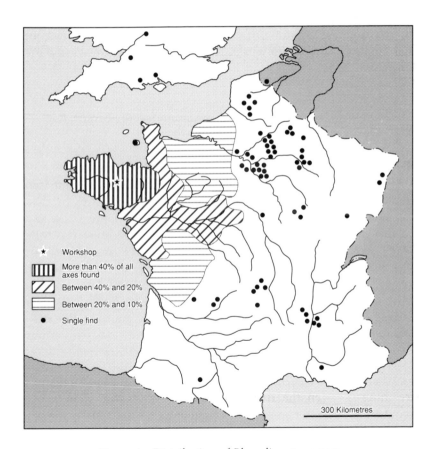

Figure 4   Distribution of Plussulien stone axes

a population of at least five persons per square km. As demographic growth entailed the development of farming activities,
much emphasis was placed on the production of pottery containers
and stone tools, the latter being made of the locally available
hardstones (dolerite, fibrolite, etc.). The most spectacular example
of increased tool production is to be found at Sélédin, Plussulien
(C-d'A), where, in the third millennium, earlier makeshift methods
of extraction and axe-preparation were replaced by more systematic
processes. This resulted in an average output of about 5000
dolerite A axes per year, accounting for more than 40% of all the
Neolithic axes found in Brittany. Plussulien tools, and to a lesser
extent hornblendite C axes from Kerlevot, Pleuven (F), were also
extensively 'traded' outside the peninsula to the whole of western
France and the Paris basin. Their overall distribution pattern
points, together with that of various pottery types, to the existence
of complex exchange networks along the Atlantic seaways and the
Loire and Seine.

The emergence of metal-using communities: the Bronze Age (2400–600 BC)

These routes were certainly the means by which, at the very end of
the period – 2800–2400 BC – Breton Neolithic cultures came into
contact with some of the metal-using communities which by then
occupied most of Europe from Bohemia to the Atlantic coast and
from the Mediterranean to the British Isles. The most revealing
clues to such complex contacts are distinctive assemblages of
artefacts. These generally include copper or poor-quality bronze
daggers and javelin heads, thin gold plaques and bone (or jet)
buttons, schist wristguards and fine flint arrowheads. The most
characteristic feature of such assemblages is good-quality bell-
shaped beakers with bands of decorative impressions (in various
regional styles). The sudden appearance of these objects – or at
least some of them – in Breton Late Neolithic funerary contexts is
still largely unexplained. We cannot be sure whether they belonged
to intrusive groups, or resulted from prestige exchange patterns
between Portuguese and Dutch Chalcolithic groups and the upper
levels of Breton Neolithic communities. The overall distribution of
flat copper axes, an entirely new type of tool, either imported from

the Iberian peninsula or imitated locally, makes it clear that at the end of the third millennium Brittany was being drawn into the metalworking network that covered most of western Europe.

The process was given a further boost by the development of bronze technology, since Armorica had fair amounts of tin, its major component, mostly in alluvial form. The tapping of such mineral resources, abundant in western Brittany, together with the development of cross-Channel 'trade' with south-western Britain and Ireland and the monopolization of bronze production, certainly explains the emergence *c*. 2400–2200 BC of powerful hierarchical chiefdoms. The evidence for the Early Bronze Age communities, closely associated with western mineral deposits, on the whole, comes from large funerary mounds, with a strong coastal distribution bias. These huge earthen mounds, sometimes 10 m high, cover single stone cairns sealing central individual inhumations placed inside wooden coffins or dry-stone cists. Those buried below these mounds clearly belonged to the highest ranks of society and were provided sometimes with a range of extremely

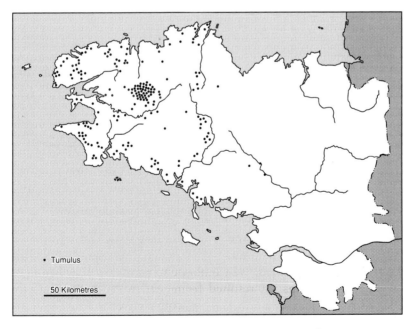

• Tumulus

50 Kilometres

Figure 5   Distribution of Bronze Age tumuli

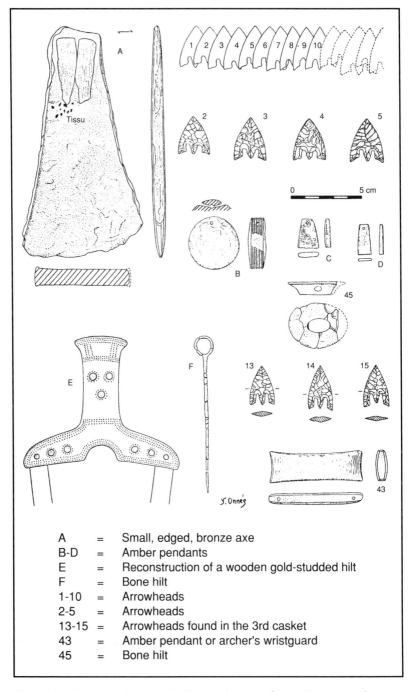

A	=	Small, edged, bronze axe
B-D	=	Amber pendants
E	=	Reconstruction of a wooden gold-studded hilt
F	=	Bone hilt
1-10	=	Arrowheads
2-5	=	Arrowheads
13-15	=	Arrowheads found in the 3rd casket
43	=	Amber pendant or archer's wristguard
45	=	Bone hilt

Figure 6   Grave-goods from the Bronze Age tumulus at Kernonen, Plouvorn

lavish grave-goods, including quivers of arrows with very fine flint arrowheads, bronze axes, swords and daggers (some of the latter having geometrically patterned gold-studded hilts), gold and silver jewels or vessels, amber beads and wristguards. Other large barrows, often sited near these 'princely' graves, may have been used for high-ranking ladies or lesser dignitaries since they contain very few or no metal objects. Such a grave, excavated at Saint-Jude II, Bourbriac (C-d'A), contained nothing more than some bronze debris, a pottery vessel and a single fibrolite axe, but it was placed inside a fine mortuary house, entirely lined with thick branches and protected by a stone cairn covered by a sloping wooden roof.

Though the wealth of grave-goods has attracted much attention, this limited series of large monuments was apparently a short-lived phenomenon on the fringe of the mainstream styles of Breton Early Bronze Age burials. Partly contemporary with these large mounds of the 'first series' is a more common 'second series', the main concentration of which is in Finistère but with an inland penetration extending to the Monts d'Arrée and the upper reaches of the Blavet. These barrows are generally sited on poorer land and often occur in groups, for instance at Berrien (F). They also overlie a central rectangular, dry-stone walled pit, a schist cist or a wooden coffin, though containing frequently no more than a pot and a bronze dagger placed near the body. Besides these barrows or *tombelles*, flat graves, often made of several well-placed schist slabs and clustering in small cemeteries as at Locquirec and Park-Mysteric, Landeleau (F), generally contain even fewer grave-goods if any at all.

This complex body of evidence may be read in a number of ways. It is, for instance, impossible to determine whether the 'princes', so lavishly buried under large mounds, belonged to immigrant groups who settled on both sides of the Channel, *c.* 2400–2200 BC, or if these elites were merely the successors of the Bell-beaker users, with whom they share a number of cultural similarities (individual burials, archer's gear among the grave-goods, etc.). In addition, although the funerary evidence indisputably points to clear-cut social hierarchies, with warrior overlords ruling over pastoral or agricultural communities, one cannot be sure whether the poorer graves described above are those of the lower-ranking sections of society or peripheral groups supplying raw materials to neighbouring chiefdoms or if, on the contrary, some of them at least point to an internal evolution of the latter. The brevity of the 'princely' phenomenon and the growing rarity of bronze weapons among grave-goods make it clear that Breton communities were evolving towards less hierarchical orders at the end of the Early Bronze Age, *c.* 1700 BC.

Whereas in the Early Bronze Age bronze technology had clearly been geared to the production of a fairly small number of prestige items, circulated among the top-ranking echelons of Breton communities, the large number of hoards of bronze objects buried in the centuries of the Middle Bronze Age, *c.* 1400–1000 BC, may indeed mean that a wider section of the population was then using metal artefacts and that the bases of power within such largely agrarian communities had to a degree shifted from war and plunder to trade and economic competition. Settlement sites of that period, either open or defended,[4] are uninformative – as are contemporary burials. But hoards of the Tréboul group show the beginnings of an intensive bronze production, making much use of the tin resources of northern Finistère and Morbihan, as well as of imported copper in the form of ingots traded from Iberia, Britain or the Alpine zone. The overall distribution of such highly distinctive ingots and of heavy gold Tara–Yeovil torques, either imported from the British Isles or copied locally, together with the strong typological affinities with other north-western manufacturing centres evidenced by Breton axes and swords and the presence of fine Tréboul-type swords in the Low Countries and near Lyon, makes it clear that Breton bronze-producing communities were being meshed into an extensive maritime and fluvial trade network. Unfortunately we can only guess at the complex social organization that must have underlain such long-distance exchanges.

At the end of the second millennium BC, new chiefdoms – called Urnfield groups because they incinerated their dead and buried cinerary urns in large cemeteries or 'urnfields' – emerged in central Europe and soon engaged in a flourishing trade with northern Italy. As the bronze production of some of the major Urnfield communities in eastern France and the middle Rhine region developed, their demand for tin grew correspondingly, boosting the exploitation of Atlantic tin resources. It may be assumed that, in exchange, the Armorican tribes received copper ingots as well as

---

[4] Open: Lividic, Plounéour-Trez (F); La Roussellerie, Saint-Michel-Chef-Chef (L-A); defended: Trémargat; Roc'h-an-Evned, Ploubazlanec (C-d'A).

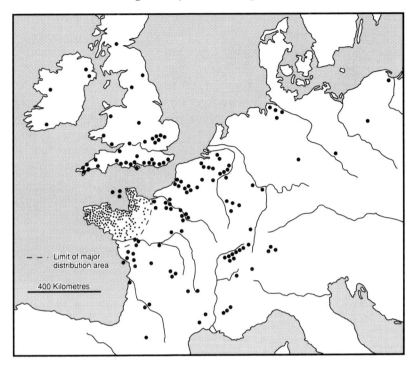

Figure 7   Distribution of Breton socketed axes

diverse ornamental weapons, which they copied and traded along the Atlantic seaways. The ensuing intensification of output may indeed be judged from the ever increasing number of bronze hoards of the Rosnoën (F, *c.* 1100–1000 BC) and Saint-Brieuc-des-Iffs (I-et-V) types buried in the early or middle Late Bronze Age. These include a range of axes, swords, spearheads, tools and personal ornaments. The presence of numerous fragments of bronze artefacts among these hoards clearly means that most were just old stock destined for recycling. This further underlines an intense demand for tools and weapons in the Late Bronze Age. Most of the latter, produced and traded along the Atlantic seaboard – the main manufacturing centres being in the lowlands of southern Britain, Normandy and Brittany – show strong typological and stylistic similarities which certainly suggest regular exchanges of personnel and technological expertise among the Atlantic communities.

Plate 4 Late Bronze Age socketed axe hoard, from Le Rest-Menou,
Plestin-les-Grèves (C-d'A)

Similar cultural and economic developments may actually be
perceived in the last phase of the Atlantic Bronze Age, characterized
by an increase in the number of large founders' hoards buried in
the west (more than a hundred). Most of these contain fragments
of 'carp's tongue' swords (a widely traded Atlantic weapon, with a
characteristic tapering blade), together with various other weapons
and tools. Many of these may have been manufactured in Nantes,
ideally placed for both maritime trade along the Atlantic seaways
and exchanges with the interior of France along the Loire.

On the evidence of such hoards, the Armorican Late Bronze Age
might then be viewed as a golden age, in which the extraordinary
boom in bronze production and trade entailed an overall prosperity
and some degree of social stability among the Armorican tribes.
The whole system was, however, extremely vulnerable, as it rested
almost entirely on its consumers' preference for bronze artefacts
and could therefore be severely crippled if metal technology or
fashion happened to change. This was precisely the case in the
eighth and seventh centuries BC, as iron metallurgy developed
north of the Alps and the demand for western tin and bronze

declined accordingly. The over-production of socketed axes, made more or less non-functional by an excessive addition of lead, together with the burying of large numbers of enormous bronze hoards in the seventh and sixth centuries BC, may therefore be regarded as a last-ditch attempt by Breton bronzesmiths to preserve their long-standing supremacy. This proved to be of no avail as their bronze technology and the weapon fashions they had helped develop were now increasingly outdated. This inability to adapt to new circumstances was, for several centuries, to isolate Breton communities from the main technological and cultural trends then developing in Iron Age Europe.

2

The Early Iron Age

The Breton Iron Age cannot be dismissed as a mere hotchpotch of events and changes, even though it is not possible to write the history of the Armorican tribes before the Roman conquest in the first century BC brings them into the limelight. On the contrary, the complex technical, social and political developments which took place during the last millennium BC must be seen as part of an intricate historical process leading to, and to some extent triggering off, the Roman intervention in western Gaul. It is true, however, that since the rich Iron Age communities of Germany and eastern France have no real counterpart in Brittany, Normandy or the Channel Islands, the systematic chronological systems elaborated for the cultures of central Europe, the Rhineland or Champagne are on the whole irrelevant in the west, where clear-cut chronological distinctions between an Early Iron Age (or Hallstatt period, *c.* 700–450 BC) and a Later Iron Age (or La Tène period, *c.* 450–50 BC) can only be used as rough guidelines.

Sharp differentiation between the current terminology of Late Bronze Age and Early Iron Age is largely formal since Bronze Age techniques and traditions persisted in the west down to the end of the sixth century BC. Various Early Iron Age 'imports' such as Hallstattian razors or 'protohallstattian' swords discovered in founders' hoards show that objects belonging to the Late Bronze Age 'carp's tongue' sword complex were still being hoarded – and perhaps made – in the seventh century BC.[1] Similarly the extremely numerous Late Bronze Age 'Armorican' socketed axes were often

---

[1] Guennoc, Landéda (F); Prairie de Mauves and Jardin des Plantes, Nantes.

associated in hoards with Early Iron Age artefacts.[2] Such hoards, consisting almost entirely of complete objects, have long been a puzzle to archaeologists, who find it hard to understand why such large numbers of non-functional artefacts (over 25,000) should have been so carefully hidden and subsequently abandoned. As the once popular theory of a massive invasion of Hallstattian iron sword-wielding riders is no longer tenable, part of the answer may be found in the redistribution of power and demand in the last millennium BC. The long-term development of European communities, beginning with the collapse of the Hittite and Mycenaean Empires (*c*. 1200 BC) and ending with the emergence of the Etruscan and Greek states on the one hand, and of the central European Hallstatt groups on the other, clearly deflected demand and trade from the Atlantic seaways to eastern and southern Europe. The disruption of copper supplies and the growing availability of iron by the end of the eighth century, together with the obvious inability of Armorican craftsmen to discard their obsolete bronze technology, resulted in a growing disaffection for Breton products, which may explain the burying of such outdated and useless artefacts, and in the increasing isolation of Armorican communities.

Trade and contacts

Exchanges between the Armorican and Atlantic communities and those of central-eastern France, still fairly active in the eighth and seventh centuries BC, became much scarcer in the next two centuries. The wide distribution of Armorican socketed axes, 'exported' to the whole of northern France and southern Britain during the Armorican Late Bronze Age and Early Hallstatt period, testifies to the permanence of a network of maritime exchanges with the Atlantic provinces, extending from the Netherlands to Spain, and also of continued trade with the Alpine zone along land and river routes. However, from the end of the seventh century onwards, the diffusion of the technology of iron and the development of a brilliant Hallstattian civilization in Burgundy polarized long-distance exchanges towards the Rhône-Seine corridor,

[2] Imported *situlae* at Kerléonet, Spézet (F); iron ingots (*Spitzbarre*) at Saint-Martin-des-Champs (F), etc.

a route served by the Phocean emporium of *Massalia* (Marseille), founded *c.* 600 BC, and the large native *oppida* of Le Pègue (Ardèche) and Mont Lassois (Côte-d'Or). In such a system, the once prosperous Atlantic communities became economic backwaters, from which the developing communities of Burgundy and the Marne acquired various commodities (tin, salt, slaves, etc.) via the peripheral arteries of the Loire and Seine. The range of Early Iron Age imports found in the west, distributed along the southern coast of the peninsula with a strong concentration of finds at the mouth of the Loire, points to limited or irregular connections with the eastern cultural groups, acting as middlemen for the Etruscans or the Greek colonies of *Magna Grecia*. There is, so far, no evidence of any direct contact between the Armorican tribes and the latter, or with the Carthaginians operating from *Gades* (Cadiz), along the routes already opened by the traders of the Tartessian kingdom. No Carthaginian settlement is known north of the river Tagus, and though Himilco's exploratory voyage, commissioned by the state in the second half of the fifth century, reached the land of the *Oestrymnides* (the *Osismi?*), rich in tin and lead, it apparently had no effect on Carthaginian commerce with north-western Europe.

Settlements

Very little is known of Early Iron Age settlements in western France, though surface surveys have revealed consistent traces of what were probably isolated farmsteads or hamlets. One such settlement has been excavated at Kerlande, Brandivy (M), showing two adjacent enclosures protected by a 1.5 m thick dry-stone rampart; against it stood a lean-to cabin, its roof upheld by a central post. The dead were apparently disposed of in low *tombelles*, sixty of which were recorded in the neighbouring fields. Similar enclosure banks have been observed in the vicinity of Early Iron Age *sépultures circulaires* (see below p. 34) and urnfields at Coat-Plen-Coat, Saint-Goazec (F), and Penfoul, Landeleau (F), where they probably protected farmsteads or hamlets.

As was common in the whole of western Europe during the Early Iron Age, many defensive sites, such as hilltops and headlands, were fortified – or re-fortified – between the eighth and fifth centuries BC, though it is still far from clear whether these settlements were permanent or temporary. Large enclosed sites have been identified at Toul-Goulic, Trémargat (C-d'A), Le Lizio, Carnac (M), and Pointe du Blair, Baden (M). Their earth and stone ramparts, first put up in Neolithic times, were apparently strengthened in the Early Iron Age. Some of them may well have sheltered permanent hamlets (Le Lizio; Pointe du Blair); others, like the windswept and weather-beaten promontory forts of Cap d'Erquy, Erquy (C-d'A), and the Pointe de la Torche, Plomeur (F), were surely temporary settlements.

Agriculture and crafts

Although agriculture was certainly the mainstay of peninsular economy during the Early Iron Age, its archaeological traces are almost non-existent. The concentration of settlements on what are now barren uplands may indicate a strong bias toward sheep- and cattle-rearing, the more probable as the climate of western Europe deteriorated in that period. But it may also be argued that a fair number of lowland farmsteads devoted to the growing of cereals have been eradicated by later agrarian activities.

Salt production was important for the preservation of food (meat and fish) and the curing of leather. The manufacturing of salt from sea-water in briquetage structures had developed in northern Brittany, for example at Le Curnic, Guissény (F), and the south, as at Le Boucaud, L'Epinette, Préfailles (L-A), in the Late Bronze Age, probably under Continental influence. There is every reason to believe that this seasonal industry, almost certainly a sub-activity of local farming, was maintained during the Early Iron Age. But few Breton briquetage sites can be securely dated before the last three centuries BC.

No pottery workshop similar to the one recently excavated in Les Huguettes, Alderney, dated to about 490 BC, has yet been brought to light in Brittany, though the wares common in both graves and settlement sites were undoubtedly produced locally. Most of this pottery was made in brown or black fabrics, often coated with a brown glossy slip. Some of these pots, however, often associated with hoards of the 'carp's tongue' sword complex, suggest typological influences derived from the Continental Urnfield cultures.[3] Breton Early Iron Age wares, or rather those buried in the graves belonging to the later part of the period, show little variation in form. The most common type – truncated pots with vertical necks and everted rims like those found at Bagatelle, Saint-Martin-des-Champs (F), and Boquidet, Sérent (M), and *situla*-shaped, round-bodied pots (Bagatelle) – were apparently modelled on imported sheet bronze vessels. Round-bodied urns with everted rims and high hollow pedestalled bases were imitated from types produced in northern Spain and Aquitaine *c.* 540–450 BC.[4] Rarer varieties include coarse ware carinated bowls (Boquidet, Sérent; Erquy), and a most interesting buff ware vessel (Kerscao, Peumerit, F), reproducing the form of a sheet bronze bowl down to the smallest details. Extra-peninsular influences also show in the decorative patterns made up of shallow depressions, either used singly as at Kerscao, Peumerit, in triangles pointing downwards (Coët-a-Tous, Carnac) or in 'daisy' designs impressed on the body or shoulder.[5] These may well derive from both Continental Bronze Age and south-western French Iron Age artistic traditions. Furthermore, the linear patterns stamped on Late Hallstatt or Early La Tène Armorican wares can be traced back to Late Hallstatt metalwork styles of northern Italy and the north-western part of the Alpine zone. The simple motifs (squares, rectangles, crosses, zigzags, circles, etc.), organized in narrow horizontal or vertical strips defining large undecorated zones and seen on various vessels from Kerviltré and Castellou-Péron, Saint-Jean-Trolimon, or Kervéo, Plomelin (F), indeed relate to those stamped on north Italian wares from Golasecca or Bologna and bronze copper belt-plaques from south-western Germany. They may have been copied, in the early fifth century BC, from bronze vessels imported into western France. Painted pottery, common in the Continental Hallstatt cultures, is rare in the peninsula. The best example is the Menez-Kervouyen, Plogastel-Saint-Germain (F), cinerary urn, decorated with brown hooks, triangles and squares painted on a haematite slip.

Armorican potters evidently came under the influence of various technological and artistic trends derived from Continental and Aquitanian Hallstatt sources. The scarcity of iron objects in local Early Iron Age contexts may however indicate that the use of iron,

[3] Vern, Moëlan (F); Parc-aux-Boeufs, Questembert (M), etc.
[4] Tronoën, Saint-Jean-Trolimon (F); Kergoglé, Plovan, etc.
[5] Penfoul, Landeleau; Lann-Tinekei, Ploemeur (M).

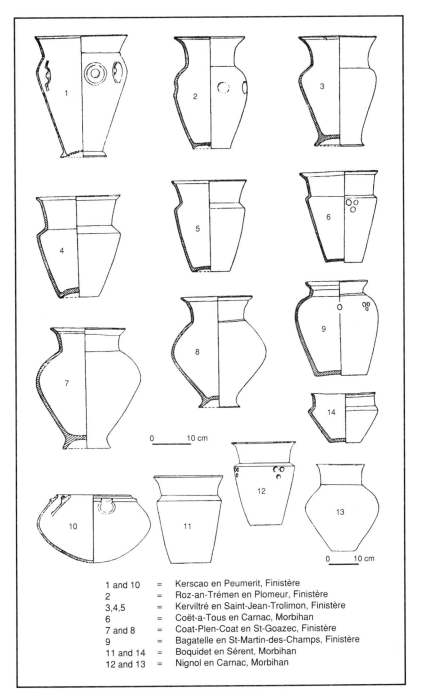

1 and 10 = Kerscao en Peumerit, Finistère
2 = Roz-an-Trémen en Plomeur, Finistère
3,4,5 = Kerviltré en Saint-Jean-Trolimon, Finistère
6 = Coët-a-Tous en Carnac, Morbihan
7 and 8 = Coat-Plen-Coat en St-Goazec, Finistère
9 = Bagatelle en St-Martin-des-Champs, Finistère
11 and 14 = Boquidet en Sérent, Morbihan
12 and 13 = Nignol en Carnac, Morbihan

Figure 8   Breton Early Iron Age pottery

a metal which had then become common elsewhere, did not spread to the west till very late in the period. The various iron trinkets – plain or bossed bracelets, nails, swan's-neck pins – found in Early Iron Age burial mounds may be accounted for by the development of small homestead industries similar to that recently identified at Penfoul, Landeleau (F).

The amazingly prolific production of Armorican socketed axes is now known to have continued into the Early Iron Age. The association of typical Hallstatt artefacts like the bronze *situlae* from Kerléonet, Spézet (F), for example, or the bossed bracelet from Saint-Bugan, Loudéac (C-d'A), with hoards of socketed axes clearly shows that Armorican bronzesmiths went on producing various sub-types of such objects down to the sixth century in very large numbers. It is far from clear why so many have such a high lead content (more than 20% in many cases, 100% in some), so that they cannot have been used as proper tools. Puzzling, too, is the relative paucity of small bronze objects at both settlement and burial sites. The ores used in this industry were, however, certainly obtained from local sources, though nothing is known about the mining techniques.

Death and burial

Our knowledge of Armorican Early Iron Age communities derives, to a large extent, from memorials to the dead rather than from traces of activities of the living. The most prominent local funerary monuments are low mounds known as *sépultures circulaires*, a small number of which have survived on the uplands of Morbihan and southern Finistère.[6] These earthen barrows, between 10 and 20 metres in diameter, cover a central circular or horseshoe-shaped wall, which can be either vertical or sloping, generally one metre high and 5 to 11 metres in diameter, built in regular courses of thin shale slabs. These structures enclose a small number of cinerary urns (up to twenty), buried in shallow rectangular pits or protected by small stone cists or slabs, together with stone stelae probably intended as grave-markers. The variety of funerary practices observed on these sites, and the presence of cinerary urns outside

---

[6] Le Rocher, Le Bono; Le Nignol and Coët-a-Tous, Carnac (M); Parc-Lostec, Scaër; Kerbascat, Tréguennec (F).

Plate 5 *Sépulture circulaire*, Kerbascat, Tréguennec

the central area (e.g. at Kerbascat), may imply long use, possibly by one family, of such burial-grounds, growing by accretion with each generation.

Most cinerary urns found in the *sépultures circulaires* are locally made and belong to one of the Late Hallstatt types defined above, the only exceptions being the two bronze *situlae* found under adjacent monuments at Le Rocher, Le Bono (M). The better preserved of the two is made of riveted sheet bronze, strengthened by iron bands; both had been buried in an upright position in layers of charcoal and ashes lying at the bottom of rectangular pits dug into the subsoil. One was covered by an upturned bronze cup, probably imported from Etruria or *Magna Grecia c.* 600–550 BC. Even these 'rich' graves, in which exotic metal containers originally designed for the mixing and serving of wine were used as cinerary urns, contained few grave-goods. This is true generally of all *sépultures circulaires*, where offerings consisted of a small number of personal ornaments such as bronze and iron bossed bracelets, beads of glass and amber.

Far less impressive than the *sépultures circulaires* derived from models fairly common in the Continental Hallstatt areas, are the humble *tombelles* preserved in the *landes* of central Brittany which

Plate 6   Bronze *situla* and basin, Le Rocher, Le Bono (M)

probably originated from native traditions and had a wider distribution than the former monuments.[7] Most of these low earth and rubble mounds are less than a metre high and 7 metres in diameter and are often found in clusters of dozens of units. Though the presence of one inhumation has been suspected under one at La Bésizais, Trébry (C-d'A), *tombelles*, all the others overlie cremations, with the body burnt *in situ*, or the ashes deposited on the ground or protected by stone or wooden cists. These cists, however, are also commonly found in isolation, for instance at Kergoglé, Plovan (F), or clustered in small cemeteries (Kériéré, Poullan, F), sometimes marked by wooden or stone stelae.

The few clues provided by the burial and settlement sites of Early Iron Age Armorica evince a strong degree of cultural continuity with the Late Bronze Age and hint at diversified communities of metallurgists, farmers and shepherds, cultivating cereals and raising sheep, pigs and cattle. Various structures and artefacts testify to intermittent exchanges between the Armorican farmer communities and the Hallstatt cultures of south-western and central France and of the Atlantic seaboard. But it is clear that these contacts were not sufficient to generate a highly differentiated elite of the kind common to most Early Iron Age cultures. The evidence provided by cemeteries, whose grave-goods are, on the whole, scarce and modest, suggests indeed that while the dead buried in 'rich' graves were certainly important personages in these communities, they were not far above the rest with whom they shared common styles of living and dying.

[7] La Grée-Minguet, Questembert (M); Menez-Hom area (F).

3

The Later Iron Age

While present evidence suggests that the Early Iron Age groups in the region were only superficially affected by the Continental Hallstattian cultures, their Later Iron Age counterparts offer a strongly contrasting picture. Their numerous monuments and settlements suggest sharp demographic growth as well as various technological advances and imply social structures which were less static and gradually opening up to external influences.

Population and settlement

The task of estimating the population of the Armorican peninsula in the Later Iron Age is difficult since data is scarce. P-R. Giot, using the figures provided by Caesar, has suggested a plausible population of 150,000 to 300,000, with a density of three to ten inhabitants per square km, but this is largely hypothetical. What is certain is that large areas, previously devoted to sheep-rearing or left uncultivated, were being cleared before ploughing and the sowing of cereals, while contemporary settlements are so commonly found on the remotest *landes* of central Finistère or Morbihan or the most exposed Atlantic islands or islets,[1] that very few areas seem to have been left unpopulated in the Later Iron Age. This, together with the probable rise in the yield of cereals brought about by a colder and wetter climate, argues for demographic growth and ensuing social and political changes.

---

[1] Talhouët, Pluvigner (M); Ile Geignog, Landéda; Ile d'Yock, Landunvez (F).

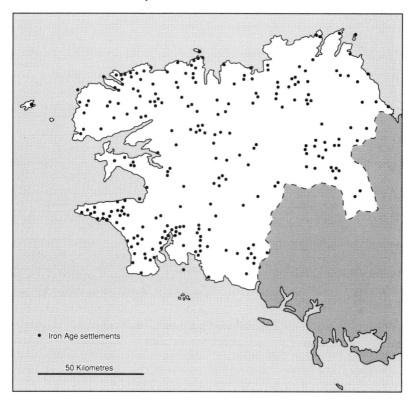

Figure 9   Population distribution in the Iron Age: the Osismi

In recent years a large number of Iron Age enclosures have been discovered by aerial survey, mostly in Côtes-d'Armor and Finistère. They generally consist of quadrangular ditch-systems, possibly with palisades, enclosing an area of less than a hectare, where buildings can occasionally be observed. The excavation of some of these settlements at Saint-Symphorien, Paule; Le Boisanne, Plouer-sur-Rance (both C-d'A), Talhouët, Pluvigner (M), and, particularly, Le Braden, Quimper (F), has revealed sequences of palisaded enclosures and/or earthen banks surrounding various agricultural buildings and structures as well as a small number of huts. Such small, scattered, nucleated hamlets, probably occupied by one or two extended families, may turn out to be characteristic of the Armorican Late Iron Age. As yet very few indisputably Iron Age

Plate 7   Vertical aerial view of the Late Iron Age settlement at Le Braden,
Quimper (F)

villages have been discovered in western Gaul. Their sites
continued in use in Roman, medieval and modern times.

Besides these open hamlets, since the palisades and banks were
clearly not designed for military purposes but simply to keep wild
animals away, fortified enclosures of various types occupied a
fairly prominent place in the Iron Age landscape. Among the most
common are cliff-forts of the type observed by Caesar during his
campaign against the *Veneti* (*BG*, III, 12). These were usually
located on high promontories cut off from the mainland by a single
or complex sequence of ditch and earthen ramparts, sometimes
stone-revetted; they are quite frequent along the coasts of Brittany
from Ille-et-Vilaine and Côtes-d'Armor to Finistère and Morbihan.[2]
Though Iron Age sherds and huts have often been reported from
these sites, it is unlikely that most of these exposed and windswept
locations were more than temporary shelters, only used in case of

[2] La Pointe du Grouin, Cancale; Le Mainga, Saint-Coulomb (I-et-V); Le Cap
d'Erquy, Erquy; Coz-Yaudet, Ploulec'h (C-d'A); Kermorvan, Ploumoguer; Castel-
Meur, Cléden-Cap-Sizun (F); Beg-an-Aud, Saint-Pierre-Quiberon; Pointe du Vieux
Château, Belle-Ile-en-Mer (M).

need. This is perhaps also the case, though less certainly so, of promontory-forts overlooking river bends like Le Camp-du-Mur, Comblessac (I-et-V), Le Camp-du-Château-Blanc, Plumelec (M), or Saint-Adrien, Arzano (F).

Hill-forts, ubiquitous features in the landscape of Iron Age Europe, are not very commmon in the west, where most enclose no more than 2 to 6 ha. Few have been excavated, but surface finds include Late Iron Age pottery and sherds of Dressel 1 A wine amphorae from Italy. Trial excavations at Kercaradec, Quimper (F), have revealed a fairly elaborate rampart and several possible hut-sites, with Iron Age pottery and about 40 sling-stones.

Larger sites, such as Le Camp d'Artus, Huelgoat (37.5 ha, F), Le Camp de Lescouais, Guénon (80 ha?, M), or Le Camp du Poulailler, Landéan (25 ha, I-et-V), are much rarer. Though their size might suggest that they should be classified among the classical *oppida* of temperate Europe, they have none of the proto-urban characteristics of these. The 1938–9 trial excavation of R. E. M. Wheeler and K. Richardson in Le Camp d'Artus indeed revealed that the large 'camp' was surrounded by a *murus gallicus* of the type described by Caesar (*BG*, VII, 23), also observed in the Beg-an-Aud promontory fort, but that the inner area had been very thinly occupied in the last century BC, a fact confirmed by field

Plate 8   Lostmarc'h cliff-fort, Crozon (F)

survey after the 1987 hurricane had played havoc with the forest covering the site.

There are actually very few traces of large pre-Roman nucleated settlements in western France, with the notable exception of Alet, Saint-Malo (I-et-V), at the mouth of the river Rance. This 30 ha promontory fort, densely occupied between 80 BC and AD 20, was probably an important political centre of the *Coriosolitae*, in which the tribal coins were minted and diverse goods gathered and prepared for trade with southern British entry ports. Future research at promising sites like Quimper and Coz-Yaudet, Ploulec'h, may, however, reveal similar nuclei.

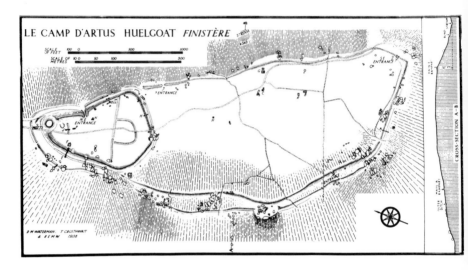

Figure 10   Plan of Le Camp d'Artus, Huelgoat

Buildings and structures

Huts have been observed and often excavated on such settlement sites. Most of them are square or rectangular in plan, but apsed (Le Braden II, Quimper) and circular buildings have also been identified recently.[3] Timber-framed walls with wattle-and-daub infill, sometimes whitewashed as at Keriner, Pluguffan (F), were

---

[3] For example, Talhouët, Pluvigner; Polvern, Hennebont (M); Le Braden I, Quimper.

apparently more frequent, and probably slightly earlier than dry-stone walls with dressed facings and rubble infill. Very little is known of roof structures, though it may reasonably be supposed that they were covered in thatch or reeds. Generally dated to the Middle or Late La Tène periods, these buildings, which may have housed human beings and/or animals, vary greatly in surface from a mere 12 square metres at Goulvars, Quiberon (M), to 60 square metres at Le Braden II, Quimper. They are, on the whole, provided with few amenities except central hearths or clay bell-ovens.

Related agricultural structures include silos at Alet, Saint-Malo, Le Braden, Quimper, and elsewhere, threshing-floors and granaries elevated on four or six posts (Le Braden II; Keriner). But the most common features of Armorican Iron Age settlements are un-doubtedly the underground structures known as *souterrains armoricains*, about three hundred of which have been discovered in western Brittany. These *souterrains*, excavated in decayed granite or schist, are between 3 and 40 metres long and consist in a single cell or a series of cells, strung along a common axis or diverging from it, connected by narrow passageways. Access to the under-ground chambers, buried from one to four metres deep under the ground surface, was provided by slanting corridors or vertical pits. In all known cases, these corridors had been carefully backfilled with refuse from nearby surface settlements such as burnt or incompletely burnt planks and timber, ashes, pottery, loomweights, grindstones, bronze and iron slag, so as to seal off the underground cells.

More than half of these Armorican *souterrains* were entirely empty when discovered or excavated. But in a few, dozens of pots, probably used as containers, had been stacked along the walls.[4] The purpose of such structures is not clear. Hearths, in which the firing of clay loomweights or the working of bronze had been carried out, have been observed in some of them.[5] As *souterrains* are often found in association with settlements,[6] it is quite likely that in most cases they were used as subterranean storage rooms or workshops. The presence of Iron Age stelae in some of them like Trézéan, Pédernec (C-d'A), and of a string of gold beads in that at

---

[4] Bellevue, Plouégat-Moysan; Kermoysan, Plabennec (F).

[5] Litiez, La Feuillée; Lamphily, Concarneau (F).

[6] L'Armorique, Plouaret (C-d'A); Saint-Symphorien, Paule; La Boisanne, Plouer-sur-Rance, etc.

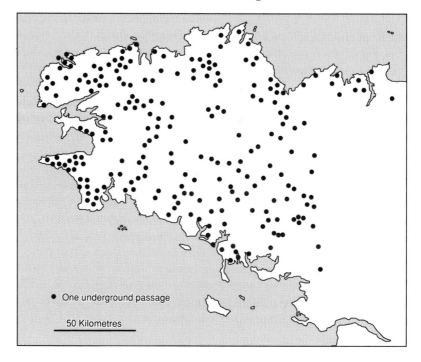

Figure 11   Distribution of Late Iron Age souterrains

Kerellen, Tréglonou (F), remind us that other uses are possible, not least since they cover a long time span from the Late Bronze Age or Early Iron Age (late sixth century BC) to the early first century BC.

Agriculture and farming

Pollen analysis carried out on the peat-bogs at Le Cloître-Saint-Thégonnec, Spézet and Brasparts in central Finistère have revealed large-scale deforestation in the Late Iron Age, connected with the clearing of land and the extension of agricultural activities. This may have been made necessary because of an overall growth of population, and assisted by the increased availability of iron, hence of more efficient iron tools such as ploughshares.

Plough-marks observed under sand-dunes at Théven and Kerbrat, Plougoulm (F), show that farm-land was cultivated in narrow strips, though no 'Celtic field' has so far been identified. As pollen analyses have shown, wheat – much used for bread and gruel – was easily the most widely grown cereal in the west, though rye and buckwheat have also been noted. The presence of granaries, silos, grindstones and rotary querns (from the second century BC onwards) on most rural sites testifies to the essential role of cereal-growing in the local economy. Leguminous plants such as broad beans were also probably cultivated as complementary resources as at Kerné, Quiberon (M). Sheep- and cattle-rearing continued; the ditched enclosures and animal bones exhumed on settlement sites suggest the breeding of pigs, sheep, oxen and goats on most farms. Milk provided butter and cheese, although finds of cheese presses are rare. The meat could be eaten fresh or preserved in salt and skins tanned, cut and sewn into shoes, straps and sails. Wild boars and stags from the nearby forests were also captured and eaten, while on the sea-shores, limpets, mussels and sea-urchins were collected and consumed, sometimes in very large quantities as is shown by finds at Moulin de la Rive, Locquirec (C-d'A), Alet and Goulvars, Quiberon (M).

Crafts and arts

In the Ancient world the Gauls enjoyed a wide reputation as gifted craftsmen, proficient cartwrights and the inventors of tinning. Most of the artefacts they produced, being made of perishable materials (apart from metal objects), have, however, disappeared and we are therefore left with limited and biased views of their activities. Little is known of the work of joiners, carpenters and shipbuilders, though Caesar admired the technical qualities of Venetic vessels (*BG*, III, 13). The crafts of spinners and weavers, which were largely, if not entirely, home-based, are slightly better documented by the discovery of spindlewhorls and clay loom-weights on a large number of settlement sites.

Crucibles are fairly frequent site finds, showing that the working of bronze was a common activity of many farms and hamlets. Bronze artefacts, such as brooches, pins, torques, bracelets and rings, are actually surprisingly rare in local Iron Age contexts. They cannot, in most cases, be attributed to individual production centres. One cannot help feeling that the striking of such complex objects as copper, silver and gold coins, however, shows the existence of a body of highly skilled craftsmen, either based in large settlements like Alet or working on demand. Both obverse and reverse sides of coins, based on gold staters of Philip of Macedonia, were transmogrified into fantastic figures. Possessing distinctive regional and tribal styles, Armorican coins display a highly idiosyncratic tradition of die-engraving that ranks among the finest examples of workmanship in the Celtic world.

The respect, mingled with awe, attached to blacksmiths in the Celtic world shows they were specialized craftsmen working within tribal communities, or perhaps moving from group to group with the secrets of their trade. Iron ore, fairly abundant in the peninsula, was collected from outcrops or perhaps even mined, before being smelted in small oval-shaped shaft furnaces of the type recently excavated at Kermoisan, Quimper. The large pair of blacksmith's tongs found at Le Braden and another in a Late Iron Age context at Lanneunoc, Plounévez-Lochrist (F), are good evidence of the techniques used for the shaping of iron ingots. These came in the form of 'currency-bars' (Kermoisan) or of the more recognizable *Spitzbarren*, that is, rhomboidal ingots with tapering extremities, weighing between five and six kilos. They were often buried in 'hoards', which may hark back to Late Bronze Age habits of hiding away 'precious' metals. In spite of such direct evidence of the use of iron as the long iron nails found in the *murus gallicus* of Le Camp d'Artus and indirect evidence from Caesar's description of the nails holding Venetic ships together, iron artefacts are uncommon site finds in this period, though admittedly more numerous than in the seventh and sixth centuries BC. It is therefore likely that discarded or broken objects were collected as scrap-metal and reprocessed in the local smelting units.

Salt being a necessary commodity for the preservation of meat and fish, as well as for the curing of leather, Late Iron Age saltworks, continuing earlier traditions, were extremely common on western coasts from the Cotentin to the mouth of the Loire. They all used salt scooped up from sand-beaches after the high tides, the salt being then washed off in clean water and the brine thus produced evaporated in ovens. In the earliest phase of the industry (800–450 BC), cylindrical pots, used for boiling brine, were placed in horizontal stone slabs supported by clay props over a fire as at L'Epinette, Préfailles (L-A). More complicated structures, derived from central European techniques, then appeared in the Middle La Tène period (third century BC). They consisted of clay fire-bars set across rectangular fire-pits, the salt-moulds being placed on the bars or on flat bricks placed across the latter. These gradually evolved into *augets* ovens in which numerous, often more than 250, salt-cake moulds in the shape of truncated pyramids (*augets*) were inserted into the clay lattice-work of rectangular ovens. Mould fragments found on a small number of inland settlement sites like Le Braden or Rosvein, Pont-l'Abbé (F), show that salt-cakes were sold in their containers. But we know nothing of the yield of such units, nor of the number of people

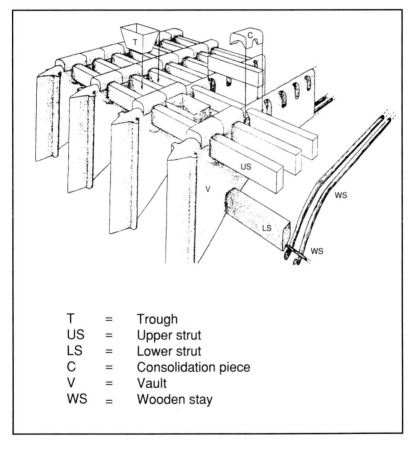

T	=	Trough
US	=	Upper strut
LS	=	Lower strut
C	=	Consolidation piece
V	=	Vault
WS	=	Wooden stay

Figure 12   Briquetage, La Tara, La Plaine-sur-Mer

involved. There is no telling, either, whether this was a specialized industry, or just one of a number of seasonal activities in a balanced community.

Much the same may be said of pottery-making, especially since the large population needed vast quantities of pottery containers to preserve, cook and eat food. Only one contemporary kiln has been discovered (at Polvern, Hennebont, M). But the wealth and variety of Armorican Late Iron Age wares are such that they certainly point to the existence of a number of pottery-making units, in which fine and coarse wares were fired at a maximum temperature of 600–700 degrees C.

Whereas the Early La Tène *situla*-shaped vessels with angular or ovoid bodies were probably reserved for funerary purposes, most of the later wares were certainly designed for domestic usage and were accordingly turned in a limited range of sizes and forms. Pots, sometimes with counter-sunk handles, bowls and jars were the commonest. They generally come in crude and thick fabrics, with very few decorative features. But finer wares, carefully burnished and/or ornamented, are far from rare in funerary contexts and on settlement sites. Down to the very end of the period, many of these wares were given a glossy sheen by a more or less uniform coating of a graphite or haematite slip, both minerals being common in the Armorican massif. Some, however, painted with red and/or black geometric patterns as at Kergourognon, Prat (C-d'A) and Rugéré, Plouvorn (F), or floral ones (Parc-ar-Groas, Quimper), may either testify to northern Italian influences from the Este culture or may hark back to the local Early Iron Age.

Evidence of a similar degree of continuity may also be seen on the stamped wares of Early Iron Age tradition, fairly common in the Early and Middle La Tène (fourth–third centuries BC) and, to a lesser extent in Late La Tène contexts. They are characterized by stylistic changes, the earlier rectilinear patterns (squares, rectangles, etc.) being gradually replaced, probably under the influence of the *Bogenstil* of Bohemia and Bavaria, by a series of tangential arcs, stamped or incised in serried succession on the bodies of shallow bowls or *situla*-shaped vessels, and often associated with 'bunches' of three or more *ocelli*.

The most remarkable ceramic productions of the age belong, however, to a limited series of carefully black-burnished vessels decorated in a characteristic style associating a small number of stamped patterns incised, either freehand or with the help of dividers, on the body and sometimes also on the feet of bowls and *situla*-shaped vessels. These stylistic elements probably originate from the designs to be seen on the bronze vessels of eastern France and the western half of central Europe, though intermediate geographical links are still missing. These influences show particularly well in the northern group of Armorican *Metalstil* vessels (second half of the fourth century BC), best exemplified by the Saint-Pol-de-Léon urn, decorated in a 'severe' style with long vertical palmettes and S-shaped motifs, the Le Blavet, Hénon (C-d'A), bowls, one of which bears a complex design closely resembling that engraved by a Celtic artist on the Etruscan Besançon bronze flagon, and the Losheim-type Litiez, La Feuillée (F), and Trézéan, Pédernec (C-d'A), embossed cups. Similar designs, sometimes associated with stamped *Bogenstil* patterns, may be seen on the rarer vessels of the southern group (Kélouër, Plouhinec, F), probably dating to the third century BC.

Though Armorican pottery styles clearly influenced the decorative repertoire of other cultural groups – such as those of south-western Britain – their various patterns rarely appear on local metal artefacts. The only notable exception is the geometric ornamentation stamped on the bronze scabbard of the Kernavest, Quiberon (M), iron dagger. The same patterns, however, appear on a small number of fifth- and fourth-century stone stelae, the best known of which is the late fourth-century stone from Kermaria, Pont-l'Abbé (F), carved on all four faces with complex designs derived from a common Celtic tradition. This finds its most remarkable expression on the Pfalzfeld and Steinenbronn pillars from Württemberg and the Truroe and Castelstrange stones in Ireland.

Even though it is likely that further examples of such decorated monuments have been lost to us by weathering of the friable granite surfaces, it must be admitted that a large majority of these stones were left plain. Where they were carved, however, the work was often carefully executed. These stones come in a variety of shapes and sizes, from low bulbous stones, sometimes less than 0.50 m in diameter, to high tapering pillars, quadrangular, polygonal or circular in section. The distribution of these sub-types, particularly the tall fluted stones, perhaps imitated from Greek columns, commonly seen in south-western Finistère, may well point to regional cultures and artistic traditions, of which little

Plate 9   Iron Age pot, Saint-Pol-de-Léon (F)

Plate 10 Bronze dagger, Kernavest, Quiberon (M)

Plate 11   Iron Age stela, Kermaria, Pont-l'Abbé (F)

is actually known. It is indeed difficult, if not impossible, to relate the two Late Iron Age statues found in western France at Lanneunoc, Plounévez-Lochrist, and Saint-Symphorien, Paule (C-d'A), to any of the latter, as they clearly have widely different artistic affinities. The Paule statue, probably dating to the late second century BC, carved in a local stone, shows a male god holding a seven-stringed lyre; arguably it may be derived from extra-Armorican models, whereas the Lanneunoc statue, though incomplete, looks far cruder and more 'local'.

Contacts, exchanges and trade

The decorative styles (*Bogenstil, Metalstil,* etc.) of both Armorican potteries and stone stelae are certainly the clearest evidence we have of contacts between the peninsular tribes and other Gaulish communities in the Early and Middle La Tène periods. Yet contemporary 'imported' artefacts are exceedingly rare and cannot be related to regular trading contacts. They must rather be seen as extraordinary gifts to local chieftains, sometimes re-used as votive offerings in tribal sanctuaries. The basis of contact and possible exchanges between Armorican La Tène groups and the contemporary cultures prospering in eastern and central Gaul remains, therefore, totally obscure.

This, of course, does nothing to help solve the vexed problem of the *Cassiterides* and of the famed tin trade between the 'barbarian' communities of north-western Europe and the Mediterranean states and city-states. These long-distance exchanges are actually well documented by the writings of three successive groups of explorers and geographers: Herodotus, Pytheas and Timaeus, before or slightly after 300 BC; Polybius and Posidonius *c.* 100 BC; Diodorus Siculus and Strabo in the first century BC. Sometimes quoted by later sources, all these refer quite consistently to southern Britain and/or to a group of islands they called *Cassiterides*, used as sources of tin by the Aegean and Phoenician communities at least as early as the fifth century BC. The tin trade involved merchants (Gaulish or Mediterranean?) coming to these remote parts to acquire the precious metal – sometimes fashioned into knuckle-bone shaped ingots – from specialized trading posts

Plate 12   Iron Age stelae: (a above) Plonéour-Lanvern (F);
(b facing) Lannilis (F)

before conveying it to Narbonne and/or Marseille, prior to
despatching it to further destinations.

Though instructive, these accounts throw little light on the
precise location of the *Cassiterides*, placed rather vaguely some-

where between Spain and Britain, or the British tin marts. They leave much unexplained as to the routes followed by traders between north-western Europe and the Mediterranean ports of trade. Most archaeologists would argue that the word *Cassiterides* was used as a blanket term to define the tin-producing areas of both Britain (Cornwall) and Gaul (western Brittany), probably to be equated with the *Oestrymnides* explored by the Carthaginian navigator Himilco in the fifth century BC. There is also some consensus about the identification of *Ictis*, a British port where the locals carted their tin to be 'bought' by overseas merchants, with either Mount Batten in Plymouth Sound or Saint Michael's Mount off Marazion, Cornwall.

The controversial question of trade routes to the Mediterranean is, on the other hand, still very much of a puzzle, though the heat of the argument has abated in recent years as the growing availability and quality of data has helped archaeologists and historians give more substance to the writings of Ancient geographers. The discovery of the princely tomb at Vix (Côte-d'Or), with its superb range of grave-goods, has shed some light on the role played by the neighbouring hill-fort at Mont Lassois. There surface surveys and trial excavations have revealed large numbers of sherds of Attic black figure wares, as well as of wine amphorae from the Marseille region, suggesting it was a major centre controlling trade between the upper reaches of the Saône and the Seine. This has therefore substantiated Strabo's account (*Geographica*, IV, 1, 14, probably using Posidonius) of a trade route following the valleys of the Rhône, Saône and Seine and crossing the Channel towards the Isle of Wight (*Vectis*), to which native coracles brought tin from *Belerion*. As has been argued by a number of historians, this short crossing would spare traders the dangers of a longer maritime journey around western Armorica, though one may equally admit that a long trek (thirty days, according to Diodorus Siculus, *Bibliotheca Historiae*, V, 22) through un-controlled territory would be as risky as any kind of sea trade.

Evidence about the use of the western seaways in the Early and Middle La Tène periods is provided by some of the texts mentioned above, though the information offered is often tantalizingly sparse. The central character in the story is, of course, Pytheas, whose name is recurrently linked to the tin trade between Britain and *Massalia* and the opening – or rather, re-opening, as they had been used in the Bronze Age and Early Iron Age – of direct routes to *Massalia*. Sailing from there *c.* 325 BC to find new supplies of tin after Carthage had established a monopoly of the Iberian sources, Pytheas explored new trade routes by-passing the Carthaginian-controlled Straits of Gibraltar. He reconnoitred western Armorica, identifying the *Ostimoi* (*Osismi*), cape *Kabaion* (Penmarc'h?) and the *Uxisama* (Ushant) archipelago, before proceeding to Britain and northern Europe. His expedition, or expeditions, the results of which were doubted by later geographers, may well have been successful in initiating a direct trade route from *Ictis* and/or the Armorican tin deposits to *Massalia*. Some archaeological evidence for these long-distance exchanges may be reflected in the gold stater, minted in Cyrene between 322 and 315 BC, found on the shore at Lampaul-Ploudalmézeau (F) and in the possible hoard of Massalian drachmas brought to light at Plouguerneau (F), though it must be admitted that such a trade was bound, owing to its very nature, to leave but few archaeological traces. It is still far from clear whether trading ships, after sailing round the western approaches of the *Osismi*, proceeded due south to the mouth of the Garonne, from which a relatively short overland route led across the Gaulish 'isthmus' to the *oppidum* of Montlaurès or, alternatively, veered to the south-east towards the mouth of the Loire and the harbour of *Corbilo(n)*, recorded by Polybius (*Historia*, XXXIV, 10, 6 under the year 134 BC). The former route, though only documented at the close of the Iron Age, was certainly used from the Bronze Age onwards, whereas the latter ran very close to the important tin deposits of the Vilaine valley and of northern Loire-Atlantique (Abbaretz, Nozay) before leading into central Gaul. It was equally frequented at a very early date, as may be inferred from the Late Bronze Age and Early Iron Age 'imports' found in Morbihan, Loire-Atlantique and Maine-et-Loire.

The existence of commercial and, no doubt, more complex contacts between Armorica and the trading ports of Mediterranean Gaul in the La Tène period cannot, therefore, be disputed as Ancient sources and, to a lesser extent, archaeological data fairly consistently document an intensification of traditional contacts from the fourth century onwards. But too much has probably been made of what is, all things considered, a mere scatter of finds. It must also be admitted that no contemporary trading post, rich in 'imported' artefacts, has yet been discovered on the Breton shores. It would thus be wholly wrong to fancy regular convoys of swarthy Mediterranean tin traders wending their way to the far reaches of north-western Europe according to some well-planned timetable. Early Mediterranean trade with Armorica and Britain must have remained largely erratic, depending on economic necessities and political circumstances, both local and external.

The latter played a major role in the recasting and intensification of traditional trade patterns in the later second century BC as, in the aftermath of the defeat of the *Saluvii* in 124 BC, the Roman province of Transalpine was established in southern Gaul. This typical colonial venture encouraged an influx of merchants and entrepreneurs, bent on exploiting the natural and commercial resources of the newly acquired territory, who soon infiltrated into *Gallia Comata* to further their trade with the northern Barbarians (*BG*, II, 15; IV, 2; VI, 24). Foremost among the merchants were certainly Italian *vinarii*, anxious to clear their surpluses of wine on the markets of Gaul, whose natives had a long-standing reputation for inebriety:

They are exceedingly fond of wine and sate themselves with the unmixed wine imported by merchants; their desire makes them drink it greedily and, when they become drunk, they fall into a stupor or into a maniacal disposition. (Diodorus Siculus, *Bibliotheca Historiae*, V, 26, 3)

They were even so foolish as to swap one of their slaves for an amphora of Italian wine. Italian entrepreneurs, given a monopoly on wine supply both by political support (Cicero, *Pro Fonteio*, 19–20) and by a decree of the Senate prohibiting wine-growing outside Italy (Cicero, *De republica*, III, 9, 16), were quick to seize the opportunity they had been given to revitalize trade with north-western Europe, made easier because the new province sat astride and controlled two major routes leading to that region – the Rhône valley and the Gaulish 'isthmus'. One may ascertain, from the large body of archaeological evidence derived from surface surveys and the underwater exploration of Ancient wrecks, that Italian wines, mass-produced on the large senatorial *fundi* of Etruria, Latium and Campania, were loaded in their characteristic containers (late 'Graeco-Italian' and Dressel 1 amphorae) onto ships sailing from the Tyrrhenian ports of *Cosa* (Ansedonia) or Ostia to *Arelate* (Arles) or *Narbo* (Narbonne). From there land and river routes took them to northern and eastern Gaul or to *Burdigala* (Bordeaux), where they were transshipped onto sea-going vessels. A few days' sailing would then be enough to take them north, to Armorica and Britain. The Dressel 1 A amphorae (the pre-conquest sub-type) found in western France have a wide geographical

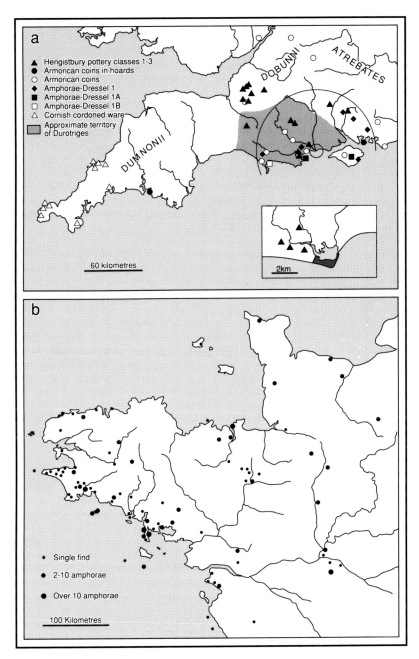

Figure 13 Distribution of Italian amphorae in southern Britain and
north-western France

distribution and, though clusters of finds in Quiberon, Quimper and Alet may point to the existence of trading ports, it is clear that most amphorae were then distributed to inland settlements such as Saint-Symphorien, Paule, by either the river or 'road' system, and to coastal sites by smaller craft. Sherds of these Late Iron Age (late second century–first century BC) containers have now been brought to light in such large numbers (over a hundred) and at such a wide variety of western Gaulish sites, from hill-forts to isolated farmsteads and from salt-producing sites to 'temples', that it must be recognized that Italian wines were popular commodities in a wide spectrum of communities and social groups.

The same cannot be said of the southern British tribes. Finds of Dressel 1 A amphorae are almost entirely confined to the ports of entry of central southern England – Barry Cunliffe's 'Wessex contact zone' – such as Hengistbury Head and Poole Harbour and their hinterland, while the small number of discoveries in Cornwall may hint at a secondary distribution pattern, emanating by coastal traffic from the central port at Hengistbury Head. Excavations on the latter site and at Green Island in Poole Harbour have, on the other hand, established the existence of an active, though probably transitory, short-haul traffic between Armorica and southern Britain. On both sites fairly large quantities of Late Iron Age Armorican pottery have been found in association with imported amphorae. This is actually given further substance by the distribution of Armorican coins (mostly silver staters minted by the *Coriosolitae*) in southern Britain. These are strongly concentrated at Hengistbury Head and Mount Batten, the obvious implication being that cross-Channel trade, continuing the long-distance traffic bringing wine and a few exotica such as the Ampurian *olpè* of Plouer-sur-Rance or the lumps of raw purple glass at Hengistbury Head, to the northern Barbarians, was controlled by Armorican shippers. With the obvious exception of wine, the precise nature of the cargoes they ferried back and forth is unfortunately beyond recovery.

The Armorican pottery vessels exported to Britain were probably used as containers for some unidentified commodity. Strabo lists grain, cattle, gold, silver and iron, together with hides, slaves and hunting dogs as the most famous British exports (*Geog.*, IV, 5, 2). The pattern thus seen emerging in the late second century and first century BC in north-western Europe is plainly that of a complex network of long- and short-haul traffic plying between southern Gaul and Armorica on the one hand, Armorica and southern Britain on the other. In the latter case, it connected communities closely bound in a nexus of linguistic, cultural and socio-economic systems. Though a few imports, such as the double pyramidal iron ingots found at Portland, and the development of the southern British decorated pottery groups collectively known as 'Glastonbury ware' certainly point to limited cultural contacts, possibly associated with the north-western tin trade, across the Channel in the Early and Middle La Tène periods, the emergence of this complex pattern must be firmly ascribed to the Roman conquest of southern Gaul and the ensuing economic and political changes it triggered off among the Armorican tribes. Political alliances between the latter and the peoples of Normandy and Belgic Gaul, well documented by both written and archaeological sources, must surely be seen as long-term effects of these central causes.

Against this intricate economic and political background, Caesar's famous statement:

Now of all the peoples of the coastal part of that area, the *Veneti* are by far the strongest. They have a great many ships and regularly sail to and from Britain. When it comes to knowledge and experience of navigation, they leave all other tribes standing. (*BG*, III, 8; trans S. A. Handforth, revised Jane F. Gardner, Penguin Classics, 1988)

supported as it is by Strabo's phrase:

The *Veneti* are those who fought at sea against Caesar, for they were prepared to hinder his voyage to Britain as they were using the emporion there (*Geog.*, IV, 4, 1)

looks very much like an over-simplification of realities, since it is far from being wholly borne out by archaeological evidence. Armorican coins and wares unearthed on British sites, minted or turned among the *Coriosolitae* or *Osismi*, point much more to the northern and western tribes of the peninsula, and to harbours such as Alet at the mouth of the Rance, than to the *Veneti* of southern Armorica. The latter may, however, have been the first peninsular tribe to mint gold staters in the late second century BC, demonstrating thereby their political sway in western Gaul. Though the discrepancy between documentary sources has often been explained away by a hypothetical control of the *Veneti* over their northern and western neighbours, the latter being used as middlemen in the transactions

with Britain, one cannot help feeling that such a simple answer is
not totally adequate and that, *in fine*, no satisfactory elucidation
will be reached until the detailed workings of the regional balance
of power and economics have been established.

Death and burial

Since the social and territorial organization of prehistoric societies
is generally extremely hard to disentangle in the absence of written
documents, archaeologists have commonly relied on the careful
examination of burial rites as a source of evidence. They assume
that status, wealth and cultural affiliation are reflected in the siting
and structure of the tomb and the nature and quality of grave-
goods. In this respect Armorican Iron Age graves, with their wide
range of tomb structures and overall paucity of grave-goods, offer
an interesting example for consideration.

Local Hallstattian tradition, still apparent in some parts of the
peninsula during the Early La Tène period (late fifth and fourth
centuries BC) in the continued use of Early Iron Age *sépultures
circulaires*, progressively weakened as new funerary rites were
introduced, pointing perhaps to more 'egalitarian' stances among
Armorican La Tène communities. Many of the age-old *champs de
tombelles* grew by accretion until the very end of the Iron Age; one
of the Kerangouarec, Arzano (F), *tombelles* overlay the sherds of a
Dressel 1 A amphora and some of the mounds at Les Grandes
Routes, Plaudren (M), even contained *tegula* fragments. However,
the most common burial structures of the Early and Middle La
Tène periods are flat, shallow, cremation graves where the ashes of
the dead were placed in stone cists and/or pottery urns. These are
found either in isolation as at Kélouër, Plouhinec and Saint-Pol-de-
Léon or, more generally, in small cemeteries of a few dozen graves.
The latter were sometimes ranged in neat parallel rows, for
instance at Kergonfalz, Bignan (M), or, more characteristically,
clustered around one or several stone stelae which may have served
as grave-markers for family groups.[7]

The gradual spread of cremation rites in the west did not,
however, entail a complete disappearance of inhumation among

---

[7] Kerancoat, Quimper; Pembrat-Vihan, Lannilis (F) etc.

the Armorican communities. Crouched inhumations in cists, fairly common in Late Bronze Age peninsular cultures, still occur sporadically in Early and Middle La Tène contexts at Kernavest, Quiberon (M) or Plougoulm (F), though by the end of the second century BC extended inhumation had become the norm. At Kerviltré, Saint-Jean-Trolimon (F) and Roz-an-Trémen, Plomeur (F), bodies were thus buried among, or next to, the older cinerary urns of the site, whereas at Locquirec, Plougasnou (F), Kerné, Quiberon (M), and elsewhere, graves were dug among the kitchen middens of nearby settlements. Such untidy inhumations were not uncommon in the late Celtic world.

One may, of course, argue that the number of Late Iron Age graves excavated in Brittany is so small that their characteristic features cannot possibly illustrate the whole range of local burial rites, especially since most inhumations, dissolved by acid soils, have been irretrievably lost. The fact remains, however, that both cremation and inhumation graves share idiosyncratic traits that cannot be ignored as mere epiphenomena. In a large majority of cases, for instance, the dead (almost certainly female) were provided with jewellery (brooches, armlets and anklets) either left on the body or placed in the cinerary urns, but with very few, if any, other grave-goods. Among this fairly undifferentiated material, probably pointing to the absence of any strongly hierarchical organization in Armorican communities, a few graves do stand out, however, owing more to their grave-goods than to the nature or size of the tombs. The most remarkable of these is certainly the Tronoën, Saint-Jean-Trolimon, inhumation grave, with a sword, spearheads, a few pots, a gold stater and smaller coins. Other lesser known examples at Guilguiffin, Landudec (F), Le Stanq, Plonéour-Lanvern (F) and Les Grandes Routes, Plaudren, also have notable grave-goods such as iron swords and shields, a bronze *simpulum* and decorated bronze fittings, while the presence of a broken wine amphora in the Kerangouarec, Arzano, *tombelle* and of miniature pots in one of the Les Grandes Routes mounds, probably testifies to the pouring of libations over the ashes of the dead.

Whether, because of the presence of weapons, these may be considered as the graves of local chieftains or of members of their retinue, is still far from clear. The range and 'wealth' of the grave-goods is notably inferior to anything found in comparable Continental and insular tombs. Furthermore, the structural variety of the 'richer' graves of Late Iron Age Armorica (inhumations, cremations under *tombelles*, etc.) does not appear to support the hypothesis of common cultural traditions. On the contrary, this small group, together with the whole body of 'poorer' graves, testifies to the existence of highly differentiated funerary rites among communities, and to the permanence of strong local and even family traditions in western Gaul during the Iron Age.

Gods and sanctuaries

The well-known 'local and anarchical' character of Celtic mythology and ritual, reflecting the decentralized structure of Celtic society, is unfortunately very poorly documented by contemporary plastic representations of myths and divinities. Armorican coins of the second and first centuries BC certainly depict religious subjects, such as the naked rider-goddess brandishing a spear and a shield to be seen on some of the staters of the *Riedones* (BN 6756). But the latter are both too allusive and elusive for any simple, straightforward explanation. Cult statues are, on the other hand, extremely rare, partly because wooden sculptures certainly formed a large part of Iron Age religious statuary. Consequently, such examples as do exist raise difficult interpretive problems. It has been suggested that the remarkable stone statuette (0.42 m high) recently discovered in a late second-century BC context at Saint-Symphorien, Paule, represents the Celtic god *Maponus* – the 'divine youth' – also worshipped in Roman Britain and Gaul, and at least once equated with Apollo *Citharoedus*. Most of these statues will have stood in small shrines located on or near consecrated sites like springs and marshes as at Pennanguer, Plonéis (F), and L'Alnay, Fay-de-Bretagne (L-A), or in sacred groves (*nemetoi*); the Forêt de Nevet, Kerlaz (F), is probably a former *nemeton*. Others will have decorated more elaborate sanctuaries of *Viereckschanze* or Gournay-sur-Aronde type, where wooden temples stood among sacred precincts enclosed by more or less complex bank-and-ditch systems like those at Sermon, Mordelles (I-et-V), and Trogouzel, Douarnenez (F). The votive offerings commonly found buried in the *temenoi* or ditches of these sanctuaries include a wide range of artefacts, often ritually 'killed' (coins, brooches, items of military equipment). Most of these never turn up among the site finds of civilian settlements and may be assumed to have been highly valued by Iron Age communities.

Cultural and political identity

Some of these cults, relating to animate or inanimate Nature, probably have their roots deep in the pre-Iron Age past. But it is clear that, on the whole, Armorican Late Iron Age mythology and rites have much in common with those of other 'Celtic' areas, such as northern Gaul and southern Britain. Cultural affinities and similarities within the western 'Celtic' world were indeed quite strong and were given increased cohesion by the use of a common language or closely related dialects. That the Late Iron Age Armorican communities actually spoke Celtic is beyond any doubt, as tribal names, anthroponyms, place-names and hydronyms unquestionably derive from Gaulish roots.[8] When and how the Celtic language in the west emerged is very much a matter of debate. It has recently been suggested that Celtic dialects originated, by a process of differentiation and crystallization, from an earlier Indo-European language which had spread to most of western Europe in the second millennium BC, or even as early as 4000 BC with the coming of farming.[9] Traces of this very early pre-Celtic linguistic layer may indeed be seen in a number of river-names (Oust, Oudon, Ille, Isac, Odet) and probably in the name of the *Veneti*.

Though still fragile, the evolutionary or processual theory, eliminating the need to explain the emergence of Celtic by either mass or elite migrations to western Europe, has the advantage of reconciling linguistic and archaeological evidence. Skeletal material from Brittany, Normandy and the Paris basin indeed shares so many common characteristics from the Neolithic to the ninth century AD that nothing substantiates a migration of Celtic-speaking communities to Armorica in the last millennium BC. Linguistic developments in Armorica, documented *c.* 325 BC by

---

[8] Tribal names: *Osismi, Coriosolitae, Riedones, Namnetes*; anthroponyms: *Agedo-virus, Argiotalus, Durneo, Meticca*, etc.; place-names: *Aregenua, Gabaion, Condate, Darioritum, Uxisama, Vorgium*, etc.; hydronyms: *Vicinonia*, Aulne, Aven, etc.

[9] C. Renfrew, *Archaeology and Language. The Puzzle of Indo-European Origins*, London, 1987.

Pytheas' exploration, should therefore certainly be regarded as a largely local phenomenon, the earlier proto-Celtic spoken in the west evolving into Celtic among long-established groups by a long process of cultural transformation. Similarly, most of the artistic and spiritual changes which characterize the Armorican Late Iron Age may be related to the effects of 'cumulative Celticity', combining internal social mutations with cultural interchange, and not to any large-scale population movement.

The political structure of Armorican tribes, difficult to recreate from archaeological evidence and insufficiently illuminated by allusions in Caesar's *De Bello Gallico*, offers another example of mutation within an otherwise apparently stable framework. Armorican Iron Age communities were basically agrarian, the 'agricultural produce, raw materials and finished goods produced . . . both by free peasants and by dependent labour [being] the principal basis of social wealth' (D. Nash).[10] The material surplus thus generated, partly appropriated by the nobility through dues and taxes, was transformed into more valuable forms of wealth through trade with both stronger (core) and weaker (peripheral) societies. In the early phases of their development such communities were undoubtedly ruled by fiercely competitive patricians reigning over a heavily exploited producing population of agricultural labourers and craftsmen with the assistance of skilled warriors recruited from the richest strata of the peasantry whose number necessarily remained small because military commitment would encroach upon productive concerns. Though some form of shared ethnic identity may have been acknowledged, it is very unlikely that before the second century BC tribes had yet formed into unified political units with centralized overlordships. Their territories must have been fragmented into a large number of petty chiefdoms.

The appearance of tribal coinages in the west, at some time during the second century BC, should therefore be regarded as a sign of major political changes. Though their exact dating and order of succession are still a matter of dispute among numismatists, it is clear that the striking of individualized series of high-value gold coins by the *Veneti*, *Riedones* and *Namnetes* reflects the emergence of tribal kingdoms or of oligarchic states, with noble

---

[10] D. Nash, 'The basis of contact between Britain and Gaul in the Late Pre-Roman Iron Age', *Cross-Channel Trade between Gaul and Britain in the Pre-Roman Iron Age*, ed. S. McReady and F. H. Thompson (London, 1984), p. 97.

Plate 13 Armorican coinage: (a) *Coriosolitae* (Class VI stater)

over

Plate 13(b) *Namnetes* (stater)

families singly or collectively ruling integrated territories. Additional evidence of this may be found in Caesar's allusions to the senates of the *Veneti*, *Aulerci Eburovices* and *Lexovii* (*BG*, III, 16–17). This may suggest the existence of constitutions modelled on that of Marseille (Strabo, *Geog.*, IV, 1, 5), with elected magistrates holding office for a limited term. Only the *Osismi* may perhaps be excepted from these developments because their coinage shows a variety of types with an unclear geographical distribution, which must have been struck for a number of pettty chiefs or minor kings. Equally the *Coriosolitae* had no tribal mint before 90–80 BC and may, for a time, have been vassals of the *Veneti* who possibly controlled the trans-peninsular trade route between the mouths of the Vilaine and Rance (above pp. 58–60).

Armorican coinages are, on the whole, confined to relatively well-defined territories within which they were certainly used in a continuous cycle of official payments (to noble retainers or to warriors) and taxation. As they seldom strayed away from their territory of origin (with the exception of late Coriosolite silver issues), it is very unlikely that such prestige coins were ever used for long-distance commercial exchanges, or even for the recruitment of foreign warriors. The gradual debasement of both gold and silver issues in the course of the first century BC, when gold and silver were alloyed with increasing amounts of bronze, together with a sharp rise in the number of coins minted may, therefore, be the

Plate 13(c) *Osismi* (stater)

Plate 13(d) *Riedones* (stater)

Plate 13(e) *Veneti* (stater)

result of the emergence of a real market economy needing large quantities of low-value issues for its daily transactions.

Trade with southern Britain, *Aquitania* and, to a lesser extent, Belgic Gaul, carried out through permanent specialized trading ports such as Alet, was also undoubtedly another key factor in Armorican Late Iron Age political developments. It strengthened traditional alliances with the communities of south-western Britain and the Belgic tribes of northern Gaul to whom the Armoricans turned for help during the rebellions of 56 BC (*BG*, III, 9). It probably also contributed to the emergence of a 'bourgeoisie' which, strongly antagonistic to the traditional aristocracy, favoured trade and contacts with Rome and the newly formed *Provincia* (roughly equivalent to modern Provence).

The Roman conquest

The conquest of southern Gaul, between 125 and 117 BC, opened the gates of northern Europe to the Roman Republic and initiated a process which was bound, sooner or later, to engulf the whole of *Gallia Comata*. It is clear, however, that Rome had at first no intention of conquering northern Gaul, as the Roman Senate was content with maintaining order in the newly conquered province and averting any threat of invasion. The *Aedui*, even though they had been declared 'Brothers and kinsmen of the Roman people' (*BG*, I, 33), were thus refused Roman help against the *Sequani* and the Germans. But the temptation was strong for the conquering power to enlarge its defensive glacis, all the more so as the equestrian order in Italy was itching for new economic ventures and urging expansion. It comes therefore as no surprise that Julius Caesar should have taken the initiative of intervening in the internal affairs of *Gallia Comata* as soon as he became governor of Cisalpine and Transalpine Gaul in 58 BC. Though largely motivated by ambition and greed (Suetonius, *Caesar*, 54), he found a plausible reason for his intervention in the migration of the *Helvetii*, who had decided to leave their ancestral lands and settle in south-western Gaul (*BG*, I, 2–6). After they had obeyed his strict orders to avoid the territory of the *Provincia*, Caesar attacked them in the Rhône valley, slaughtering a large number of them and forcing the others to retreat (*BG*, I, 7–29). This facile victory certainly helped Caesar present himself as champion of Gallic freedom and independence and encouraged the Gallic council to entreat him to engage the Germans of Ariovistus, who had settled on Sequanian territory and were threatening the *Aedui* (*BG*, I, 31). The ensuing victory over the Germans in the summer of 58 BC (*BG*, I, 33–54), drawing the legions further north, offered Caesar the opportunity of conquering the whole of northern Gaul in one operation. He quickly seized it in the spring of 57 BC when he marched his legions against the Belgic confederation and the Armorican tribes (*BG*, II, *passim*).

The campaign against the *Belgae* was long and difficult, whereas the conquest of the Armorican tribes by Publius Crassus appears to have been a mere walkover, since Caesar mentioned no battle in the final communiqué:

About the same time Caesar was informed by Publius Crassus, whom he had sent with one legion against the *Veneti* and the other tribes on the Atlantic seaboard – the *Venelli, Osismi, Coriosolites, Esuvii, Aulerci* and *Riedones* – that all these had been subjected to Roman rule. (*BG*, II, 34).

According to military tradition, hostages were taken from among the conquered tribes and Publius Crassus left to winter his troops on the territory of the *Andecavi* (around Angers), leaving no garrison behind him.

The campaign of 57 BC against the Armoricans may arguably be ascribed to military strategy, to the necessity of cutting off the rebellious *Belgae* from their Armorican allies and of rounding out the conquest of Gaul. But one cannot help thinking that Julius Caesar also had a future invasion of Britain in mind, which would isolate the Continental *Belgae* from their insular supporters and give the Romans sway over a major trading system between Britain and Gaul, hitherto under Armorican control (*BG*, III, 8; Strabo, *Geog.*, IV, 4, 1). The reconnaissance of the Scillies by Publius Crassus (Strabo, *Geog.*, III, 5, 11) confirmed the misgivings of Armorican entrepreneurs, who feared they would lose their highly profitable trade to the Romans. They had perhaps also learnt about the decline of Marseille. Such events prompted them to encourage their fellow citizens to revolt against Roman rule.

The opportunity was soon found as in the early spring of 56 BC the Roman army began requisitioning grain and food on the territories of the *Esuvii, Coriosolitae* and *Veneti* (*BG*, III, 7). The

Roman envoys were detained and the restitution of the Armorican hostages demanded from Publius Crassus. This being refused, the *Veneti, Coriosolitae* and *Esuvii*

secured the alliance of various tribes in the neighbourhood (the *Osismi, Lexovii, Namnetes, Ambiliati* and *Diablintes*) and of the *Morini* and *Menapii*, and summoned reinforcements from Britain, which faces that part of Gaul. (*BG*, III, 9).

Since this vast coalition of maritime tribes threatened to disrupt Roman control of the whole protectorate, a massive military intervention was necessary. As Caesar was held up in Italy, he ordered his lieutenants to have warships built on the Loire and to enlist crews and pilots. Meanwhile, the allies had gathered a large fleet of 220 ships in Venetic waters and were busy reinforcing their strongholds and preparing for long sieges (*BG*, III, 9).

Events accelerated on the arrival of Caesar in Gaul in the late spring of 56 BC. As he feared the revolt would spread to the other Belgic tribes and to *Aquitania*, the proconsul despatched Labienus towards the *Treveri* and Publius Crassus to the south of the Loire, while he led the main body of the army towards western Gaul. As soon as he entered Armorica from the south, Caesar sent Sabinus with three legions against the *Unelli, Coriosolitae* and *Lexovii*, gave Decimus Brutus the command of the Roman fleet with orders to sail as soon as possible, and marched towards the territory of the *Veneti* with the rest of the army (*BG*, III, 10–11).

The first phase of the land operations did not prove a success because

Most of the *Veneti*'s strongholds were so situated on the end of spits or headlands that it was impossible to approach them by land when the tide rushed in from the open sea, which happens regularly every twelve hours; and they were also difficult to reach by sea, because at low tide the ships would run aground on the shoals. For these reasons, the strongholds were hard to attack. Sometimes the Romans made them untenable by building huge dykes, which both kept the sea away and enabled the besiegers to get on a level with the top of the walls; but as soon as the defenders saw that their position was hopeless, they would bring up ships, of which they had an unlimited supply, transfer all their property onto them, and retire to neighbouring strongholds equally well situated for defence. They found it easy to pursue these tactics during most of the summer, because our ships were weather-bound and sailing was very hazardous in that vast, open sea, where the tides were high and harbours almost non-existent. (*BG*, III, 12)

In fact, the decisive engagement was fought out at sea, probably in the Bay of Quiberon, the account given by Caesar of the resounding defeat suffered by the allies being one of the best-known documents of Breton history:

After taking several strongholds, Caesar saw that all his labour was being wasted; capturing their strongholds did not prevent the enemy from escaping, and he was not in a position to cripple them. He decided, therefore, that he must wait for his fleet to be assembled and brought up. Directly it hove into sight, some two hundred and twenty enemy ships, perfectly equipped and ready for immediate action, sailed out of harbour and took up stations facing it. Neither its commander Brutus nor the military tribunes and centurions in charge of the individual ships could decide what to do or what tactics to adopt. They knew that no injury could be inflicted on the enemy by ramming, and when they tried erecting turrets they found that they were still overtopped by the foreigners' lofty sterns and were too low to make their missiles carry properly, while the enemy's fell with great force. One device, however, that our men had prepared proved useful – pointed hooks fixed into the ends of long poles, not unlike the grappling-hooks used in sieges. With these the halyards were grasped and pulled taut, and then snapped by rowing hard away. This of course brought the yards down, and since the Gallic ships depended wholly on their sails and rigging, when stripped of these they were at once immobilized. After that it was a soldier's battle, in which the Romans proved superior especially as it was fought under the eyes of Caesar and the whole army, so that any act of special bravery was bound to be noticed; all the cliffs and hills that commanded a near view of the sea were occupied by the troops.

When the yards of an enemy ship were torn down in the manner described, two or three of ours would get alongside and the soldiers would make vigorous efforts to board it. When the natives saw what was happening, and after the loss of several ships could still find no answer to these tactics, they tried to escape by flight. They had already put their ships before the wind when suddenly such a dead calm fell that they could not stir. Nothing could have been more fortunate for us. It enabled us to complete the victory by pursuing and capturing the vessels one after another, and only a very few managed to make land when night came on after a battle that lasted from about ten o'clock in the morning until sunset.

This victory ended the war with the *Veneti* and all the other maritime tribes, for besides assembling all their men of military age, and indeed all the older men of any standing or reputation for good judgement, they had also concentrated every one of their ships; and now that all these were

lost, the survivors had no refuge left and no means of defending their
strongholds, so they surrendered themselves and all their possessions to
Caesar. He resolved to make an example of them in order to teach the
natives to be more careful in future about respecting the rights of
ambassadors; he had all their councillors executed and the rest of the
population sold as slaves. (*BG*, III, 14–16)

Meanwhile, on the northern front, the three legions of Sabinus,
encamped in the Avranches area, had to face 'a host of desperadoes
and bandits, to whom the prospect of fighting and plunder was
more attractive than farming and regular work' (*BG*, III, 17), led
by the *Unelli* chief Viridorix. The two armies joined battle near the
Petit-Celland *oppidum* and the Armorican allies were once again
routed. What was left of their host fled towards the north of the
Cotentin and the Channel Isles.

The western half of the Gallic confederation having thus been
defeated and subjected, Caesar tried to engage the *Morini* and
Menapii of northern Gaul who, alone among the Gallic tribes, kept
up the spirit of rebellion against Rome. His expedition came to
nothing and after withdrawing his troops, Caesar quartered them
among the apparently pacified Armoricans (*BG*, III, 28–9).

The resounding defeats they had suffered had not, however,
annihilated all spirit of resistance to annexation among the western
Gaulish communities. Thus, as early as 54 BC, encouraged by the
revolt of the *Eburones* and the news of the destruction of Sabinus'
army (*BG*, V, 24–37), the Armoricans marched against L. Roscius'
thirteenth legion, then wintering among the *Esuvii*, and only
retreated on hearing of Caesar's victory over the *Nervii* (*BG*, V,
53). In 52 BC Coriosolite, Osismian, Riedone and Venetic
contingents joined the vast army sent to help Vercingetorix loosen
Caesar's grip on the besieged stronghold of Alesia (*BG*, VII, 75).
Though they were once again defeated, the Armoricans did not
hesitate in 51 BC to rise up in arms against Roman rule (*BG*, VIII,
24) and to side with Dumnacos, leader of the *Andecavi*, against the
pro-Roman party of Duratius, king of the *Pictones* (*BG*, VIII, 26).
This new uprising concluded with yet another disaster as the rebels
were routed by the legions of C. Fabius (*BG*, VIII, 31) and forced
to give hostages. It is quite likely that this ultimate fiasco proved
too much for the communities of western Gaul, who eventually
settled for an uneasy peace and a sullen acceptance of the destiny
imposed on them.

4

Roman Armorica: Aspects of Colonization

It would be quite wrong to assume, on the strength of Caesar's testimony, that Armorica had suffered irreparable damage during the years of the Gallic wars, that its countryside and townships had been laid waste and its population slaughtered. On the contrary, the numerous archaeological remains of the Roman period known in the peninsula witness to the permanence of human occupation and to a considerable economic and cultural growth in the first four centuries AD.

The early period of Romanization

In the years that followed the Gaulish defeat at Alesia, the country does not seem to have been agitated by any renewed political or military turmoil. This apparent calm may, of course, be seen as the legacy of the long years of war which, according to Plutarch (*Caesar*, XV, 2–3), had cost the tribes of *Gallia Comata* more than two million people, either killed on the battlefield or taken into slavery, but also as a direct consequence of a deliberate policy of appeasement. It is indeed extremely likely that Caesar, much preoccupied with the approaching end of his proconsular functions, as well as with the unavoidable power struggle awaiting him in Italy, should have wanted to end a war which nothing could apparently conclude. When he departed for Italy in December 50 BC, Caesar left a fairly peaceful country behind him, protected by the legions stationed along the Rhine.

Furthermore, the annual levy of a military contingent in the new protectorate allowed the Gauls to gratify their taste for combat and strife. It channelled the energies of the local hotheads, all too ready to foster disturbances or foment sedition. Renewing the old Mediterranean tradition of recruiting mercenaries among the Celts, Caesar built up a new legion, named *Alauda* (skylark), entirely manned by Gauls, who were subsequently granted Roman citizenship and many of whom became relatively wealthy in the troubled years of the Civil War. The best of these men, distinguished and promoted by the dictator, often took the same *nomen* and *praenomen* as Caesar and founded the Gaulish 'aristocracy' of the *Iulii*, linked to the Julio-Claudian dynasty by strong bonds of friendship and gratitude.

As a clever politician, Caesar knew how to ingratiate himself with the Gaulish upper classes and how to exploit the evident rivalries in Gaulish society, by upholding here the 'feudal' clans and there the 'modernistic' factions like the pro-Roman senates of the *Lexovii*, in the Lisieux area, or of the *Aulerci Eburovices* around Evreux, for instance, exploiting with consummate skill the age-old feuds between clans and tribes. The extent of his success reveals the deep social and political divisions of the Gauls.

We are very poorly informed about the years intervening between the defeat of the Armorican allies and the early years of Augustus' reign (i.e. the last decades of the first century BC). There is, however, no reason to think that the Armorican tribes were treated more harshly than their neighbours, or that their territorial limits suffered much change, though the *Namnetes* apparently lost their lands lying south of the Loire to the pro-Roman *Pictones*. Very small bronze coins of Gaulish style, less than 1 cm in diameter, minted on the territory of the *Veneti* (in the Brech (M) hoard, for instance) or in the vicinity of Morlaix (F) during those years point to the permanence of some form of native rule or authority. Its nature and structure are, of course, largely unknown to us. Such small cash clearly made up for the lack of proper Roman currency. As it would only be used in small everyday transactions, it provides very few clues as to the state of the local economy before the end of the century. The sharp decline in the number of imported wine amphorae (Dressel 1 B of Italian origin) in the peninsula as well as the hoarding of Roman silver *denarii* in the years 30–20 BC such as those discovered at Guingamp and Plestin-lès-Grèves (C-d'A), Locronan and Plouguerneau (F) and

Guer (M) may, however, testify to some kind of economic slump generated by the shift towards the Rhône–Rhine axis of the old trade route between the Mediterranean and Britain. This was, perhaps, aggravated by unrestrained exploitation of the economic and financial resources of Gaul by Roman 'carpetbaggers'.

It comes as no surprise that Gaul should have been restless under various popular movements between the early forties and the last visit of Augustus to the new province in 8 BC. One may indeed appreciate the intensity of provincial resentment towards Rome in the defacement of the imperial effigy on *all* the Roman coins – *asses* of Augustus – of the Port-Haliguen, Quiberon, hoard, dated to that same year. Only such a strong-willed and talented emperor as Augustus could ease these social tensions by applying himself to the task of integrating Gaul into the Roman Empire. This entailed, among other things, laying down a coherent and efficient administrative framework (the three provinces of *Aquitania*, *Lugdunensis* and *Belgica* were created in 27 BC). Secondly, a comprehensive road system was developed, the first elements of which were built or refurbished from older trackways during Agrippa's first governorship of Gaul, *c.* 39–37 BC (Strabo, *Geog.*, IV, 6, 11). Lastly, the leading citizens of the sixty Gaulish *civitates* were granted the real, if strictly controlled, opportunity of expressing themselves and of giving vent to their grievances against the provincial administration at their annual meeting and festival in the first days of August held near the large marble altar dedicated to Rome and Augustus, overlooking the confluence of the rivers Rhône and Saône at *Condate*.

This policy of acculturation and integration of the local aristocracies, so well exemplified in Britain less than a century later by Tacitus' father-in-law Agricola, also rested to a large extent on the development of urban centres. Some were expanded from native settlements, others were created *ex nihilo*; both were used as showcases for Romanity and as administrative and economic focal points for the surrounding *civitas*. Many of them were granted a title reflecting the patronage of the imperial house, like *Iuliomagus Andecavorum*, Angers, for example.

Though no Armorican town was given this honour, all *civitas*-capitals – Rennes, Corseul (C-d'A), Carhaix (F), Vannes (M) and Nantes – as well as some lesser townships like Quimper have provided evidence of a regular street-grid (Rennes) or of large public buildings (Carhaix, Quimper). These suggest a determined, systematic policy of urbanization and Romanization, put to work in carefully chosen 'tribal' centres, even when native traditions endured in the rural world and in most small towns. The policy, apparently carried out with some diplomacy under Augustus, was vitiated in the early years of Tiberius' reign by such clumsy and oppressive measures as the suppression of druidism and the revocation of the tax-exempt status accorded to the most important *civitates*. This clearly hurt feelings and ran counter to the interests not only of the most archaic and conservative elements in Gaulish society, but of the most important citizens. Soon they were bitterly complaining about 'endless taxation, crushing rates of interest and the brutality and arrogance of governors' (Tacitus, *Annals*, III, xl).

In AD 21 general unrest swelled to outright rebellion, principally inspired by two Gallic noblemen, *Iulius Sacrovir* and *Iulius Florus*. Although they tried to stir up insurrection among the Gaulish *civitates*, Tacitus' account leaves us in no doubt as to the ultimate failure of their attempt, as the two ringleaders were routed by the legions and committed suicide. Both literary and archaeological sources show, however, that many *civitates* of northern Gaul were affected by the uprising and the subsequent retribution. The destruction both of public buildings at Quimper and Carhaix and of a large native settlement at Alet apparently demonstrates the spread of revolt to westernmost Gaul. The events of AD 21 were thus undoubtedly extensive and serious, but there is no sign that they impaired in any way the developing Romanization and growing material prosperity of the Three Gauls.

The administrative structure

At the time of Caesar's conquest, Gaul had no central government that could have united Gallic resistance to military aggression, and though some large communities like the *Averni* and the *Aedui*, in particular, controlled smaller peoples, most of its numerous tribes formed independent units, which would only join forces in time of imminent military danger. The imperial administration was careful not to modify this structure which, by dividing the Gaulish ruling class into rival groups, prevented any inopportune concentration of power. *Gallia Comata* was divided, for administrative convenience, into three roughly equal districts (*Aquitania, Belgica* and *Lugdunensis*), placed under the emperor's direct control. There is every reason to believe that the Gaulish *civitates* of the High Empire, though they lacked political independence, did not suffer much in their everyday life from the burden of central authority. Rather they enjoyed a high degree of autonomy, the provincial administration being commissioned only to settle disputes between communities, to supervise compilation of the census, to register properties, and to ascertain that local budgets were properly balanced. If there was need, it could appoint a *curator rei publicae*, entrusted with the audit and restoration of public finances, such as Caius Decimus Sabianus of the *Senones*, charged with the examination of the budget of the *Veneti* in the early third century AD (*CIL*, XIII, 2950).

In western *Lugdunensis*, as throughout Gaul, the *civitates*, originating from the old Gaulish tribes within the same territorial limits, constituted the basic political and administrative units. It comes as no surprise therefore that some local patriotism should have survived the conquest. Thus the epitaph of Saturninus Macarius, who died at Dompierre-les-Eglises (Haute-Vienne), tells us that the deceased belonged to the 'nation of the *Namnetes*', and the tombstone put up for Donata by her husband in Bordeaux records that he was a *civis Coriosolis* (*CIL*, XIII, 616). Besides, the very size of most *civitates* meant that they had to be subdivided into smaller units, called *pagi* (such as the *pagus Matans*, the *pagus Sextanmanduus*, the *pagus Carnutenus*, in the territory of the *Riedones*), protected by their tutelary divinities (*Mars Mullo* and *Mercurius Atepomarus* for the *pagus Matans*), administered by *magistri pagi*, perhaps operating from the *vici* (townships), and probably organized in some kind of federal structure. Many of these tribal subdivisions, reflecting the continuing strength of a local identity within the larger communities, have given birth to our modern *pays*. The name of Corps-Nuds (I-et-V), a village to the south of Rennes, has thus been shown to derive from that of the long-vanished *pagus Carnutenus*.

The five Armorican *civitates* of the *Riedones, Coriosolitae, Osismi, Veneti* and *Namnetes*, though placed in the less 'privileged' category of the *civitates stipendariae* or 'tributary states', were probably administered, in imitation of Roman municipal forms, by assemblies of leading citizens. That of the *Riedones* was called

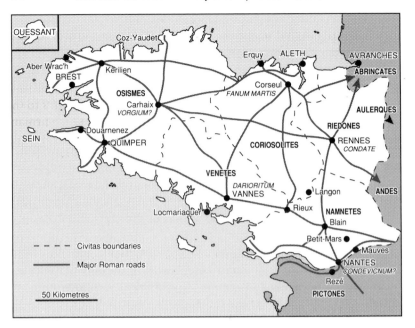

Figure 14   The Armorican civitates *and road network*

senatus in AD 135 and *ordo* in AD 238. They met to discuss community affairs in the senate house (*curia*) of the *civitas*-capital. Such elected *decuriones* had to see to the financial and administrative business of the *civitas*, manage municipal finances and distribute taxes amongst the citizens. Executive magistrates, generally elected for one year by the Senate from among its members, held the top local offices and were entrusted with the executive charge of the *civitas*, administration of justice, maintenance of law and order and the collection of taxes. These offices were often organized in a series of three ranks (quaestorship, aedileship, duumvirate), that local senators could hold successively in a fairly common *cursus honorum*.

Several inscribed statue bases, discovered in Rennes in 1968, provide much information as to the career of Titus Flavius Postuminus, a member of the *senatus* of the *Riedones*, a priest of the official cult of Rome and Augustus and a perpetual *flamen* of *Mars Mullo*, who had 'held all official charges in his native land'

and had been honoured twice with the title and charge of *duumvir*. We have here a very important member of the local aristocracy, one of the fortunate and powerful Gauls who achieved full integration into the Roman world and had been granted Roman citizenship (in this case in the late first century AD). From such people were recruited the representatives sent by the *civitates* to the *Concilium Galliarum*, and the *sacerdos* (priest and chairman) elected annually among its members.

The high offices held at some time in the *Concilium* by two members of Armorican *civitates* (the *Veneti* and *Coriosolitae*) – Lucius Tauricius Florens, the chairman (*patronus*) of the corporation of *nautae* (boatmen and traders) of the rivers Saône and Loire, became the chief treasurer of the council (*allector arkae galliarum*) and [. . .] Lucanus Canius, the *patronus* of the *nautae* of the Confluence, the *sacerdos* of the Gallic council – are thus most interesting clues as to the Romanization of the peninsular elites and hint, beyond this, at the full integration of the communication and trading system of the Three Gauls.

The road system

Most Breton (or French) *communes* boast of possessing at least a short section of a 'Roman road' on their territory. These are often associated in collective memory with great figures of a bygone or mythical past like Charlemagne or Princess Ahès. Though many rural tracks have thus been exalted above their true nature, archaeological research has shown beyond doubt that, in spite of the small number of routes mentioned by the Peutinger Table or the Antonine Itinerary (*Itinerarium Antonii Augusti*), the Armorican peninsula was densely covered by a complex network of Roman roads and ways.

The layout of the system was largely determined by the geological structure of the peninsula, in which coastal plateaux and Hercynian upfolds, running roughly from east to west and separated by a fractured depression (the 'fosse armoricaine'), alternate from north to south. Three major roads, connected to the networks of *Aquitania*, central and northern *Lugdunensis*, and heading from east to west, may thus be found running lengthwise across the central depression and along the coastal plateaux, some distance away from the long tidal estuaries – rias – indenting the coastlines of the Channel and the Atlantic Ocean:

- a northern route, linking *Suindinum* (Le Mans) to the northern extremity of Finistère, running through Jublains (Mayenne), Corseul, Saint-Brieuc, Guingamp, Morlaix and Kérilien-en-Plounéventer (F)
- a central trunk road, connecting *Suindinum* and *Vorgium* (Carhaix, F) through Rennes, Loudéac, Mûr-de-Bretagne and Rostrenen (C-d'A), and perhaps running on as far as Camaret (F) on the Crozon peninsula
- a southern route, connecting with the major road heading for *Lugdunum* (Lyon) through Poitiers, and running from *Condevicnum* (Nantes) to Quimper, through *Darioritum* (Vannes), Hennebont and Quimperlé.

Such major axial routes were, however, supplemented by a dense network of minor roads, characteristically radiating from the *civitas*-capitals towards all parts of the tribal territories. More than twelve roads, leading to Corseul, Tréguier, Lannion, Morlaix, Kérilien, Landerneau, Châteaulin, Douarnenez, Quimper, Quimperlé, Hennebont, Vannes and Rennes thus diverge from *Vorgium* to serve the whole *civitas*, while smaller townships, such as Quimper or Morlaix, played a similar role on a local scale. This well-integrated system was, moreover, completed by trans-peninsular routes such as those from Corseul to Vannes or to Quimper.

Contrary to popular opinion, Roman roads hardly ever run in a perfectly straight line. The slight or major changes in the direction of their courses, fairly common in the Breton peneplain, are generally accounted for by the need to avoid steep slopes or marshy valley bottoms. Most rivers were apparently forded, since not a single bridge of Roman date has yet been identified in western France. Travellers, as they crossed the stream, usually threw a coin into it to propitiate the water divinity: 30,000 Roman coins, from Augustus to Valentinian II (AD 375–92), have been discovered in the river Vilaine at Rennes.

Since fords were places where traffic had to slow down or even stop when the rivers were swollen with rain or when the tide was running, *tabernae*, wine shops and various stalls generally clustered near river-crossings, often to develop into small townships. Many Breton towns like Morlaix, Landerneau, Quimperlé or Visseiche

(*Vicus Sipiae* on the river *Sipia*, I-et-V) indeed owe their birth in the Roman period to their situation as first fording sites across rivers or tidal estuaries.

The Roman roads of the peninsula, including their shoulders and ditches, were commonly between 5 and 8 m wide (10 m at La Louzais in Langon, I-et-V). They sometimes used the natural surface with hardly any preparation; more commonly they are constituted of layers of locally available materials, piled up so as to form a resilient structure. Quite easy to build and repair, they were obviously meant for light traffic with vehicles weighing less than half a ton.

Few of the stone (and perhaps wooden) milliary columns that once stood every mile (1480 m) or *leuga* along the Roman roads of Armorica have actually survived weathering, defacement or total destruction. But the survivors are an invaluable source of information as to the structure, layout and maintenance of the regional road system. This may have developed from Iron Age trackways but major developments occurred from as early as the reign of Augustus and continued during the first century AD as milestones of Claudius (AD 45–6) at Kerscao, Kernilis (F), and of one of the Flavian emperors at Mespaul (F) show. Milestones of Postumus at Rennes, of Victorinus at Saint-Méloir (C-d'A), Surzur (M), Nantes and Rennes, and of Tetricus at Saint-Gondran (I-et-V), Nantes and Caro (M) suggest that the system was kept in good repair down to the economic collapse of the late fourth century. Medieval peasants, tradesmen and pilgrims still used it many centuries later, before new roads, geared to the defence of the province, were laid out by the duc d'Aiguillon in the eighteenth century.

As they provided easy and regular connections between the countryside and the towns, the areas where raw materials were produced and those where the latter were transformed and consumed, the roads of Roman Armorica were an essential element in an integrated economic system. By allowing new fashions, tastes and techniques to penetrate the westernmost *civitates* of Gaul, they contributed greatly to the Romanization of the peninsula. The role they played in the spread of Breton during the Middle Ages and early modern period is indeed a further indication of their major importance as axes of dissemination of a new culture (cf. below p. 146).

Towns and urbanization

Towns are undoubtedly the best symbols of the emergence of a new order in the west. Though in the Late Iron Age the western tribes had developed a few 'urban' nuclei like Alet, coherent and rational urban planning only emerged under Roman influence some time after the conquest. Townships that had come into existence in Late Iron Age Armorica, as long-distance trade produced major changes in its socio-economic structures, expanded during the Roman period. But recent archaeological work has shown that while some were chosen to become *civitas*-capitals or the chief towns of *pagi*, most urban centres remained small.

The *civitas*-capitals of the *Riedones* (*Condate*, Rennes), *Coriosolitae* (*Fanum Martis*, Corseul), *Osismi* (*Vorgium*, Carhaix), *Veneti* (*Darioritum*, Vannes), *Namnetes* (*Condevicnum*, Nantes) were probably all laid out early in the first century AD, on a regular street-plan, based on the intersection of two major axial routes (the *kardo* and *decumanus*), and secondary streets branching off at right-angles to form a 'chequerboard' pattern of blocks (*insulae*) occupied by private and public buildings or left undeveloped. The difficulties of excavating the built-up areas of Breton towns account for our very patchy knowledge of the internal organization of Armorican *civitas*-capitals. Though some inscriptions found at Rennes and Nantes provide limited information about the buildings included in their *forum*-complexes (*basilica* and probably temple of *Mars Mullo* in Rennes, *tribunal*, temple and vaulted *portico* at Nantes), none of these central spaces, generally located at the crossing of the *kardo* and the *decumanus*, has so far been excavated in western France.

Public baths, catering for the needs of a Romanized elite looking for diversion and relaxation in pleasant and comfortable surroundings, were one of the major amenities of urban life, and bath-buildings like the Thermes de Cluny at Paris or the Barbarathermen at Trier are among the best preserved and best known monuments of Roman Gaul. Public establishments of this type have been identified in most of the Armorican *civitas*-capitals. Two of them, excavated in Rennes (Rue de Dinan) and Corseul (Champ Mulon), have indeed shown the usual range of rooms (*caldarium*, *tepidarium*, *frigidarium*, etc.) through which bathers would progress.

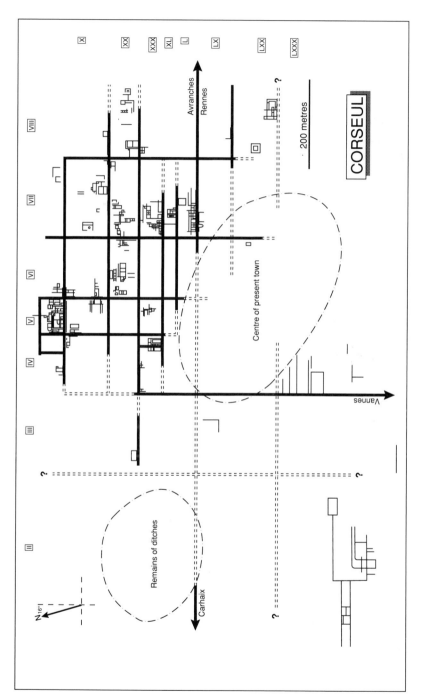

Figure 15 Plan of Roman Corseul (Fanum Martis)

Such buildings, and indeed Romanized towns as a whole, required large and regular supplies of water, which had to be brought in from outside. Water leats, running below ground level for the greater part of their course, have been observed in Rennes and Carhaix. The water supply of the latter town has been particularly well studied and has been shown to come from the southern slopes of the Montagnes Noires, across the communes of Paule, Glomel, Maël-Carhaix and Le Moustoir (C-d'A), before reaching a *castellum divisiorum* located in the eastern suburbs. Excessive expenditure was avoided by a very clever use of the contours, eliminating the need for bridge-aqueducts similar to the one to be seen at Jouy-aux-Arches (Moselle).

Important towns generally had several centres of worship, besides the temples of their *forum*-complexes. The plan used was not Roman but Celtic, that is built on a square (at Carhaix and Corseul), rectangular, circular or polygonal design, with a central chamber (*cella*) surrounded by a lean-to ambulatory, the whole structure often being enclosed in a sacred precinct. Such sanctuaries were probably patronized by visiting *pagani*, as well as by the local *urbani*. The same is certainly true of the public shows held in theatres (Corseul) and amphitheatres, or in hybrids of the two.

Some minor towns apparently aped the public amenities of the *civitas*-capitals or, because of their particular status as the main townships of the *pagi*, were given important public monuments. This is a fairly common occurrence in the Three Gauls, as has been recently shown by the excavations at *Alesia*, a small town of the *Aedui*. 'Romano-Celtic' theatres are indeed to be seen at Loc-mariaquer (M), where the small settlement was also provided with an aqueduct running across the *rivière d'Auray*, and Kérilien-en-Plounéventer. This latter township was replanned in the second century AD and given a regular street-plan.

Though most of these townships and roadside *vici* show no trace of formal urban planning, the presence of such public amenities as theatres, aqueducts and even 'native' temples, such as those at Taden and Erquy (C-d'A), Quimper or Rieux, bear witness to the impact of the Roman concept of urbanization on the Armorican *civitates*. Cantonal capitals and minor settlements certainly played a key role in the administration of tribal units and sub-units, and in the diffusion of new techniques and tastes. This does not mean, however, that towns were nothing but artificial and unproductive parasites, devouring the whole agricultural surplus of the surrounding *pagus* or *civitas*. Indeed, all of them have produced evidence of commercial activities: a *vicus portensis* is known at Nantes (cf. *CIL*, XIII, 3105–7). Various entrepôts, where ships could be loaded and unloaded, have been identified and/or excavated at Quimper, Taden and Vannes. Urban industrial production is also fairly well documented.[1] By transforming the raw agricultural products of their territories and channelling them into wider markets, towns actually generated wealth that the *civitas* or *pagus* could share in, by being able to sell its goods to regular and dependable purchasers and to buy the commodities available in the towns. Whenever an Armorican *paganus* came to town to sell his corn, vegetables, cattle or sheep in the marketplace or at the fair, to buy a few tools, pots and trinkets in the shops, worship his favourite deity at the local temple and enjoy a show or pantomime at the theatre, he was actually sharing luxuries that he had helped to provide.

The countryside

In all western societies prior to the Industrial Revolution, agriculture was the chief source of economic activity, and in the Roman world 'most adults . . . worked in the fields; most wealth was based on landownership' (Hopkins).[2] The Armorican peninsula being, on the whole, a region of moderately good pasture and arable land, the number of Roman rural sites identified by fieldwork, aerial survey and excavation in western Gaul is proportionately high; the low-lying plateaux extending on each side of the central hill ridges and the Rennes basin are particularly densely settled. These concentrations can be readily explained by the overall quality of the land they occupied, though fair numbers of Romanized settlements have also come to light recently on barren, windswept hills (Goënidou, near Berrien, F), rocky headlands (Troguer, Cléden-Cap-Sizun, F) and even tiny islands like Lavret off Bréhat (C-d'A).

[1] E.g. potteries making coarse wares, *terra nigra*, *mortaria* and pipe-clay statuettes in Rennes; buildings used for the working of iron and bronze in Nantes and Kérilien-en-Plounéventer.

[2] 'Economic growth and towns in Classical Antiquity', *Towns in Societies*, ed. P. Abrams and E. A. Wrigley (Cambridge, 1978).

Most of the rural sites recorded so far, generally identified by surface clusters of building materials (*tegulae, tubuli,* mortar, etc.) and Roman pottery, apparently correspond to free-standing villas, though it must be admitted that we still know very little of native homesteads and villages, which may well have existed in the most Romanized areas. Future, much-needed, work on such settlements and their field systems will certainly provide us with new insights into the spread of Romanized techniques and tastes among the Armorican peasantry. As many western villas, like those at Keradennec, Saint-Frégant and Le Cavardy, Saint-Evarzec (F), have yielded evidence of a Late La Tène occupation and shown traces of pre-Claudian structures associated with imported wares, such as Lyons and south Gaulish Samian, it is quite likely that a number of them developed directly from Late Iron Age *aedificia* (cf. *BG,* VIII, 7, 2). Largely built of wood in the early phases of their development, many of these native farms seem to have been turned into stone villas in the second half of the first century AD and to have gradually grown in size and complexity until the dark years of the late third-century crisis.

The archaeologists of the north-western provinces of the Empire have long considered that most of the villas of Roman Britain and Gaul fell into three categories, the 'simple' home or 'cottage', the 'winged-corridor' type and the 'courtyard' villa. This division holds true in western Gaul, though with variations on the basic plans. Some small rectangular farmsteads of the 'simple' type have been excavated or identified in central Finistère, for instance at Kergréac'h, Sizun, and southern Ille-et-Vilaine at Binon, Bains-sur-Oust, while most villa dwelling-houses belong to one of the variants of the 'winged-corridor' type, very common in the north-west of the Empire. An interesting example of this type, consisting in a rectangular structure, 25 m long and 12 m wide, subdivided into a series of rooms ('kitchen', 'living-room', 'bedrooms'), served by short corridors opening onto a verandah flanked by 'storerooms', has been fully excavated at Le Valy-Cloître, La Roche Maurice (F), and others explored.[3] Beside the living quarters proper stood other buildings such as barns, stables, a smithy, a bath-house and so on, the whole being protected by a high wall.

---

[3] Le Guilly, Malguénac (M); Le Bosséno, Carnac (M); Le Pérennou, Plomelin (F).

Plate 14   Decorated slab, Caulnes (C-d'A)

Larger and more complex villas, either built on the horseshoe plan common in *Gallia Belgica* and *Gallia Lugdunensis* or on the 'courtyard' plan known in Britain and Gaul, are far less common and only a few examples are known in western Gaul.[4] Standing in most cases in the vicinity of cantonal capitals or of important townships, better planned and decorated than other neighbouring units, they clearly belong to a superior class of rural residences.

This does not mean, however, that 'inferior' types of villas were left plain and unadorned. Stone columns are far from rare, and most villas were provided with some form of interior decoration. Though mosaics are not frequent, painted plaster was commonly used from the first century AD onwards, and floors laid with slate and limestone slabs arranged in patterns, stucco arches and colonnades, wall plaques carved with *peltae* shields, dolphins and sea-monsters, became fashionable in the late second and early third centuries.

Because attractive and sometimes dramatic elements of that kind are almost entirely contained in the living quarters of villas,

[4] Keradennec, Saint-Frégant; Kervéguen, Quimper (F); La Gauvenais, Corseul; La Guyomerais, Châtillon-sur-Seiche (I-et-V).

archaeologists have generally devoted much of their attention to the better-built residential structures of the *pars urbana*, and have neglected most of the subsidiary agricultural buildings, constructed of poorer materials. The 'total' excavation of a villa, including a thorough investigation of the farm buildings of the *pars rustica*, is a fairly recent development in Gallic studies. Few sites have had the benefit of such a comprehensive exploration. The evidence of agricultural activities in Roman Armorica, as in most of the provinces, is therefore largely indirect. It may be inferred from the balanced sickles and ubiquitous rotary querns, made either of granite or of imported lava, found on rural sites, that the basic cereals, such as wheat, barley and oats in the staple diet of bread and gruel, were common crops in western Gaul, as they were indeed in most northern provinces. But it should also be borne in mind that cash-crops of that type would almost certainly be

Plate 15   Model of the third-century extension of the Roman villa at La Guyomerais, Châtillon-sur-Seiche

complemented by the growing of fruit, vegetables, flax and hemp, which leave few or no recognizable remains.

Gaul was also famous in the Empire for the size of its herds and the excellent quality of its *charcuterie*. All sources of evidence indeed testify to stock-keeping as well as to the breeding of pigs, sheep and fowl. Animal bones occur in large numbers of rural middens and urban dumps, and specialist studies have generally revealed a strong predominance of pigs and sheep among the animals butchered and eaten. Oxen and cows are rare as slaughtered animals on rural sites and may have been preserved for the draught force needed on the farms. Ducks, hens and perhaps geese were also common in the yards of villas (cf. Pliny, *Naturalis Historia*, X, 53). Cattle were probably reared in Iron Age-type enclosures, with or without antennae ditches flaring out at the entrance, and fed on hay or turnips (Columella, *De Re Rustica*, II, x, 22). They were overwintered in stables, simple rectangular buildings, possibly of basilican plan as at La Guyomerais, Châtillon-sur-Seiche (I-et-V).

Animals were providers of meat, eaten fresh or preserved by salting or curing, which in part may explain the development of the Gallic salt 'industry'. They also provided milk, used for dairy products such as cheese (though cheese presses are not common site finds), leather and wool. Cropping shears are not very frequent on rural sites, but pottery spindlewhorls occur in most excavations and point to the home spinning of wool (and perhaps of flax and hemp), presumably by women (cf. Catullus, *Poems*, 64, 310–19). Such wool, woven on upright frame looms with the warp suspended by clay loomweights, was apparently not worked at villas, as such artefacts are not common there, but in the neighbouring *vici* and towns. Armorican villas, like all northern Gallic villas, produced only raw materials, and the so-called 'evidence' of industrial activities on rural sites has generally proved, on re-examination, to be largely misleading.

Since Roman villas were probably self-supporting in terms of food, one should not be surprised at the mixed economies evidenced in almost all units. It is clear that the prominence of wheat, or the nature and role of the animals reared on such farms, will have varied from one region to another, because villas, being geared also to profit-making, had to specialize in a particular type of farming related to the natural potential of the area in which they were situated. As vital pieces of information, like the balance between arable and pasture, are irretrievably lost, we can never be quite certain as to the type and level of specialization reached in a particular region or site.

The sheer size of some of these units and the general trend towards standards of comfort and taste distinctly superior to those of the Iron Age huts, evidenced by the use of hypocausts and bath-houses, the presence of ornate floors and painted wall-plaster, have usually been regarded as indicative of a general drive towards Roman mores and manners among the landed gentry and lesser farmers. This is scarcely debatable, but it is equally clear that the outlay involved in the setting-up, furnishing and maintenance of such large and sometimes luxurious buildings testifies to the integration of villas into a market economy and to the generation of some surplus, even if landowners probably had 'their fingers in many pies' (Rivet),[5] part of which was re-invested in the rural estates. Some historians have analysed the Romanization of Gaul, the growth of towns and the development of the villa system in terms of a swift change from a subsistence to a market economy. One should, however, consider that the development of *oppida* or the large-scale importation of Italian wine plainly show that the phenomenon had gathered impetus well before the conquest of Gaul, though it is equally clear that the creation or expansion of urban centres and the demands of the legions stationed in central-eastern Gaul, on the Rhenish *limes* or in Britain cannot but have speeded up the process, directly or indirectly. Since the obligation to supply the army was probably discharged in the form of cash taxes, it is clear that the money needed had to be earned through the production of an agricultural surplus. This was exchanged for money in the course of trade, thus generating an overall stimulation of economic activity, especially in areas having more or less direct access to the military consumption zones. Towns, often considered as parasitic on the countryside, certainly acted as an added incentive. Proof of this impetus lies in the greater number of coins, especially *aurei*, in circulation, and in the overall prosperity of the west during the High Empire.

In his recent work *Roman Gaul* (1983), John Drinkwater has argued that most agricultural products – and other raw materials,

[5] A. L. F. Rivet, *The Roman Villa in Britain* (London, 1969).

for that matter – had to undergo further processing (wool, for instance) and that, before being traded on the open market, 'most goods would have to be moved from the place of their production to a place more suitable for their wider distribution'. Commerce in agricultural products thus brought about the birth and development of various entrepôts and artisan-centres, loosely called *vici* and conveniently located near land, river and sea routes, for further transportation of the finished products towards the centres of consumption. Such intermediate centres, developing along trunk roads like Iffendic (I-et-V), for example, or main rivers with waterside harbours (Taden) and even the sea coast (Douarnenez, Quimper), were indeed quite numerous in western Gaul under the High Empire. Some of them had already developed in the Late Iron Age. A fair number of these townships have provided evidence of the storage of grain before transport, in silos (Quimper) or *horrea* (Taden?) and the working of wool (Blain), as well as various industrial activities such as metalworking at Kérilien-en-Plounéventer and pottery and tile-making at Quimper and Landerneau (F).

This also makes it clear that, very much like the larger *civitas*-capitals, such townships supplied the surrounding countryside with the goods and commodities which the rural estates did not provide, such as wine in the non-producing areas, or *terra sigillata*, common on all rural sites. This could be bought in the shops lining their streets or in the marketplace on fair days. Their temples, such as those at Rieux, Erquy and Taden, and theatres (Locmariaquer or Kérilien-en-Plounéventer – this last being clearly designed for a much larger population than the *vicus* could possibly hold), also show that, very much like the large *conciliabula* common in the countryside of northern Gaul (Mauves and Petit-Mars, L-A, for instance), townships served as worship and recreation centres for the vicinity. They were thus relay stations between the *civitas*-capitals and the *rus*, contributing to the spread of Romanized manners and fashions in the rural districts.

This integrated economic system has often been thought to have its origins in the existence of hierarchically organized estates, worked in part by the resident or absentee owner or his bailiff (*vilicus*), and in part by his tenants (*coloni* or *cultores*), and either derived from the large estates of Caesar's Gallic nobility of the Later Iron Age or created *ex nihilo*, and geared to the production of a large agricultural surplus, by the wealthy bourgeoisie, investing in land the benefits accrued from trade or industry. The large, comfortable villas would therefore be the country homes of the great landlords, and the less luxurious, admittedly more numerous, smaller units, the dependent farms worked by their tenant farmers. Though this view may, to a certain extent, be substantiated by a degree of continuity between Iron Age farms and Roman villas, both in plan and location, as well as by the well-established fact that the urban elites and local magistrates did derive most of their wealth from their estates – 'the *villa . . . a* means by which the townsman can exploit the countryside', as Leo Rivet put it – it is, in the light of present evidence, far too sweeping and general to describe a complex reality.

Extensive estates, probably corresponding to large bipartite villa-buildings, are quite common in the rich wheat-producing plains of Picardy or the Beauce. They may well testify to an intensive agricultural exploitation of fertile soils, linked to the needs of the military or civilian markets. They made use of slaves housed in the *pars rustica* of the villa, and/or of *coloni* living in hamlets (*loci*), or in various types of buildings scattered on the estate. The sheer size of such villas, the luxury sometimes displayed in their living quarters, certainly reflect the existence of some kind of rural aristocracy, somehow connected with urban centres, from whom were recruited the magistrates running the *civitas*. It may also be argued that the remarkable growth and embellishment of some units, obviously involving a large outlay, are indicative of the growing prosperity of the curial class in the second and early third centuries: the Saint-Frégant and Pont-Croix villas thus developed, though at different dates, from simple wooden huts to large courtyard units. It should, however, be realized that large bipartite villas of that type are rarer elsewhere in *Lugdunensis*, where lesser units, at various levels of Romanization and sophistication, occur in substantial numbers or are even the commonest type. As John Drinkwater has recently pointed out in his *Roman Gaul*:

Any picture of an extreme polarization of wealth in High Roman Gaul must be put in question by the undoubted existence of medium-sized villas with relatively well-appointed dwelling houses, which it is impossible to fit into a general scheme of great landlords and their downtrodden petty tenants.

The once generally accepted picture of a large class of land-tied and oppressed *coloni*, believed to be depicted on the famous 'rent-paying' scenes of eastern Gaul, thus fades, to be replaced by one of a consistent and relatively affluent class of freeholders, working medium-sized estates (100–150 ha), either singly or jointly, and for whose amusement, well-being and edification, numerous *conciliabula* were deliberately founded in the open countryside of Gaul by local notables. The pendulum, however, should not be allowed to swing too far; there probably existed a large, and largely submerged, population of agricultural labourers and other marginal workers, 'eking out a precarious existence at the beck and call of landowners of any size or status' (Drinkwater), who in the late third century probably formed the main component of the insurgent *Bagaudae*.

Salt and salt-related industries

The many miles of the Armorican coastline were profitably exploited for fishing and shell-gathering, both traditional local activities. Salt-recovery in briquetages, a thriving industry during the Iron Age, has, however, long been thought to have disappeared in the late first century BC or the early first century AD as a result of the Roman invasion, being either prohibited by the Roman authorities or brought down by the more competitive products from salt-marshes. New evidence from Hirel (I-et-V), as well as the overall distribution of the salt-consuming *garum* (fish-sauce or fish-paste) and salted fish industries of north-western Gaul, however, tend to challenge this hypothesis. One may well wonder whether the traditional techniques of salt-winning had not been modified, at least in some areas, by Roman technology, the old salt-making hearths being replaced by more efficient structures of tile-kiln type, such as the one excavated at Camézen, Plonévez-Porzay (F). Salt was a state monopoly in the Roman Empire, control of production and distribution devolving upon *conductores salinarum* (known from Dacia, for instance: *CIL*, III, 1209, 1306). But it is equally clear from two inscriptions from Rimini (*Ariminum*), dedicated to the centurion L. Lepidius Proculus by the *salinatores civitatis Menapiorum* and *salinatores civitatis Morinorum* at the end of the first century AD (*CIL*, XI, 390–1), that salt was still produced on a tribal basis in *Gallia Belgica* and hence probably in other parts of Roman Gaul.

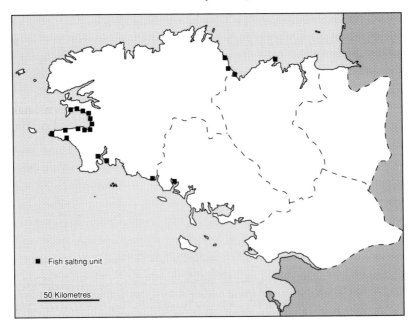

■ Fish salting unit

50 Kilometres

Figure 16   Distribution of fish-salting units

Though some of this salt was certainly used to flavour food, most of it must surely have gone to salt meat, fish and other commodities for winter supplies. Classical authors also mention its use in the making of cheese and the preparation of leather. Gallic salt pork and sausages were renowned in the Roman world, even before the conquest (Strabo, *Geog.*, IV, 3, 2). It is quite likely that the abundant fish and other sea-foods from the Atlantic and the Channel, as well as the locally bred cattle and pigs, were processed in this fashion in Late Iron Age Armorica.

The existence of such traditional activity in western Gaul, as well as the presence of large shoals of sardines off the peninsula in late spring, certainly account for the growth of an extensive salting industry in Roman Armorica. For about two centuries this produced and sold large quantities of salt fish and *garum*. The techniques used to produce these items were apparently first developed in the seventh century BC by the Greek colonies of the Black Sea and Propontis and gradually spread westwards towards *Gades* (Cadiz) and the Straits of Gibraltar. There, the remains of a very extensive salting industry, dating from the first century BC to the third century AD, have been identified on the Moroccan and Spanish coasts where the famous *garum sociorum* (Pliny, *Nat. Hist.*, XXXI, 94) was produced.[6] From the Straits of Gibraltar, the fish-salting industry progressed towards the Algarve and Setubal in southern and western Portugal, as well as north-western Spain (Barés and Espasante), to reach western Gaul in the second century AD.

Plate 16   Fish-salting tank, Le Caon, Telgruc (F)

About thirty such sites have so far been identified or excavated in western France. They are distributed between the Bay of Saint-Brieuc in the north and the river Blavet in the south, but are mainly concentrated on the territory of the *Osismi*, especially on the shores of the Bay of Douarnenez where nineteen sites, more than 60% of the total, have been found. They are all characterized by the presence of batteries of two to twenty square tanks, 2 to 4 m deep, with cemented sides and floors made entirely watertight by

---

[6] At Lixus, Tahadart and Cotta in Morocco and Torremolinos, Alcantara, Belo and especially Cartagena – *Cartago Nova* – in Spain.

cement quarter-round mouldings, buried up to their top in the subsoil. Tile roofs, placed over the lines of parallel tanks, prevented the contents from being diluted by rainwater. Nearby premises, generally simple structures with earth floors, were probably used as packing-rooms and stores, whereas more complex and luxurious buildings, situated at some distance from the tanks, served as living quarters for the owners. Most of these sites are located between four and fifteen metres above sea level, on the low cliffs running along the long sandy beaches common in these parts, generally near a source of fresh water.

The osteological examination of the fish bones found in the tanks has shown that the fish used in the Armorican salting industry consisted almost exclusively of very small sardines, three or four centimetres long, probably trawled offshore or caught in nets set at some distance out from the coast and then pulled to the beach. The catch was then dragged (this was probably the purpose of the ramp leading from the beach to a battery of tanks identified at Le Ris near Douarnenez) or carted to the tanks before being tipped inside in layers with enough salt to ensure 'une autodigestion du poisson par les distases de son propre tube digestif, en présence d'un antiseptique, le sel, qui empêche toute putréfaction' (R. Etienne).[7] The mixture of fish and salt was then crushed, mixed and left for about five or six weeks, at the end of which the finished product, *garum*, fish-paste or salt fish, could be packaged in wooden casks or pottery containers and sold.

The total volume of the Armorican salting tanks is so large that their whole annual production could certainly not be consumed locally or even regionally. It is very likely, therefore, that at least some of it was shipped, through ports like Douarnenez, towards other parts of Gaul or the Empire, Britain being a distinct possibility. Salt fish and *garum* – often served as *hydrogarum*, watered-down *garum* – were popular delicacies throughout the Empire. As they were included in the basic diet of the legions, one may well wonder whether the northward migration of the salting industries in the course of the second century AD was not intended to bring such productions closer to the military markets of the British and Rhenish *limites*.

The development of such an extensive industry in western Gaul

---

[7] R. Etienne, 'A propos du *garum sociorum*', *Latomus*, xxix, 2 (1970), 297–313.

obviously implies much more than any straightforward personal venture, as the capital needed to build and maintain such a large concern as the Plomarc'h unit at Douarnenez must have exceeded the private means of any individual. Should it then be supposed that the general economy of Armorica could generate enough capital to be re-invested in such a venture, or that the birth and rapid growth of the industry should be ascribed to a public *societas* of 'foreign' entrepreneurs?

A pointer towards an answer to this question may perhaps be found in the inscription on a base discovered in 1948 on a Douarnenez beach and now in Quimper museum. Though much weathered it is still legible:

> N.AVG
> NEPTVNO HIPPIO
> C.VARENIUS VOLTIN.
> VARVS C.C.R. IIII
> POSVIT

This may be developed as: *N(umini) Aug(usti),/Neptuno Hippio,/ C(aius) Varenius Voltin(ia tribu),/Varus, c(urator) c(ivium) r(omanorum) IIII (quartum)/posuit*, and translated as: To the divinity of Augustus and to Neptune Hippius, Caius Varenius Varus, of the Voltinia tribe, curator of the *conventus* of Roman citizens for the fourth time, has erected (this statue).

This most important text refers to the presence of a community of Roman citizens (*conventus*) in Douarnenez, which was probably formed on the territory of the *Osismi* in the second or early third century, that is before Roman citizenship was granted by Caracalla to all his subjects (AD 211). Such 'clubs', whose membership consisted of the Roman citizens isolated in peregrine *civitates*, were generally based in cantonal capitals, which is obviously not the case here since Douarnenez was the main town of a *pagus* and not of a *civitas*. Caius Varenius Varus, the chairman of the *conventus*, was probably not a native of Armorica, as the name *Varenius* is rare in the Three Gauls (though common in the *Provincia*). Perhaps with fellow members of the *conventus*, he had settled at Douarnenez as an entrepreneur in the salting industry or as a shipowner or trader.

Neptune *Hippius*, the tutelary god of the *conventus*, is certainly not a Romanized Celtic deity, but the Greek *Poseidon Hippios* (sometimes called *Neptunus Equestris* by later Latin writers), the husband of Amphitrite, dashing over the waves on his chariot and worshipped at Epidaurus and Olympia in classical times. The meaning of two statues of Hercules found in salting units in Douarnenez is not as clear, as the Mediterranean god appears to have been assimilated to Celtic deities. He is associated with Neptune and *Nehalennia* in many inscriptions found in the maritime sanctuaries of Domburg and Coilinjsplaat at the mouth of the Rhine.

It is unlikely that a purely local environment created the Armorican fish-salting industry, strikingly similar in its approach and techniques to that of Morocco and southern Spain, employing a 'foreign' personnel, both human and divine. The excavation of the Plomarc'h, Douarnenez and Le Resto, Lanester (M) units, together with a study of the pottery found during surface surveys, show that all sites came into existence *c.* AD 120 and developed considerably between AD 150 and AD 250 as did the whole Armorican economy.

Mines and quarries

The Romanization of the western *civitates*, the quick development of towns, townships and villas entailed the need for very large quantities of building materials, especially stone. Though no Roman quarry comparable to the one 'excavated' at Saint-Boil (Saône-et-Loire) has yet been brought to light in western France, a detailed study of the stone used for the villas of Le Valy-Cloître, La Roche Maurice, and Sables d'Or-les-Pins, Pléhérel (C-d'A) has shown that the builders made use of the material available locally, whereas the contractors of the large Kéradennec unit, Saint-Frégant, exploited the Loc-Brévalaire (F) granite, some 5 km to the south.

This was apparently a standard practice in the erection of urban and rural buildings, but areas where stone was scarce, like the Rennes basin, had to be supplied from distant sources, with materials carted or shipped to the sites. Soft limestone (*tuffeau*) from the Loire valley and ornamental marbles, imported rough (as at Kervenennec, Pont-Croix, F) or already fashioned into slabs to make columns, pavements or bath-linings, as at Keradennec, probably followed the same sea and river routes. But granite (or granulite) architectural elements, fairly common on urban and rural sites, must have been carved in local 'workshops'.[8]

The Armorican massif has abundant mineral resources of iron, gold, lead and tin, many of which were tapped as early as the Middle Bronze Age and were still in use in the post-Roman period. Lead was mined on many sites and traces of Roman workings have been identified at Trémuson and Pont-Névez, Plélauff (C-d'A), and at Donges-Crossac (L-A). At Pont-Névez, a research shaft bored into the deposit came across a series of galleries, 36 to 70 m below the ground surface. These gave radiocarbon dates of AD 460 and AD 750, and a Roman pit, backfilled in the early first century AD, was subsequently discovered nearby.

As a necessary ingredient for bronze-making, tin was exploited in western France, where it appears both in seams and in sedimentary levels. The latter deposits, in the vicinity of Saint-Renan (F) or at the mouth of the Vilaine, still show slight traces of Roman workings, whereas the long seams of Abbaretz-Nozay were mined by the open-cast method. A trench 2 to 18 m deep and 25 to 100 m wide was dug along the line of the deposits. Numerous finds of tools, coins and pottery were made in and near the trench, which point to an interesting permanence of mining techniques during the first six centuries AD.

Iron ore is no longer mined in Brittany, though the total resources of the region may be estimated at about 1000 million tons of magnetite and haematite, with a relatively low iron content (about 36.5%). Since such low-quality ores were commonly used for early or 'primitive' iron-smelting (that is before the widespread use of the blast-furnace), the large number of slag heaps scattered all over Brittany comes as no surprise. Though many of the tips are the result of medieval and early modern works, a fair number may be dated to the Roman period. They clearly correspond to small-scale mining, the working of outcrops and shallow seams by pits or by the open-cast method, and to the subsequent reduction of the iron ore in smelting installations similar to the one excavated at Kermoisan, Quimper, with its ore-roasting areas and oval-shaped shaft furnaces.

---

[8] For example, at Rennes, Carhaix, Nantes and Quimper or at Kervadiou, Plomelin and Beuz, Le Trévoux (F).

Though some of the Abbaretz-Nozay tin may have been exported, it is quite likely that mining and metal-smelting were largely local or sub-regional concerns, worked for the needs of villas, *vici* and towns, where tools, instruments and various small objects were fashioned from the rough ingots bought from neighbouring industries.

Crafts

The many small objects found on Roman sites can give us only a limited insight into an extremely active industry, often praised by Latin authors, since the various objects made from perishable materials have left no archaeological evidence. We thus know next to nothing about the working of wood, leather and bone in Roman Armorica, though these activities must have been of paramount importance in the economy of its villages and *vici*.

As towns and villas appeared and expanded, a new class of craftsmen came into existence, since the overall development of building activities now required specialists able to put up complex architectural structures. The private and public buildings they erected in stone or brick, bound by strong mortar, were generally decorated with painted plaster applied to their walls and ceilings (sometimes vaulted, as in the bath-house, Rue de l'Aqueduc, Carhaix), stucco-work, as at Keradennec or Mané-Véchen, Plouhinec (M), and carved wall-plaques. Mosaics were uncommon, but floors were often ornamented with pavements of slate and limestone slabs arranged in geometrical patterns.[9]

Beyond the standardized tastes they revealed, these various decorative elements certainly show the existence of specialized teams, either itinerant or working within the limits of a *civitas* from a fairly small stock of patterns. Their names remain unknown; the single exception, a signature painted on the wall-plaster of the Keradennec villa, has not yet been deciphered.

Bronzesmiths certainly held a central place in the local industry, as bronze objects are very common site finds. Urban workshops-cum-shops, similar to the ones excavated at Nantes and Kérilien-en-Plounéventer, manufactured a wide variety of brooches, rings,

[9] For example, at Kervenennec, Pont-Croix (F); Mané-Bourgerel, Arradon (M); Curin, Gâvre (L-A), etc.

bracelets and diverse trinkets from wiredrawn, cast or sheet metal. But it is likely that such plastic works as bronze statuettes and statues, involving complex technical skills, such as the lost-wax process, could only be produced in a small number of manufactories. None of these has, however, yet been identified. The Celtic personal names – *Boduos*, *Litugenus*, *Tituris*, etc. – stamped on some Armorican brooches, especially on the early pseudo-La Tène II type, may point to small family concerns of native origin, akin to those smelting lead for the production of water-pipes and coffins.

The Roman world made extensive use of clay, either fashioned and baked into bricks, tiles and various hypocaust elements (all these were necessary for the building and roofing of various constructions), or modelled and fired into diverse pottery containers designed for the transportation, preservation, cooking and consumption of liquids and solid food. These industries, geared to the needs and tastes of local customers, were generally located near centres of consumption, in townships (Quimper, Landerneau) or the suburban confines of larger towns (Place des Lices, Rue de Dinan and Rue de Saint-Martin in Rennes). Building materials were fired in rectangular kilns like those at Saint-Julien (C-d'A) and Redon, whereas potters used oval-shaped or circular ones (Glomel and Pabu, C-d'A). Most of the pottery produced on these sites may be categorized as coarse ware; made in a dark grey or brown thick fabric and rarely decorated, it was clearly intended for daily domestic usage. Armorican production centres, however, though they never manufactured any Samian, did also produce finer tablewares, such as flagons and *terra nigra* containers, as well as pipe-clay statuettes, distributed throughout western Gaul.

Textiles were another basic necessity, and though some may have been imported from the famous 'mills' of *Gallia Belgica*, most woollen and linen clothes worn in Armorica were spun locally and woven on vertical looms. Numerous finds of spindlewhorls in rural settlements and town houses may indicate that spinning was largely a cottage industry, whereas weaving was apparently carried out in specialized units at Nantes, Vannes, Quimper and elsewhere.

Transport and trade

The wine- and olive-oil containers (amphorae) imported from the lands bordering the Mediterranean, together with various other commodities, which occur quite commonly on Armorican sites, are probably the best examples one can use to demonstrate the vitality of the old trade route running across the 'Gallic isthmus' and along the coasts of *Aquitania* towards north-western Gaul and southern Britain. The ships (tramps, quite probably) used the many Armorican ports mentioned by Ptolemy or discovered by archaeologists. Though *Condevicnum* (Nantes) vaunted its *vicus portensis* and Taden may have been provided with large *horrea*, most Armorican ports were probably little better than mere havens, in which ships would moor at a wooden quay to load or unload cargoes brought from the hinterland or distributed into it by merchants using the dense road network.[10]

This coastal trade route was complemented by the dense commercial traffic going down the Loire and transporting central Gaulish and Mediterranean wares to western Gaul and Britain. As many inscriptions demonstrate, this was largely controlled by Armorican *nautae*. At some stage in their history, they probably controlled the Rhône and Saône traders, and formed a powerful corporation, whose members, like M. Lucceius Genialis, M. Gemellus Secundus and G. Sedatius Florus in Nantes, belonged to the urban elites and were wealthy enough to put up monuments to their tutelary god Vulcan.

Nothing, on the other hand, is known of the Armorican *navicularii*, which is all the more surprising as such open sea sailors and merchants were certainly important members of the local trading companies. Our knowledge of the ships they used is similarly limited by the almost total lack of identifiable wrecks in the Atlantic and Channel, the only ones known so far being those discovered at St Peter Port, Guernsey, and Ploumanac'h (C-d'A).

There can be no doubt that our appraisal of the imports and exports of Roman Armorica remains incomplete because it cannot take account of the perishable goods, but must necessarily rest on

[10] Nantes: *Portus Namnetum*; *Portus Brivates*(?), Vannes; *Vindana Portus* (Port-Louis, M?); Quimper, Douarnenez, *Gesibocrate* (Brest?), *Portus Saliocanus* (Morlaix?), Alet, Saint-Servan, Taden, etc.

the identification and attempted quantification of non-perishable commodities. These include such items as marble or porphyry brought from Greece, Italy or Tunisia, soft limestone from the Loire valley, Volvic lava quernstones, metal ingots from Britain, southern Spanish oil from the Guadalquivir valley in Dressel 20 amphorae and wine from Italy, *Tarraconensis* (north-eastern Spain) or *Narbonensis* in Dressel 2–4, Pascual 1 or 'south Gaulish' amphorae. Pottery (Samian ware in particular) was imported from many production centres such as Italy, Lyons, southern and central Gaul, as well as from *Aquitania* ('à l'éponge' ware), the Argonne forest and British wares (essentially New Forest and 'black-burnished') in the fourth century.

The prosperity of western Gaul, demonstrated by the imports listed above, by the distribution of *aurei* and, above all, by the growth and embellishment of towns and rural residences alike, clearly implies that some of the agricultural, maritime and, perhaps, mineral surplus of the five *civitates* was sold outside the peninsula for hard cash. It is, however, almost impossible to establish the nature and geographical distribution of these exports. This means that the goods sold outside Armorica are neither directly recognizable nor transported in containers that archaeology has yet been able to identify. There can, nevertheless, be little doubt that they consisted largely in cereals and meat, *garum* and salted fish, the staple productions of the west.

This long-distance system of exchange was complemented by local commerce, draining the raw materials of the countryside towards ports of trade and distributing imported wares to the remotest parts of the peninsula. The presence of second-century central Gaulish Samian ware (often in large amounts) on all western Roman sites is a most interesting testimony to the vitality of this exchange.

Religion

It is common knowledge that the Roman authorities carefully avoided persecuting the native deities of the lands they conquered. They contented themselves with suppressing the bloodiest ceremonies of local cults, showing in this respect a remarkable tolerance and pragmatism that few other colonizers have imitated. The Gauls very soon adopted the Roman, Greek and oriental gods and goddesses brought by the soldiers, traders or administrators, but interpreted them in their own way, using the names and images of those who best suited their beliefs or most resembled their favourite deities. This complex interfusion of polytheisms and pooling of the divine personnel of various peoples and races engendered Gallo-Roman religion.

Like all Ancient societies, the Gauls peopled their environment with gods whom they located in the salient features of the landscape, rocks, mountains, streams and springs. Belief in such primitive and localized deities was not washed away by the conquest and indeed persisted during the whole Roman period and even into the Middle Ages. Hill- and mountain-tops, like Ménez Bré, Ménez Hom and the 'Montagne de Locronan' (F), were thus venerated in Armorica as they were in the whole of Gaul (Puy-de-Dôme, Donon, Vosges). In addition, traces of a very archaic water-cult may be seen in the presence of a temple dedicated to the goddess *Viccinonia* (the river Vilaine) near the latter's source, or the large numbers of coins thrown into streams by travellers fording them, for example, the Vilaine at Rennes or the Blavet at Saint-Gelven (C-d'A). Furthermore, obscure superstitions associated with Neolithic barrows and dolmens certainly account for the magical rites performed in their underground corridors and chambers, traces of which, in the form of hearths surrounded by broken pipe-clay figurines, have often been recorded by excavators.

Primitive beliefs of this kind, certainly quite widespread among the Gauls, did not exclude more elaborate creeds. The writings of classical authors (admittedly rare and allusive) and the numerous religious monuments of the Three Gauls testify to the existence of a large and complex pantheon, in which native gods were granted a new existence by written dedications and plastic representations.

Most common in western Gaul, for example, are pipe-clay statuettes showing mother-goddesses (*Deae Nutrices*) sitting in high-backed wickerwork armchairs and nursing one or two sucklings, as well as various types of naked goddesses. These are either moulded in the round (sundry variations on Venus) or included in a clay plaque stamped with different geometrical patterns and with the Gaulish phrase: REXTVGENOS SVLLIAS AVVOT (*Rextugenos* of *Sullias* has made this?). These cheap figurines, mass-produced in local 'factories' at Rennes, Tréguennec

(F) and elsewhere, were personal objects of devotion. They were intended for popular worship in private chapels (*sacella, larariae*), used as ex-votos in public shrines or buried with the dead. They certainly had protective functions and were clearly connected with a native domestic fertility cult.

Other purely native deities like the horned god (*Cernunnos?*) found at Blain, the hammer-god (*Sucellus*) at Saint-Brandan (C-d'A), or the ithyphallic god at Plougastel-Daoulas (F), were, oddly enough, rarely portrayed in Armorica. This is in contrast to Romano-Celtic divinities, displaying both Roman identity and substantial Celtic influence.

Lug-Mercury and *Teutatès*-Mars, sometimes provided with Celtic subnames (*Mercurius Atepomarus*, the Great Rider; *Mars Mullo*, of the mule drivers?, *Mars Vicinnus*, of the river Vilaine, in Rennes and Nantes), were particularly popular gods in western Gaul, not only in their classical roles, but also as protectors of the tribe, merchants and traders. They were often depicted in stone like the statue of Mercury at Saint-Adrien (C-d'A) and bronze.[11]

The Romano-Celtic sky-god (*Jupiter Optimus Maximus – Taranis*) is known to have been portrayed in two main forms, both of which occur in Armorica. Fragments of 'Jupiter columns', consisting, when complete, of a stone base carved with deities, above which rises a high column topped by a carved group representing a horseman riding down, or being supported by, a monster with snake limbs, have been identified at Plouaret (C-d'A), Briec, Plomelin and Landudal (F), while a bronze statuette found at Kérilien-en-Plounéventer, resembling that discovered earlier at Le Châtelet (Haute-Marne), shows a naked Jupiter probably holding a spoked wheel and thunderbolts. The attributes of this divinity are still far from clear, though representations of the first type are generally interpreted as an allegory of the conflict between light and darkness, life and death or good and evil.

This protective role was similarly assumed in the west by various deities: Vulcan, Hercules, Minerva, Diana and Cupid.[12] As these

---

[11] Statuettes of Mercury at Dol, Corseul and Carhaix, and of Mars at Goulien, Plonévez-Porzay, and Carhaix (F) and Mauves (L-A).

[12] *Volkanus* (Vulcan): worshipped in Nantes by the inhabitants of the *vicus portensis* (*CIL*, XIII, 3105–7); Hercules: marble and stone statues have been found at Douarnenez and bronze statuettes at Trégueux (C-d'A) and Trégunc (F); Minerva: stone statue in the private shrine of the Le Balac villa, Langon (I-et-V); Diana: stone statue at

Plate 17   'Anguipède', Plouaret (C-d'A)

divinities are all represented in classical garb, it is, however, impossible to tell whether or not they correspond to anonymous native religious entities. Most of these Celtic and Romano-Celtic gods actually testify to the importance given to Nature and to the preoccupations of an essentially rural society. The complex but resolutely native pantheon evidenced by Armorican finds indeed intimates the immanent desires of a peaceful population of craftsmen and ploughmen, imploring their gods for civil peace, prosperity and the perpetuation of the race.

Native gods and goddesses were worshipped in highly characteristic sanctuaries ('Romano-Celtic temples'), built on square, circular or polygonal designs.[13] A central chamber (*cella*) holding the divine image was surrounded by a lean-to ambulatory, the whole structure being generally combined with auxiliary buildings, possibly for the clergy in charge, and enclosed by a sacred precinct (*temenos*). Such temples, stone-built, decorated with painted

Mauves (L-A), bronze statuette at Carhaix; Cupid: bronze statuettes at Crozon (F), La Bouillie (C-d'A) and Bieuzy (M).

[13] Square: Allaire, Rieux, Taden and Carhaix; circular: Crozon; polygonal: Douarnenez, Plaudren and Carentoir (M).

Plate 18   Bronze statue, Kerguilly, Dinéault (F)

plaster and tile-roofed, were certainly distinctly Roman in appearance. But their typically non-Mediterranean plans, having their origins in the Gaulish and British Iron Age (the Maiden Castle, South Cadbury and Heathrow shrines), together with the fact that they quite frequently lie above the remains of pre-Roman sanctuaries (Trogouzel, Douarnenez), reflect the continuance of 'La Tène' rites and beliefs into the Roman period.

The exception is the cult of the Spirit of Rome and the Emperor. This is attested by numerous public and private dedications to the *Numen* of the Emperor (often linked with other divinities) as at Nantes, Rennes, Corseul, Douarnenez and elsewhere, and by the presence of priests of the Imperial cult in Rennes, or the bronze statuettes of *Victoria* (Victory) discovered in Carhaix, Kerlaz (F) and Corseul. These portray an exclusively Roman divinity (or rather personification of a concept), especially beloved of soldiers. All these elements actually witness to the political and cultural assimilation of the western *civitates* and to the loyalty of the Gauls to the Empire.

The oriental mystery religions involved a more personal relationship between the individual and his god, since their devotees, after a process of secret initiation, could hope to attain happiness and salvation in the life to come by striving for perfection. They therefore held greater appeal than the native or Roman cults. The most prominent of these exotic religions in western Gaul is undoubtedly the Egyptian cult of Isis, Sarapis and their son Harpocrates, which involved initiation, baptism and salvation.

No structural remains of their shrines or temples having yet been brought to light in Armorica, oriental mystery religions are only represented by bronze and gold statuettes, found most commonly in towns or *vici*,[14] though five faience *oushabti* occur as gravegoods in a rural context at Plougonven (F). Among religions of salvation, Christianity, promising everyone, regardless of wealth or social position, a better world, could be expected to have converted large numbers of Armoricans, especially in times of political and social crisis. The few traces connected with the new faith in Brittany have been found mainly in urban contexts. This suggests that Christianity, like the other 'foreign' religions, appealed mostly

---

[14] Bronze: Carhaix, Corseul, Saint-Brieuc, Saint-Jean-Trolimon; gold: Locmariaquer.

to the 'happy educated few', while the majority of the population still adhered to its age-old beliefs.

Death and burial

Whereas Iron Age communities seem to have buried their dead at a short distance from their settlements, Romanized Gauls, according to Roman law and customs, buried theirs outside the residential area of towns, townships and villas, along the sides of roads or lanes leading to them. Cemeteries, sometimes containing hundreds of graves, have been examined on the outskirts of all Armorican towns. Some, such as Carhaix or Rennes, had several burial-grounds, probably serving different urban districts, while smaller groups of graves, scattered across the Breton countryside, apparently correspond to agricultural settlements – villas, hamlets – or 'industrial' ones – mines, fish-salting units and so on. In these loosely organized cemeteries, the means used to locate and protect the grave appear to have varied considerably from tomb to tomb. They range from a sherd of amphora or a bit of tile laid over the grave to the inscribed stelae of Nantes and Corseul, from the low heap of stones on a Quimper grave to the large barrow at Kerlan, Goulien (F). Roman-style gravestones and monuments are very rare in western Gaul and are almost exclusively found in urban contexts, for example, at Nantes and Corseul. The only notable exception is the small *cella memoriae*, consisting in a rectangular *cella* (8.10 m long and 3.50 m wide) and a semicircular apse decorated with a wall-painting showing Venus *Anadyomenae* sitting on the back of a dolphin, still standing today at Langon (I-et-V).

Cremation was, of course, the most common funeral rite in Gaul during the Higher Empire, the dead body being cremated on a pyre built in the cemetery and the ashes collected and washed in water and milk before being buried. That apparently simple rite is, however, complex in its many variations and the Créac'h-Maria cemetery, excavated near Quimper, included both *Brandgruben-gräber* (that is, unprotected cremation graves, the ashes simply being tipped into a shallow pit) and common *Urnengräber*. The former type accounts for 2% of the graves at Quimper (as against

11% at Jublains) and is probably the more archaic of the two, though a fair number of its examples postdate urn graves.

Protected graves are the most common burials in cremation cemeteries. The ashes were enclosed in a wooden casket or in an urn of stone, metal, glass or pottery, buried in a shallow pit dug into the substratum and propped up with stones or bits of tile, the pit being subsequently backfilled with the remains of the funeral pyre. It must be added that, in many cases, cinerary urns, whose openings were generally stopped by lids (stones, pottery platters, bits of tile, etc.), were doubly protected by a box made of tile or stone or even a wooden chest fitted into the grave-pit.

Cinerary urns were often buried with various offerings, either thrown broken onto the pyre or deposited intact in the grave, both reflecting, however, the same eschatological background. The first category includes animal bones, glass *unguentaria* used to pour perfumes on the pyre, bone hinges from small wooden caskets and sherds of various pottery vessels (among which Samian Dragendorf 35–36 cups and water jugs are the most common) that had been broken over the pyre. This echoes the idea of death as something dirty and corrupting, which stands in utter contradiction to the general feeling that the dead body or its ashes were somehow connected with the survival of the soul in the world beyond. The latter belief accounts for the deposit, in or around the cinerary urn, of various votive offerings, such as food and beverages left in pots and jugs (10% of the graves at Quimper), coins (usually one or two) and other objects (personal trinkets, pipe-clay statuettes etc.). These clearly show that the 'soul' of the deceased was believed to survive in the grave itself or in an ill-defined subterranean world. There was, however, no apparent ritual norm in the case of cremation graves (only 2% of the Carhaix ones had one or two coins, as against 4% at Quimper, 7% at Jublains, and 15% at Blicquy, Belgium). One is left with the feeling that some particular aspects of funerary rites were not common to all and sundry, but only to fairly small family and social groups, thus continuing Iron Age structures and habits. But it also establishes that Armorican burial customs are hardly different from those of northern Gaul as a whole. The only dissimilarity is that Armorican votive offerings are generally mediocre or extremely poor, even though the region was reasonably prosperous in Roman times.

Roman inhumation graves found in western Gaul are so rare

(fewer than a hundred) and so varied that conclusions as to their nature and archaeology cannot be anything but tentative, though all of them undoubtedly belong to the Later Empire. Unprotected inhumations are infrequent and generally include no grave-goods, which would provide closer dating, like wooden coffins, which are never furnished with votive offerings. On the contrary, tile-lined tombs, either triangular or rectangular in section, though also devoid of grave-goods are fairly well dated to the late fourth and fifth centuries, the fashion having spread northwards from the Mediterranean.

Lead coffins, having regard to the total number of inhumations so far discovered, are relatively common in Armorica with twenty currently known. They are well dated to the first half of the fourth century. Though rarely decorated, they usually hold 'rich' grave-goods, such as glass bottles and various trinkets. They mainly appear in the vicinity of towns and near large, wealthy villas.

The particular rituals associated with inhumation burials are not very varied. One should take into account the presence of a plaster burial in Rennes and the traces of a ritual fire in one of the graves of the small Laetic cemetery at Guer (M), but the most obvious and common ritual consists in the arrangement of grave-goods, the vessels containing food and drink always being placed at the foot, near the head or close to the hand of the body. This is inhumed fully dressed and adorned with brooches, pins, bracelets, belt-buckles and so on; for example, there was gold-braid cloth in the Douarnenez coffin. Surprisingly, coins are extremely rare, even in the 'richest' graves, and there seems to be no correlation between the practice of placing a coin in the mouth or hand of the corpse and the wealth of the social group concerned.

Though a detailed survey of the burials and burial customs of Armorica provides us with a vast amount of much-needed information about the tribes that inhabited the peninsula, about their degree of wealth, culture and Romanization, it cannot be denied that the signs are often hard to read. One may reasonably conclude, after a close examination of the archaeological evidence, that the Romanized peoples of Armorica believed in the survival of the 'soul' of the dead in the grave or in the underworld, where it experienced common earthly feelings and desires that had to be satisfied by means of the offering placed in the grave. The respect and awe felt by the living must have mingled, however, with a feeling of apprehension of the dead, as the presence in many graves of long iron nails meant to 'fasten' the dead soul to its *demeure certaine* demonstrates.

Celtic and Roman eschatological approaches, derived from a common cultural background, are basically so similar that it is extremely difficult to discriminate, in local burial customs, between typically pre-Roman rites and possible new rituals. A survey shows, however, that the latter never reached deeply into Armorican society, as the very limited spread of such Romanized monuments as stelae and mausolea testifies. The influence of new techniques and myths on local Gallo-Roman burial groups never extended beyond limited urban and rural groups such as major landlords, traders, *nautae* and freedmen. They apparently made few inroads outside main trade routes like the Loire, Vilaine and Rance valleys. The burial customs of western Gaul indeed reveal a wide gap between the economic and social changes that had transformed the structure of pre-Roman Armorica and the slow mutation of moral and psychological patterns, which evince a strong regional conservatism.

5

Roman Armorica: Society and Politics

Integration or assimilation?

It is a well-known fact that the integration policy conducted by the Roman administration rested on persuasion, on the acculturation of local elites rather than on brute force. It is also manifest that the non-native elements (traders, soldiers, etc.) were a tiny minority in western Gaul. As the study of personal names revealed by public and private dedications or graffiti shows, a vast majority of the Armorican population bore either purely Celtic names (*Vertros, Rextugenos, Boduos*) or Romanized Celtic names (*Moricus, Smertulitanus, Meticca*). Similarly, the hypothesis of a complete Latinization of the western *civitates* and, therefore, of a total eradication of Gaulish, once advocated by J. Loth (1883), has been rejected following the demonstration that a fair number of Gaulish place-names with characteristic *-acos* endings survived the progress of Brittonic. Indeed, it was a change still in progress at the end of the fourth century AD if we consider that the troops stationed at *Osismis* (Brest) were called *Mauri Osismiaci* not *Mauri Osismienses*; Brittonic, moreover, was influenced by the native dialects. There is every reason to believe that while towns, and perhaps large rural estates, accommodated a mixed population, using either Latin, sometimes quite debased, or Gaulish (or both), the very large and almost totally illiterate rural proletariat still spoke Gaulish.[1]

---

[1] The case of *Rextugenos* and *Caius Frugus*, the two contemporary potters known in *Condate* (Rennes), is most interesting in this respect as the former used Gaulish for his stamps and the latter Latin (cf. above pp. 103, 106).

Though Armorica, possessing a developed economy and a relatively large and prosperous population during the High Empire, appears to have been fully integrated into the Roman world, the fact remains that many particular features – notably the small number of Roman inscriptions found in the west – induce us to discriminate between a manifest economic integration and an equally limited ideological assimilation. It is obvious that such habits and tastes as were conveyed by Roman culture percolated only very slowly into the western *civitates*. They did not affect all parts of the peninsula with equal strength. The circulation and contact zones of the Loire valley and eastern Armorica were, on the whole, more Romanized than the west. Besides, regional contrasts of that kind were coupled with vast differences in the penetration of new ideas and tastes, which depended on rank and social class.

This may be exemplified by the case of the local funerary art which, if it testifies in part to the high degree of Romanization achieved by some social groups, on the other hand also reveals the deep conservatism of rural and urban masses. It is quite likely that this large, almost entirely illiterate, population, deeply attached to its age-old religious traditions, constituted a formidable block to the progress of the new ideology. The same *rusticani* or *pagani* were, actually, some centuries later, the staunchest opponents to the intolerance of the Christian Church. This largely submerged rural and urban proletariat regularly exploded into the social violence of the Bacaudic uprisings, mostly aimed at Romanized towns and villas. It is therefore clear that the unquestionable progress of techniques and tastes during the Roman period did not necessarily result in an enduring change of linguistic and mental habits in all parts of the peninsula and all social classes.

Armorica under the High Empire

Although it had certainly started under Augustus and Tiberius, the movement of economic and cultural integration of western Gaul was given new impetus in the reigns of Claudius (AD 41–54) and Nero (AD 54–68), as the main elements of the Armorican road network were completed, while towns such as Quimper and Corseul expanded and the first villas were built.[2] This major

---

[2] For example, Kervennec, Pont-Croix, and Persivien, Carhaix (F); Keran, Arradon (M).

advance, also perceptible in the leap forward in imports (Samian ware in particular) and the growing number of coins in circulation, is to be noticed in the whole of northern Gaul. Though it quite probably results in part from the clear interest of Claudius in Gallic affairs, his interest was no doubt stimulated and greatly assisted by the opening of the British market in the mid-forties.

The extension and refurbishment of numerous villas like Le Vuzit, Concarneau (F), and La Faroulais, Pléchâtel (I-et-V), or the building or rebuilding of some temples (Mauves, Trogouzel, Douarnenez) in the later first century AD, furthermore testifies to the continuation and even acceleration of this movement under the Flavian emperors. Their liberal policy towards the *peregrini* allowed large numbers of decurions to obtain Roman citizenship, as in the case of Titus Flavius Postuminus mentioned above (p. 80).

The century that elapsed between the accession of Nerva (AD 96) and the assassination of Commodus (AD 192) has been rightly regarded as a golden age, an unequalled period of growth and wealth for the Gallic provinces. This is indeed verified in the west by the development or remodelling of towns as well as villas,[3] while new farming units were established on sites so far unoccupied like Ile de Lavret, off Bréhat, or Binon, Bains-sur-Oust (I-et-V). All this, together with the material success revealed by the funeral monuments and stelae to be seen at Nantes and Corseul, for instance, clearly points to increasing wealth. This probably was more broadly spread than previously and rested on an undeniable economic vitality perceptible in the growing number of villas, the establishment of the *garum* and salt-fish industry on the coasts of the *Osismi* or the dynamism of inter-provincial trade, bringing large quantities of central and south Gaulish Samian cups and platters to all western sites.

In the course of that long period of peace and prosperity, the first cracks did, however, start showing. The invasion of northern Italy by the *Quadi* and *Marcomanni* (AD 166) opened a long series of wars. These were, in the long run, to engulf an anaemic Empire. Even more threatening, in this respect, were the endemic brigandage

---

[3] The township of Kérilien-en-Plounéventer was provided with a regular street-grid and a large theatre built on its western outskirts and a large bath complex was erected at Rennes; as for villas, among many others the case of Keradennec, Saint-Frégant, is most striking, since it was turned from a medium-sized 'corridor' type into a very large 'courtyard' villa in the late second or early third century.

and revolts of ruined artisans, landless farmers and army deserters. Bands of these, under the leadership of the deserter Maternus, played havoc in *Lugdunensis* (AD 185–7). Though this widespread social agitation has left few recognizable traces in Gaul, the temporary or final abandonment of a small number of villas,[4] together with the Stobrez (Yugoslavia) dedication mentioning the intervention of the *legio VI Victrix* and of British *alae* against rebellious Armoricans, may be considered as strongly indicative of the impact of that unrest on western *civitates*. In spite of a new period of peace and expansion in the first half of the third century, everything had already combined to trigger off the crisis that was to transform radically the economic structure of western *Lugdunensis*.

The third-century crisis

Matters changed for the worse in the second half of the century. The assassination of Gordian III in March 244 opened a long era of political and military instability in the western provinces, all the more so as climatic changes, resulting in a marine transgression, may have prompted the Franks, Saxons and Frisians to start migrating. This difficult situation may have triggered off serious revolts. According to Eutropius (*Historia romanae*, 9, 4), Decius had to suppress a *bellum civile* in Gaul in the years AD 239–51, while an outbreak of plague made things even worse. The revolt headed by Postumus in the spring of 260, with the help of the Bonn and Xanten legions, severed Gaul from the Roman Empire for a period of fourteen years. Though Postumus fought vigorously against the North Sea raiders and may have succeeded in stabilizing the western front (as the *Comes* and *Redux aurei* minted for him suggest), a number of coin hoards buried during his reign along the shores of Gaul from the Pas-de-Calais to the Vendée bear witness to a growing sense of insecurity, due to either the political or military situation. At least one Armorican site, the farm at Binon, Bains-sur-Oust, has a *sestertius* of Postumus as its last coin, and while three milestones dated to his reign (*CIL*, XIII, 8955–7) and later incorporated in the city walls of Rennes may simply be

---

[4] Le Valy-Cloître, La Roche Maurice, or Keradennec, Saint-Frégant.

Plate 19   Gold patera from Rennes

pledges to the new regime, the elements of a rich hoard discovered at Rennes in 1774 prove far more interesting. Probably buried during the reign of Aurelian, it includes a gold *patera* weighing 1.35 kg, a gold cruciform brooch, several gold medallions minted for Postumus' *quinquennales* of AD 263 and 94 *aurei*. Both the golden brooch and the medallions are of especial value, being the kind of objects emperors were wont to offer to their closest friends and to the highest officials of their administration. As this hoard had been hidden in the very heart of the Roman town, probably not very far from the *forum*, it is not unlikely that a high official in Postumus' service may have resided in Rennes, possibly as a coordinator of military activities in western Gaul.

In the winter of 269, Postumus was succeeded by Victorinus. The seven milestones put up in the west during his reign, at Saint-Méloir (C-d'A), Surzur (M), Nantes and elsewhere, suggest that his grip may have been as strong as his predecessor's, though not sufficient to protect it from sea-raiders. Numerous hoards were buried along the coasts of Gaul in the years 269–70.

Puzzling out the events of the years 270–80 proves a very difficult task. The abdication of Tetricus in 274 and the restoration of Aurelian and Probus could not put a stop to the uncertainties of that dark time. Hardly any official coins reached western Gaul between 269 and 290, while local imitations of the *antoniniani* of Tetricus were being minted as late as 280. The many hoards hidden between 270 and 280 point to a widespread panic, possibly caused by a combination of raiding, pillaging and depressed economic conditions; a large number of them, composed of imitations of Tetricus' coins, were probably buried in the late 270s.

One should not, however, imagine that all life had been eradicated in western Gaul in these years as a result of ferocious piratical onslaughts. Commerce, though probably on a small scale, was still practised, the dearth of official coinage between 269 and 281 causing local (semi-official?) mints to produce large quantities of imitations, generally called 'barbarous radiates' since 'commerce demanded means of exchange':

> On pourrait croire *a priori* que celui-ci devait être nul ou presque. Or, il n'en était rien. L'examen des trésors monétaires révèle au contraire une certaine activité, une circulation monétaire sur tout le territoire de la Gaule, notamment dans les régions qui furent le plus touchées par les razzias des Barbares . . . Ce monnayage correspondait à une nécessité, il fallait absolument approvisionner le marché local en moyens de paiement.[5]

Besides this, the fact that milestones were still being put up for Tetricus Senior, for example at Saint-Gondran (I-et-V), Rennes and Nantes, Tetricus Junior (Caro, M) and Aurelian (Elven, M), together with the find of a well-used coin of Claudius Gothicus under the bath of the *frigidarium* of the villa at Keradennec (which incidentally shows that rural buildings were still being repaired in the early 270s), point to a succession of hit-and-run raids rather than to massive and devastating invasion. The cumulative effect of these inroads was, however, a total collapse of the traditional social and economic structure of the region before the end of the century.

[5] 'One might believe, *a priori*, that this would have been absent or nearly so, yet this is not the case. On the contrary, the examination of hoards reveals a certain activity and the circulation of money throughout all Gaul, notably in the regions which were most affected by barbarian raids . . . This coinage corresponded to a necessity, since it was absolutely imperative to provide the local market with means for payment.' (J-B. Giard, 'La monnaie locale en Gaule à la fin du IIIe siècle, reflet de la vie économique', *Journal des Savants*, Janvier–Mars 1969, 5–34).

By AD 300, the agricultural system of western Gaul, like that of *Belgica*, seems indeed to have completely broken down. Some villas were finally abandoned *c.* 270–80 (for instance, Pen-ar-Creac'h, Pleudaniel, C-d'A), while in most others standards of life deteriorated dramatically. Costly pavements, for example, were robbed and main buildings were deserted in favour of bath-houses, the latter being turned into rough-and-ready shelters.[6] Though this might, of course, be related to a possible flight of landlords to safer spots, leaving their estates in the hand of bailiffs, the sharp decrease of cultivation in the late third century and the corresponding encroachment of forests, revealed by pollen analysis, and the fact that none of these villas was rebuilt in the fourth century, emphasize the acuteness of the crisis. This severe disruption probably resulted from a deep disorganization of the integrated economic system of the province. A heavy depopulation of the Empire due to war and epidemics, a general climate of terror and breakdown of traditional commercial networks, may well have caused the ruin and flight of the *honestiores*, a disintegration of rigid social structures and growing number of idle peasants, sparking off a social explosion in the 280s. According to Eutropius (*Historia romanae*, 9, 20, 3) and Orosius (*Adversus paganos*, 7, 25, 2), the Gallic *rusticani* revolted during the reign of Carinus (AD 283–5). Their *Bacaudae*, whose strong separatist tendencies foreshadow the early fifth-century Armorican uprising (Zosimus, *Historia nova*, VI, 5), wreaked havoc for a few years in the *Tractus Armoricanus* between the Seine and Loire, before being put down by regular troops.

Stretching all along the coasts of the *Osismi*, the *garum* and salt-fish industry that had developed in the second century seems to have shared in the decline. All the bay of Douarnenez installations had come to a standstill by AD 280–5. A coin hoard dated to 275 has recently been found in a fish-salting tank at Morgat (F), while at Plomarc'h, Douarnenez, the third-century destruction level, containing *antoniniani* of Tetricus, was sealed by a thick sterile layer. This perfectly viable branch of the local economy seems to have withered and died in a very short time. Since most of its prosperity depended on seaborne exports, the permanent presence

---

[6] As at Kervennec and Keradennec; Le Clos Lory, Plouasne (C-d'A); Mané-Véchen, Plouhinec (M).

of pirates in the Channel and the Atlantic (Eutropius, *Historia romanae*, 9, 21; Aurelius Victor, *Epitome*, 39, 20) must have severed its commercial networks, while the disruption of Armorican society hastened its decline.

Towns, a capital element in the integrated economic system, suffered much from its disruption. While some *civitas*-capitals, like Rennes, Vannes and Nantes, protected the remains of their past grandeur behind high walls, generally built from materials quarried from neighbouring monuments, archaeology has shown a dramatic deterioration of living standards in unprotected centres and suburbs. The aqueduct supplying *Vorgium* (Carhaix), for example, had fallen into disuse before the end of the century. The time was clearly ripe for the elaboration of a coherent and comprehensive defensive system which would allow the Gauls to lick their wounds in peace and salvage what they could from the ruins of the past.

From Armorica to Brittany

A new era of peace and stability opened in western Gaul in the first decades of the fourth century. The Emperor Diocletian (284–305) and his successors, for a time, succeeded in holding back barbarian pressure at the frontiers of the Empire by refurbishing and strengthening its defences. Progressively evolving from the *Litus Saxonicum* system of forts and naval bases established on both sides of the Straits of Dover under the Tetrarchy, in order to stop the raids of North Sea pirates, the Armorican defensive line, incorporated in the comprehensive *Tractus Armoricanus et Nervicanus* (extending from the Straits of Dover to the mouth of the Gironde), consisted in a series of *points d'appui*. These were interconnected by good roads which mobile troops could use to oppose any enemy landing, with smaller garrisons stationed in sensitive districts to hold a hostile force before the intervention of regular troops. This was a standard pattern of defence used on most *limites* of the Empire.

Though the Armorican strongpoints show no structural unity, having either made use of late third-century urban defences (Rennes, Vannes, Nantes) or been built *ex nihilo* on the site of Iron Age promontory forts like Alet, Coz-Yaudet, Ploulec'h (C-d'A), or Brest(?), their location on important river estuaries or tidal inlets (with the obvious exception of Rennes) hints at common strategic functions. They were indeed first and foremost static defences, protected against any direct attack by their high walls and artillery. Yet it is clear that flotillas harboured nearby could intercept raiders at sea, while the garrisons manning these fortresses (the *Martenses* at Alet, *Mauri Osismiaci* at Brest, *Mauri Veneti* at Vannes and *Superventores Iuniores* at Nantes) all belonged to the *legiones pseudocomitatenses* stationed in Gaul. They were placed under the high command of the *Dux Tractus Armoricani et Nervicani* and must have been able to contest any enemy landing in their zone of intervention.

Surprisingly, the various artefacts (belt-buckles, cruciform and late penannular brooches, etc.) generally connected with the

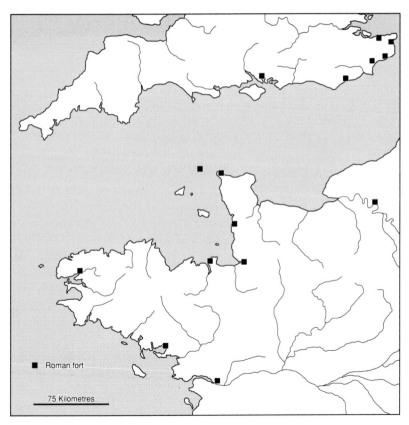

Figure 17   Distribution of Late Roman forts in the west

Plate 20   Walls of the Late Roman fort at Brest

presence of soldiers in fourth-century contexts are few in number and oddly distributed, since few (15%) come from the fortresses themselves or their vicinity. Most were actually found in the late occupation levels of villas and temples, in isolated graves and small cemeteries.[7] All of these locations are, however, situated at a short distance from major Roman roads. It is thus tempting to relate them to a complementary defensive system consisting of a network of 'foreign' communities settled on deserted estates and along main arteries after they had been 'recruited' among barbarian Germans. The late fourth-century(?) administrative document known as the *Notitia Dignitatum* thus lists Frankish *laeti* billeted on the territory of the *Riedones* (*in partibus Occidentis*, XLII, 36) and very probably among Romanized Britons, as the earliest Brittonic settlements in the Armorican peninsula are now largely thought to date from the Later Roman period.

Sheltered behind this protective curtain, the western *civitates* were able to recover for a while. Numerous finds of imported

---

[7] Villas: Keradennec, Saint-Frégant; Le Bosséno, Carnac; and Gorré-Bloué, Plouescat (F); temple: Trogouzel, Douarnenez; graves: Sables d'Or, Pléherel; Goaz-an-Eyec, Pont-du-Buis (F); and Etel (M); cemetery: La Hérupée (M).

pottery from the Argonne, *Aquitania* ('à l'éponge' ware) and Britain ('black-burnished' from Dorset and New Forest wares), as well as a few 'rich' graves and the rebuilding of a large bath complex in Corseul point to a short-lived renaissance, though social and economic conditions had clearly changed from what they were under the High Empire. This brief revival apparently came to an end in the 350s, perhaps with the usurpation of Magnentius and the barbarian onslaught on the Rhine (AD 352). From that time onwards, the military and economic situation of Armorica seems to have gradually got worse. Most, possibly all, villas were deserted before the end of the century. The local economy largely moved from a coin-economy to barter in the 360s, though Romanized ways and manners may well have been preserved in walled towns as late as the early fifth century. On the other hand, the curial class, whose vested interests were no longer protected by a strong political system and whose prosperity had largely evaporated in the economic collapse of the province, must progressively have lost faith in a far-away government that could no longer safeguard its own citizens. It is no wonder that in the early 410s:

All Armorica and other provinces of Gaul copied the British example and freed themselves in the same way, expelling their Roman governors and establishing their own administration as best they could. (Zosimus, *Hist. nova*, VI, 5)

Nothing is known, however, of this new authority which must have faced insuperable problems, as the usurpation of the British general Constantine (Constantine III, AD 406–11) combined with the barbarian invasion of Gaul and Bacaudic uprisings to accelerate the disruption of a fragile political and social order. Though the control of north-western Gaul was regained in 417 by Roman troops led by Exuperantius (Rutilius Namatianus, *De redite suo*, 1, 5, 216ff.), anarchy prevailed again after the latter's untimely death in 424. Both the *Querolus* (a comedy composed in the 420s) and the major Bacaudic revolt of 435–7 (*Chronica Gallica*, 435, 437) point to the distintegration of the traditional social structures and to renewed autonomist trends in western *Lugdunensis*, probably given added vigour by the settling of numerous British contingents.

The second half of the fifth century thus appears as a crucial

Plate 21   Fifth-century gold coin from Saint-Nicodème (C-d'A)

period in the history of western France, though it is extremely obscure because of the almost total lack of relevant historical information and archaeological material with the exception of a small group of *solidi* minted for Iulius Nepos (474–5) and Zeno (474–91) found in western Côtes-d'Armor. This is all the more unfortunate since in the midst of those dark years the old Roman order faded into oblivion and a new world was born.

After the Romans: Britons, Bretons and Franks

Britons and Bretons

The transition from Roman Armorica to Celtic Brittany was a gradual process which took place between the late fourth and early seventh centuries AD, largely because of an important influx of population from Late and post-Roman Britain. In succeeding centuries these *Brittones* merged with the indigenous *Armorici* to become *the* Bretons. This migration had profound effects on the Armorican peninsula, most obviously in dividing it linguistically between those who preserved Brittonic speech and those who spoke Vulgar Latin and its Romance successor. Political and cultural consequences also stemmed from this division though a precise chronological account of what occurred is impossible to establish from the fragmentary evidence that has survived.

The archaeological record is as yet meagre in comparison with the relative abundance of information on Roman Armorica. Contemporary historical records are also miserly with unambiguous detail. Many pose huge interpretive problems or, in the case of Gildas, even of sheer comprehension. The same is true of the numerous Breton saints' lives recounting the tribulations and triumphs of the earliest missionaries, abbots and bishops down to the seventh century. There are more than fifty of them, but against the plethora of evidence they provide (and for material conditions or attitudes it is undoubtedly valuable) has to be balanced the fact that even the earliest (the first life of St Samson of Dol) was written considerably after its subject's death around 565. Most date from the ninth century or later, several centuries after their subject's lifetime. Though containing older traditions, they much more obviously reflect conditions at the moment they were written. Moreover, as an exemplary genre, hagiography obeys rules in which historical as opposed to spiritual truths rank low in their authors' concern. This is shown by the use of earlier non-Breton lives as models, like that of St Martin of Tours by Sulpicius Severus. Hagiography thus often tells us more about later writers and their resources than about the saints themselves. Another rich source which also causes serious problems of interpretation is place-name evidence.

It is thus not surprising that the question of what weight should be attached to earlier Roman, Celtic or Gaulish traditions in the formation of Breton society in the early Middle Ages receives differing and frequently conflicting answers. There is also the matter of proximity: in contrast to other contemporary migrations, by the Goths and Vandals, for example, who ranged over huge distances and came into contact with peoples from whom they differed radically in custom or material culture, Britons and Armoricans had been neighbours since prehistoric times. They had long shared, thanks to seaways which aided rather than hindered communication, similar political and material circumstances. In his life of Agricola, Tacitus first commented on the closeness of language and the fact that tribes with similar names could be found on both sides of the Channel. Initially, the migration of large numbers of Britons reinforced aspects of a long-standing relationship.

By the third century AD Britons and Armoricans were Roman citizens. From the fourth they were nominally Christian in faith. They considered themselves 'Romans', sharing and preserving *romanitas*, despite disenchantment with Imperial rule evidenced in still mysterious Bacaudic revolts. If, as analysis of burials at Saint-Urnel-en-Plomeur (F) suggests, Britons were already settling in Armorica in the mid fourth century, it may be assumed that they were likely to have done so with the cooperation of the civil and military authorities there (cf. above p. 124). Elsewhere, lacking specifically differing characteristics, it is hard to distinguish easily in an archaeological context between newcomers and natives. Here, however, only a summary account can be presented of the many debates which have centred on why and when the Britons left Britain for Armorica and what the consequences were as they became Bretons.

Recent work, notably that of Léon Fleuriot, has emphasized that following the conquest of Britain by the Romans, Romano-Britons travelled and settled widely throughout the Empire for many reasons. Traces of their presence have been found in place-names or inscriptions from such widely dispersed locations as the Rhineland and Dalmatia as well as from Gaul, where they can be discovered chiefly in the region between the Somme and Loire. The collapse of the Empire, far from discouraging such movements seems only to have intensified them. Britons from the late fourth century joined the *Völkerwanderung* that characterized the early Middle Ages. A colony, for example, seems to have been established in Galicia in the fifth century. In the mid sixth century the abbey of St Maria de Bretona near Mondenedo and the presence of a bishop called Mailoc at a council at Braga in 572 are two signs of an active Brittonic community in Iberia. Borrowings from the Visigoths observed in Irish art may also stem from this link. A few chance finds of coins both in Brittany (before 575 from Saint-Quay Portrieux, C-d'A) and in Kent testify to early Visigothic trading links though these, like contacts with Galicia, then fade away.

It was Gildas (writing around 540) who first graphically described how some Britons, after the earliest fifth-century Anglo-Saxon invasions of England, 'made for lands beyond the sea [where] beneath the swelling sails they loudly wailed, singing a psalm that took the place of a shanty: "You have given us like sheep for eating and scattered us among the heathen"' (*De Excidio*, 25, 1, trans. Winterbottom). A few years later the Byzantine historian Procopius, who first applies the description *Britannia* to the region known previously as Armorica, recounts that people from Britain were still moving to Francia in the mid sixth century though he blames over-population rather than external enemies for their migration (*De Bello Gothico*, 8, 20). But since the majority of Britons who settled in what became Brittany seem on linguistic and religious grounds to have come from south-western England and Wales, regions initially far distant from those first affected by the Anglo-Saxons, this poses a conundrum. There is also the fact that the Anglo-Saxons' arrival and expansion westwards in England does not entirely synchronize with what is known of British migrations to Armorica.

This led scholars like Ferdinand Lot and Nora Chadwick to

emphasize the role of Pictish and Scottish (i.e. Irish) raids along the western seaboard of Britain from the late third century as a spur to migration. It has been pointed out that Late Roman defences in Wales were raised not to suppress the native population but to protect the coasts, an equivalent to the forts of the Saxon shore in south-east England and those across the Channel in the *Tractus Armoricanus et Nervicanus*, the great sweep of territory from the Seine basin to the Gironde (cf. above p. 122). Native British troops gained a reputation which led to their increasing use on the Continent in defence of the Empire, or by individuals like Magnus Maximus in 383 or Constantine III in 406–7 who took large numbers with them in a bid for Imperial power.

Such authentic troop movements to the Continent provided material for a long-accepted explanation of the origins of the Breton state (equivalent to the Anglo-Saxon Hengist and Horsa legend). This achieved its apotheosis in Geoffrey of Monmouth's *History of the Kings of Britain* (*c.* 1136), though elements were also independently incorporated into the *Dream of Macsen Wledig*, a story in the great medieval Welsh cycle known as the *Mabinogion*. According to this tradition, it was after the final defeat of the Imperial pretender Maximus in 388 that the remnants of his army, now under the leadership of Conan Meriadec, stayed behind in Gaul, where Conan founded a long-enduring dynasty and his men also took wives. Unfortunately no convincing historical proof of Conan's existence has ever come to light and the story has, since the eighteenth century, been rejected for the myth it is. In reality, whatever the extent of earlier movements, evidence currently available suggests that it was from the mid fifth century that Britons began to arrive in Gaul in increasing numbers, whilst proof of their political organization in Armorica is later still.

The written record is quickly summarized: in 461 Mansuetus *episcopus Britannorum* attended a church council at Tours. Whether he was a pilgrim from Britain to the shrine of St Martin rather than a pastor of Britons already domiciled in Gaul is unknown, though in support of this latter view Fleuriot has drawn attention to the presence at an earlier council in 453 at Angers of Chariato, whose name may also be rendered as Mansuetus (charitable). More directly, the chronicler Jordanes relates that in 469–70 a force under Riothamus (a Celtic name or title signifying supreme king or leader) was fighting for Emperor Anthemius in the

Loire valley against Euric and his Visigoths, whilst shortly afterwards the Auvergnat bishop and poet Sidonius Apollinaris mentions plans to attack the Bretons *supra Ligerim sitos*. Fleuriot has energetically championed the idea that Riothamus may be equated with Ambrosius Aurelianus, named by Gildas and Nennius as leader of the native Britons against the Saxons and the most obvious historical candidate for King Arthur. He has also attributed· to Ambrosius/Riothamus a cross-Channel thalassocracy, largely on the basis of later delphic statements in saints' lives about the existence of an analogous Brittonic joint-kingdom linking Devon and Cornwall with northern Brittany. These adventurous views, shared by other Arthurian enthusiasts, have yet to gain general support. But we may accept that British (or Breton) troops continued to fight in Gaul, perhaps under the general command of Syagrius (cf. below p. 139). Clovis, king of the Franks, is reported to have defeated such a force around 490 and as late as 530, if the life of St Dalmas, bishop of Rodez, may be trusted, a *legio britannica* was based at Orléans.

Although the *Vita Tutguali* recounts the settlement in Dumnonia of Riwal and his followers in the early sixth century, the presence of Britons in Armorica at this period has proved difficult to document. They were apparently established within the jurisdiction of Melanius, bishop of Rennes, *c.* 511–20 when he and his fellow bishops of Angers and Tours despatched a remarkable letter to two peripatetic Breton priests, Lovocat and Catihern. It expressed the bishops' deep concern at their use of women (*conhospitae*) in distributing the sacrament in two kinds as they moved from house to house, both common Celtic practices. The ministry in northern Gaul of Samson, probable founder of the abbey-bishopric of Dol, may be dated to the middle decades of the sixth century. A council held at Tours in 567 decreed that neither 'Romans' nor 'Bretons' were to be consecrated bishop without the consent of the metropolitan and his fellow bishops. Since the bishops of Rennes, Nantes and Vannes already acknowledged the authority of Tours and had attended councils from at least the mid fifth century, it may be assumed that the 'Bretons' lived further to the north and west. There the evidence of rigorously ascetic monasticism, use of the Celtic Easter, tonsure, bells, church dedications and so on, points to the predominance of insular religious practices until Carolingian reforms of the ninth century. Surviving extracts from an early law code once known as the *Canones Wallici* but found in manuscripts mainly of Breton provenance and bearing the title *Excerpta de libris Romanorum et Francorum*, may also provide a glimpse of conditions in Armorica when 'Romans' (i.e. Britons) were living alongside the Franks in relative harmony. For a distant observer like Procopius, by the mid sixth century the name *Britannia* for the province in which they lived seemed appropriate; it was adopted soon afterwards by Frankish writers and has remained in use to the present.[1]

Settlement and society in the Dark Ages

It is possible only to surmise the role of state authorities in promoting the earliest movements, probably for military purposes; it cannot be documented. Where soldiers led, civilians were encouraged to follow, officially or otherwise. Later, as central control in both Britain and Gaul broke down, the role of local secular and religious leaders in organizing migration appears paramount. Political and social fragmentation increased the importance of family and kinship. Many of the 'saints' (the eponymous founders commemorated in so many Breton place-names) to whom later tradition assigned a directing role in the exodus, were members of aristocratic or princely families. Some clearly went to Brittany as *peregrini* and hermits or as the spiritual heads of small monastic communities, anxious to shun the world. For them the harsh conditions of life on the Breton coastline were an ideal challenge as the remains of small religious sites like those on Ile Lavret and Ile Modez (C-d'A) reveal. Others may have been forced by political circumstances to seek their fortunes abroad with their families and followers. Where they can be traced, most seem to have come from south Wales. St Samson's original home,

---

[1] For Celtic-speaking peoples the form *Letavia* and its derivatives was used from an early period to describe the region to which the Britons had gone (cf. Modern Welsh *Llydaw*). One traditional explanation of its meaning harks back to the legend of Conan Meriadec and his men who took wives in Armorica but cut out their tongues 'lest their descendants should learn the language of their mothers, and that is why we in our language call them "Letewicion", that is half-silent . . .' (*Dream of Macsen Wledig*). The form 'Letewicion' is already found in the *Historia Brittonum* attributed to Nennius, whilst the Anglo-Saxon chronicle occasionally refers to Brittany as 'Lidwiccium'. *Armor* was now restricted to the coastline as opposed to *Arcoët*, the wooded and more sparsely settled interior of the province.

Llantwit Major, was an important centre from which monks later scattered along various routes, many of which led ultimately to Brittany. But Ireland and south-western England also provided leaders. Linguistic evidence especially supports the idea of a very strong late wave of migrants from Devon and Cornwall (below p. 146). Some historians have sought to trace the emigration of particular family groups by plotting the current distribution of Celtic church dedications like those to St Maudez, St Guénolé and St Gildas in Brittany.

At first new homes could probably be found without much difficulty in a province which in late Roman times suffered a decline in population. But in time, increasing numbers and urgency in the competition for good land, of which there is not a superabundance in western Brittany, caused dissension. This is most clearly seen in the military conquest of the Vannetais in the late sixth century (below p. 140). It may also be revealed in the destruction of villas and the way in which former Gallo-Roman sites offered shelter to later inhabitants in very different circumstances. It is perhaps significant that the *Excerpta* (above p. 133) make provision for compensation to be paid in slaves, for memories of Breton conquests and the expulsion or enslavement of natives haunted the Franks for many centuries. In addition, some tantalizing archaeological evidence for resistance to possible Breton advances has been discovered in fifth-century rural fortifications in the region between Quintin and Callac (C-d'A) where for a time a frontier may have lain with surviving Gallo-Romans, increasingly caught between two hostile forces, the Bretons to the north-west and the Franks to the east. In other areas, too, it is likely that violence between the indigenous population and newcomers turned peaceful infiltration into military occupation.

The best guide to the otherwise incalculable density and spread of settlement is provided by place-names. It has long been recognized that like the province itself the major political divisions of early medieval Brittany acquired new names from the migrants. Dumnonia (Domnonée), stretching from the Bay of Saint-Michel westwards and ruled for a period by a royal dynasty, and Cornovia (Cornouaille), where early political history is impenetrably shrouded in myth, indubitably owe theirs to migrants from Devon and Cornwall. The way in which Broërec took shape can be traced with some confidence, thanks to Gregory of Tours's account of the campaigns of the Breton chieftain Waroc from whom it took its name (below p. 141). But the impact of insular Brittonic-speakers on local toponomy is equally dramatic. Even a cursory glance at a map reveals close parallels between Cornish and Welsh names and those in Brittany where the same ones occur, often in identical form. Explanation of these similarities has, however, led to very different conclusions about the character of the migrations. A classic example is analysis of the element Plou.

Plou (from Latin *plebs*, people, cf. Welsh *plwyf*), later interchangeable with Gui/guic (Latin *vicus*), is very common in Brittany. Of all the place-names beginning with Plou and its many alternative forms (pla, plab, plan, ple, pleb, plo, ploe, ploi, poul, etc.) some 75% are compounded with a personal name (without exception male). About a third of these are fairly well attested as later cult figures. Another third are otherwise unknown saints whilst the rest appear to have been laymen. Where they can be traced, the majority of these eponyms have an insular origin; moreover, the way in which Plous are clustered most densely along

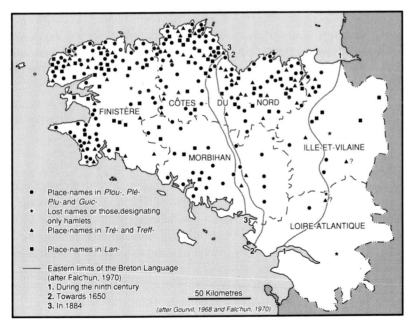

Figure 18   Distribution of place-name elements Plou-, Guic-, Tré- and Lan-

the northern littoral and diminish in numbers to the east or south
has been seen as mirroring the likely direction of much migration.
Accordingly, René Largillière (in 1925) stated categorically that
the *plou* was in essence a 'petite république autonome', formed by
missionaries following the migrations. The fact that many Plous
were parishes, a status they conserved till the Revolution, after
which they became civil communes, was taken as further proof of
their religious origins and antiquity.

More recently, however, whilst acknowledging the important
role likely to have been taken by priests in creating a parish
structure that was both in position at a very early date and also
remarkably independent of episcopal control, the secular aspects of
the *plebs* have been re-emphasized. On the one hand, studies of the
distribution of Plous in relation to the Roman road system,
Imperial administrative divisions, geographical location and size,
reinforce the view that for some at least, especially those
combining Plou with a common name (such as castle, Plougastel,
or wall, Ploumoguer), origins must be sought in the pre-migration
period. On the other hand, the existence of numerous Plounevez
(new parish or community) underlines the obvious fact that Plous
were not all created simultaneously. Moreover, when organization
and structure can be studied from contemporary records in the
ninth century the *plebs* appears as a lay community rather than as a
'community primarily associated for religious purposes' (Wendy
Davies). Whilst in most cases it had a church at its centre, it was by
then a 'social unit, with clearly defined characteristics, and the
territory that that unit occupied'. It remains to be seen whether
these arguments will carry the day.

Less controversially, two other elements, Lan (cf. Welsh *Llan*)
and Loc (Latin *locus*), do have obvious ecclesiastical significance.
Like Plou, the majority of later parishes including the element Lan
are to be found along the north coast. They are thus probably
indicative of the earliest stages of colonization. Loc, however,
represents a later period since such names are particularly
associated with settlements around priories (e.g. Loctudy, the
church or place of St Tudy, F) which subsequently formed a
nucleus for urban development in the central Middle Ages (below
p. 210).

Among other terms relating closely to the post-migration period
may be cited: Tré (Welsh *Tref*), a subdivision of a parish, a

settlement of varying size; Lis or Lez (Welsh *llys*, translated as Latin *aula*), a court or hall, the residence of a person of note as well as a village or hamlet; Ker (Welsh *Caer*), a hamlet; and Lan or Lann, with the meaning 'estate', a piece of open or common land (*lande*). Some have origins contemporary with Lan used in its religious sense and Plou names. Tré, for instance, is frequently found in conjunction with the same personal names as those used for Plous. Many were parishes and have retained their status as communes. Lis has seldom been perpetuated in parish names (the major exception is Lesneven, F) but refers, often in association with the element Coët (Welsh *Coed*, wood) or individual tree names, to minor settlements literally cut out of the forest as colonization progressed. Like Loc, Ker is also associated with later settlement rather than the migration period. It appears, at least in eastern Brittany, to replace Tré from the tenth century onwards; overall, more than 18,000 Ker names have been identified.

In addition to these elements of Brittonic origin, there is one other normally considered of major importance in connection with

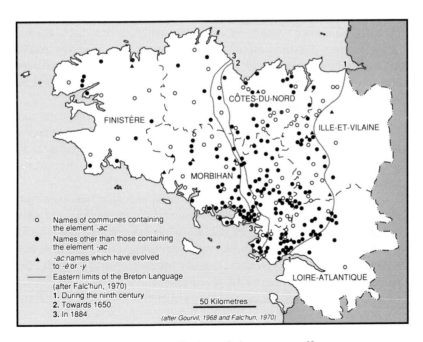

Figure 19   Distribution of place-name suffix -ac

the British settlement in Armorica and the fate of the former inhabitants: the case of names terminating in -ac, -é or -y. When plotted on a map they appear as a reverse image of Plou names. As the density of these latter decreases from north to south and from west to east, the opposite is true for -ac, -é and -y names. For Joseph Loth (d. 1934) and his disciples this fact provided both a measure of the Romanization of Armorica and evidence for the furthest limits of Breton-speaking. During the Roman period many place-names terminated in -acum. As Vulgar Latin evolved this changed in northern Gaul to -ay, -y, or -é endings. In Brittany the vast majority of parish names terminating in -é or -ay are located in the dioceses of Rennes and Nantes, whilst suffixes in -ac chiefly occupy an adjacent zone just to the west with a thin scatter into Finistère. It was, Loth argued, the migration of Bretons into this 'mixed zone' that slowed down the normal evolution and helped to preserve the intermediate form -ac (later, -oc, -euc, -uc and -ec). Where -ac names survived, it also indicated the survival of Romance-speaking populations interspersed among Brittonic-speakers. More recently it has been stressed that Gallo-Roman -acum names are a modification of the primitive Gaulish suffix -acos, while since -acum was seldom compounded with a clear Gallo-Roman personal name, this further suggested the hypothesis of a much greater survival of the Gaulish language than had been previously postulated (cf. below p. 145). Here all that need be said is that while it now seems unwise to take -ac suffixes as an index of Romanization, there still appears to be some force in the argument that the way Plou names shade into a zone where -ac, -é and -y suffixes gradually increase is a measure of the interpenetration of Breton- and Romance-speaking populations in the period immediately following the migrations.

The location of that 'mixed zone' and the question of where exactly the frontier between Breton and French lies has attracted much attention. Atlases since the late sixteenth century have shown a division between Upper and Lower Brittany. This reflects earlier administrative arrangements, which in turn once broadly approximated to the linguistic division of the province between Bretagne Gallo and Bretagne Bretonnante. But by the nineteenth century the advance westwards of French at the expense of Breton had displaced this 'frontier', usually depicted starkly as a line crossing the peninsula from a point on the north coast to one on the south. In these terms, the limit of spoken Breton currently runs south from near Saint-Quay Portrieux on the Bay of Saint-Brieuc, leaving Noyal-Pontivy (M) to the west, to strike the base of the Rhuys peninsula near Ambon (M). In Loth's day it ran parallel but some 10 to 15 km further east. Using the evidence of place-names Loth showed that the maximum extension of the 'mixed zone', in which considerable numbers of Breton-speakers at one time lived alongside French-speakers, was fixed by a line from the mouth of the Couesnon, passing to the west of Rennes and then sweeping down to the Loire at Savenay (L-A). This should not, however, be considered a fixed or water-tight boundary; just as there were enclaves of Romance-speakers in Cornouaille until well into the Middle Ages, so early colonization as well as conquest of the March of Brittany (below p. 156) saw a surge eastwards that carried some Breton-speakers into Maine and Anjou as well.

To sum up, the pattern of settlement revealed by place-name evidence suggests a considerable colonization of much of the Armorican peninsula by Brittonic-speaking migrants from the fourth century onwards that eventually extended well beyond the current limits of the Breton language. Geographically, it appears to have been densest along the northern coastal fringe, where the centres of many Plous, future parishes and *bourgs*, lie just inland on the plateau rather than on the littoral itself. In addition many small vills and hamlets were established, especially as new land was cleared. During the earliest period poorer regions like the Monts d'Arrée and Montagnes Noires do not appear to have attracted many settlers. Likewise the southern part of Cornouaille and the adjoining western parts of the diocese of Vannes were apparently lightly settled by Brittonic-speaking migrants. Overall, a pattern of dispersed dwellings, with mixed arable and pastoral farming, was established. It remained characteristic of the Breton countryside until the mid twentieth century.

Bretons and Franks

In the fifth and sixth centuries whilst the Bretons were settling Armorica, the rise of the Franks under the Merovingian dynasty was the major political development in Gaul. For Gregory of Tours a decisive step was the defeat in 486 of Syagrius *rex Romanorum* and his subsequent murder by Clovis who thus acquired Soissons, opening the way for Frankish expansion west of the Somme. As early as the fourth century Franks had served as *laeti* in Armorica, where the *Notitia Dignitatum* shows them based around Rennes. Under Clovis they gradually began to return: his defeat of a Breton force on the Loire has already been mentioned. Later Gregory of Tours wrote that 'from the death of King Clovis onwards the Bretons remained under the domination of the Franks and their rulers were called counts not kings', though the evidence seems to be that bold Frankish thrusts into Aquitaine, culminating in victory at Vouillé (507), which brought control of the middle Loire, for the moment left Armorica untouched. In the reign of Clovis's immediate successor Childebert (511–58) Frankish relations with those holding authority in Armorica, whether Bretons or the Gallo-Romans of the eastern *civitates* of Rennes, Nantes and Vannes, remained friendly if the hesitant appearance of Frankish place-names and the general absence of Frankish archaeological remains is a guide to the Franks' westward progress. The Frankish cemeteries recently excavated at Bais and Visseiche (I-et-V), for example, were apparently only brought into use from the late sixth century.

After 558 vicious family quarrels changed all this. They led to a kaleidoscopically changing series of alliances between many Frankish and Breton factions, resulting in armed attacks from either side. These are described in lurid detail by Gregory of Tours. The rebellion of the Merovingian Chramn against his father Lothair I and his flight to Brittany around 560 where he allied with Chanao is an early example. According to Gregory, Chanao himself had already killed three of his own brothers and outlawed a fourth, Macliaw, who at one point was forced to seek shelter in a hurriedly constructed barrow, breathing through a little air-hole, whilst his pursuers sat drinking on what they had been informed was his grave (*Historia Francorum*, IV, 4).

In other words, political power among the Bretons as amongst the Franks was fragmented in the hands of several chieftains. This remained normal until much later. The Brittonic title *Ri*, usually translated by Frankish chroniclers as Latin *Rex*, king, gives a misleading impression of the authority exercised by most early Breton leaders. On this occasion, Macliaw appears to have been the innocent party; later he seized the bishopric of Vannes and made a treaty with another Breton chieftain, Bodic. This he typically failed to keep, thus provoking a feud with Bodic's son, Theuderic, which resulted in his own murder and that of his son Jacob. His second son, Waroc, now succeeded and it was under his dynamic leadership that the Bretons advanced by force into the Vannetais, impelled perhaps by pressure from migrants searching for new lands and more obviously by a thirst for booty. The Gallo-Romans, especially those of Nantes, still possessed considerable material wealth as recent finds of pottery, metal-ware, sarcophagi and the remains of the cathedral, which Bishop Felix (d. 582) built, testify. The attraction for the Bretons of the Nantais in one particular respect is clear from Gregory's statement that they several times carried off the wine harvest from that region.

In 578 Chilperic attacked the Bretons in his turn. A treaty arranged with Waroc was soon broken by the Breton leader. Both sides launched new attacks which the bishops of Nantes, Felix and Nonnechius, tried to terminate in order to halt the escalating violence. In a development that curiously prefigures the Frankish March eventually set up by the Carolingians to contain the Bretons (below p. 148), King Guntram in the 580s appointed Beppolen as *dux* and committed Rennes, Nantes and Angers to his keeping. But fighting continued, especially after Beppolen's death in 590. Ebrachar, his successor, had a brief moment of triumph when he captured the city of Vannes and forced Waroc into agreeing never to cause trouble again. Hardly had the promise been given than it was broken. Ebrachar's retreating army was harried and shortly afterwards Waroc once more possessed Vannes, where Bishop Regalis lamented that his flock was forced to accept the 'Breton yoke'.

In this painful fashion the zones of Frankish and Breton influence in the south-east were defined. In territorial terms the division came to lie along the course of the Vilaine river, where it remained for nearly two centuries until Pippin III recaptured Vannes (below p. 148). But the concept of a 'political frontier' was for much of this period as fluid as the linguistic one (above p. 139). Frankish influences continued to penetrate the Vannetais, where refugees found occasional asylum. Bretons settled around Guérande (L-A) and in the Brière, the great peat-fen to the north of the Loire estuary, where pockets of Breton-speakers have remained until modern times. In many respects the Bretons of Broërec remained closer in habits and style of life to the surviving Gallo-Roman population than the Franks themselves. Unfortunately, no Frankish writer after Gregory of Tours has left us a comparable account of events. From *c.* 600 to 750 the political history of the Vannetais is an almost complete blank.

Relations between Bretons and Franks in northern Brittany from the mid sixth century do not appear to have changed as dramatically as they did in Broërec. The silence of Gregory of Tours on events in Dumnonia may be taken as an indication of this. If, as seems most probable, Bishop Samson, who attended a church council in Paris in 563, is indeed the founder of Dol, his *Lives* reveal that he was on good terms with King Childebert whose court he visited on several occasions. Once he apparently did so to obtain the release of the prince of Dumnonia (unless this story is based on events which actually occurred in the seventh century – below p. 143). His ministry was exercised over a wide region from the Trégor to the valley of the Seine as the many churches later dedicated to him and the numerous scattered enclaves and parishes acknowledging obedience to Dol in neighbouring dioceses demonstrate. In the opposite direction, there are also now more positive signs of Frankish penetration into northern Brittany. When in 616 Bertrand, bishop of Le Mans, left his possessions to his church they included *villa Colonica sita in territorio Tricurino*, usually identified as the Trégor, given him by Beppolen. A stela of Frankish type has been found at Pléherel (C-d'A) whilst place-names containing Germanic elements have been identified around Saint-Brieuc, such as Lannebert, Trohibert, Cesson (= Saxon) and Hénon (from the personal name Haymo).

Later, in 635, there is one celebrated occasion when the Frankish ruler Dagobert I (622–38) intervened directly in Breton affairs. In the absence of other evidence of comparable precision, the chronicler Fredegar's account deserves to be quoted in full:

Dagobert, then at Clichy, sent a mission into Brittany to require the Bretons to make prompt amends for what they had done amiss and to submit to his rule. Otherwise, he said, the Burgundian army that had been in Gascony would at once advance on Brittany. When he heard this, the Breton king Judicael went at once to Clichy with a quantity of gifts to ask pardon of King Dagobert . . . and undertook that he and his kingdom of Brittany should always remain under the lordship of Dagobert and the Frankish kings. However he declined to eat or sit down to table with

Dagobert, for he was religious and full of the fear of God. When Dagobert did sit down to table, Judicael left the palace and went to dine at the residence of the referendary Dado, whom he knew to lead a religious life. On the following day King Judicael took leave of Dagobert and returned laden with gifts to Brittany. (*Chronicle*, trans. Wallace-Hadrill)

The life of St Eloi by St Ouen (Dado the referendary mentioned by Fredegar) provides a different version of the same events: Judicael on arrival at Creil (not Clichy) made an alliance with Dagobert rather than a submission. Ingomar's eleventh-century *Life* of Judicael (he later became a monk at Saint-Méen) adds further details. It includes a eulogy of Judicael boasting of his martial ardour and celebrating his victories over the Franks 'who wished to subjugate Brittany'. Though it has come down to us disguised in a Latin prose version, Fleuriot recognized its similarity to an archaic Welsh *gorchan* or epic poem. If he is correct, it is one of the few identifiable remnants of what was probably once an extensive early Breton poetic literature.

Putting all this together, it may be deduced that Judicael was a typical warrior prince, that he exercised his authority over Dumnonia from a base in the vicinity of Paimpont, and that he was subject in an honourable though largely indefinable fashion to King Dagobert. Then the moment of illumination passes. For the next hundred years the history of Dumnonia remains as obscure as that of Broërec save for one revealing comment: the Annals of Metz note under the year 691 that the Bretons, who had once acknowledged Frankish supremacy, now enjoyed freedom thanks to Merovingian dissensions. That freedom was next seriously challenged by the Carolingians.

The Breton language

In modern times four principal dialects of Breton have been recognized: those spoken in Cornouaille, Léon and Trégor (with Goëllo), collectively referred to as KLT or KLTG (K standing for Kerneu, cf. Cornish *Kernow*), and Vannetais which differs markedly from the other three in accentuation and palatalization. There has been heated debate over when and how these differences first arose. They can certainly be demonstrated in the fifteenth century

and are particularly clear in surviving literature from the seventeenth
century onwards. It is also agreed that Breton evolved through two
earlier stages: Old Breton (fourth–eleventh centuries), most of the
evidence for which comes from the ninth century and later; and
Middle Breton (eleventh–sixteenth centuries), on which the powerful influence of French is acknowledged, though it otherwise
displays remarkable continuity from Old Breton. Again most of the
evidence comes from late in the period, after the mid fourteenth
century. Modern Breton, on the other hand, developed a great
diversity of form that was still proliferating in the early twentieth
century.

Old Breton, apart from place- and proper names, now only
survives in the form of glosses on Latin texts, a total of some 6000
individual words or brief phrases. A major issue in recent years has
been whether it represents the language spoken by the migrant
Britons or whether it is simply a revived form of Primitive Gaulish,
the language of earlier inhabitants of Armorica which had been
overlain but not entirely eradicated during the Roman period. The
first view was that developed in modern scholarly form by the great
Celticist Joseph Loth. Whilst admitting the possibility of some
Gaulish or earlier Celtic influences, he saw the migrants introducing
Breton which replaced the Vulgar Latin spoken by the Romanized
inhabitants of Armorica. This argument is most fully developed by
Kenneth Jackson in his monumental *Historical Phonology of
Breton* (1967). In this he documents how Breton, in close parallel
with Cornish and Welsh, developed to its present state from
Primitive Brittonic roots common to all three later languages at the
time of the migrations. Breton and Cornish, in particular, remained
very close, speakers of the one being intelligible to speakers of the
other until the extinction of Cornish. Jackson believed that the
internal differences between the various Breton dialects only
gradually emerge after the eleventh century. Most importantly, he
attributed great formative influence to developments in the
sixteenth and seventeenth centuries (or even later) for the
characteristics of KLT.

Against this must be set the views of Chanoine F. Falc'hun.
Beginning from maps in P. Le Roux's *Atlas linguistique de la
Basse-Bretagne* (1924–63), which plot usages in modern spoken
Breton in the first half of the twentieth century, and seeking reasons
for these differences, Falc'hun became increasingly sceptical of the

Loth–Jackson interpretation of dialect origins. In a series of challenging publications, culminating most recently in his *Perspectives nouvelles sur l'histoire de la langue bretonne* (1981), a third augmented version of his original thesis (*Histoire de la langue bretonne d'après la géographie linguistique*, 1951), he has argued with great panache that Breton 'preserves the last living vestiges of the first national language of France, that of Vercingetorix' as well as that of the Druids! Although admitting that the migrant Britons had considerable influence on northern Brittany (the area of the closely connected dialects of KLT), he nevertheless maintains that the origins of the different dialects can be traced to a period before their arrival. He places particular emphasis on Vannetais as closest to Gaulish and least contaminated by the movement of Celtic-speaking peoples from Britain. In its latest guise, his argument (based on contrasts in accentuation between KLT and Vannetais which all scholars acknowledge) is that these have extremely remote origins, indeed that they first occurred before the Roman conquest of Armorica and reflect a division already apparent then between Celts sharing a common language but living on either side of the Channel.

It would be rash of someone lacking phonetic and linguistic training to pronounce a verdict on these complex issues. Falc'hun's idea that a substratum of an earlier Celtic language survived the Roman conquest of a region that lay far distant from major centres of Roman influence in Gaul, and was revived by the migration of Britons speaking a closely related tongue, is not inherently improbable. As discussion of the evolution of -acos suffixes showed (above p. 138), in place-name study an important place for Gaulish must now be recognized. There is evidence for its survival as a spoken language after the fall of the Empire in regions like the Auvergne, whilst the progress of Romance westwards into Brittany was slow. Although he arrived at the same conclusion by a different route, Fleuriot in his last years was willing to posit a greater survival of Gaulish elements in Breton than scholars of the Loth–Jackson school.

On the other hand, voicing some of the many methodological problems raised by Falc'hun's approach, Fleuriot has pointed out several important weaknesses that vitiate any simplistic progression from Primitive Gaulish to Modern Breton. For instance, Falc'hun's analysis is based almost exclusively on a study of Modern Breton.

He uses no Old Breton forms and his remarks on Middle Breton
stem exclusively from the use of the *Catholicon*, a late fifteenth-
century dictionary. He largely ignores the findings of other scholars
on the remarkable continuity between Old and Middle Breton and
their explanations, based on historical evidence, for the perceptible
differences between the two main dialects of the Middle Ages,
which eventually split to become KLT and Vannetais. There is also
the embarrassing absence of direct evidence for Gaulish in
Armorica, apart from names: one possible inscription survives on a
stela at Plumergat (M) and there is a graffito at Le Valy-Cloître (F),
though some experts consider this to be in Latin! Whatever the
merits of the respective arguments over phonology and dialectology,
many of which depend on hypothetical reconstructions of ancient
forms, much of the historical substantiation claimed by Falc'hun is
curiously unconvincing and mechanistic such as his views on two
distinct waves of migration, AD 300–400 and AD 550–650. His
treatment of the history of Carhaix (F), to which he attributes a
pivotal position in the spread of KLT, is similarly cavalier. That it
was the *civitas*-capital of the *Osismi* and had long been an
important nodal centre for communications is generally accepted.
But that it maintained throughout the Middle Ages the kind of
economic, cultural and political role which Falc'hun attributes to it
as the 'carrefour et marché central' of Lower Brittany (at one point
extravagantly comparing it to Paris as the centre of Capetian
power) is to go far beyond what can be squeezed from the exiguous
surviving records that are an almost complete blank between
c. 350 and 1100 and really only begin to yield a thin harvest
after 1300.

Finally it may be remarked that whereas Jackson in his *Historical
Phonology* provides a detailed examination and refutation of
Falc'hun's ideas as expounded in the second edition (1963) of his
thesis, Falc'hun, though acknowledging some of Jackson's earlier
work, provides no comparable critique in *Perspectives nouvelles* of
the *Historical Phonology*, a work recognized by other scholars as
of seminal importance. Indeed it is not even mentioned, although
the bibliography was allegedly revised to 1980. In such circumstances an impartial reader will feel that while the debate may
continue, at present the arguments favour the traditional interpretation. These were summarized as long ago as the late twelfth
century by Gerald of Wales:

In both Cornwall and Brittany they speak almost the same language as in Wales. It comes from the same root and is intelligible to the Welsh in many instances, and almost in all. It is rougher and less clearly pronounced, but probably closer to the original British speech, or so I think myself. (*Description of Wales*, I, 7, trans. Thorpe)

A couple of final points may be made. First, for most of the Middle Ages Old and then Middle Breton was predominantly an oral not a literary language, a characteristic of all contemporary Celtic languages. The tradition of the bard, poet or story-teller who transmitted his learning and techniques to future generations simply by word of mouth or song rather than by literary means was a powerful one which the Continental Bretons shared. In the sixth century Venantius Fortunatus, for example, commented that the harp was their chosen instrument. It remained so in the eleventh and twelfth centuries when stories of Arthur were also clearly spread by Breton *jongleurs*. As a result no developed piece of Old Breton imaginative prose or poetry has come down to us, although such works did apparently once exist. The same is largely true of Middle Breton. It is only from the mid fifteenth century that more extensive works begin to appear. For most of the Middle Ages what is known about the Bretons from literary sources comes through the distorting medium of a language other than Breton itself.

7

Carolingian Brittany

An imperial power: the Carolingians

After a long period of obscurity when the Bretons lived (as far as we can tell) largely undisturbed on the fringes of the Frankish world dramatic events brought the two peoples into violent conflict. The ancestors of Charlemagne, the Arnulfing mayors of the palace, rose to power initially in regions far distant from early medieval Brittany. A critical point was reached in 751 when Pippin the Short deposed the Merovingian Dagobert III and began to rule as the first Carolingian. Shortly afterwards his attention turned to the west. A campaign was fought in which Vannes was sacked and occupied. Pippin's action may have been prompted by Breton raids into the counties of Rennes and Maine, where monasteries like Saint-Denis and Prüm, closely associated with the new dynasty, had estates at risk. Whatever the cause, it provoked tension between the Bretons and the Franks, now ruled by a succession of predatory rulers, most famously Charlemagne himself, at the head of a powerful warrior aristocracy eager for plunder. The formal establishment of the March of Brittany is further evidence of deteriorating relations. The March united the Frankish counties of Rennes, Nantes and Vannes, backed up by those of Le Mans and Angers. It was certainly in existence by 778 when Roland, 'prefect of the March' and hero of the later *chanson*, was killed by the Basques at Roncesvalles. It lasted until Emperor Louis the Pious (814–40), acknowledging stubborn Breton resistance, designated a native aristocrat, Nomenoë, as *missus* in Brittany in 831, re-arranged comital offices in the former March and incorporated the

Bretons by peaceful means into the empire. His choice proved a wise one. Nomenoë remained loyal to the Emperor (below pp. 152–3). Thereafter Carolingian political and cultural influences, which since the mid eighth century had already begun powerfully to shape Breton society, became increasingly obvious.

Royal Frankish annals provide, after the silence of the late Merovingian period, relatively plentiful information on Breton affairs from *c.* 751. The story they tell is of imperial campaigns in search of tribute and booty which in turn sparked Breton revolts (786, 799, 811, 818, 822, 824, 825). Sometimes led by the Emperor himself, more usually by the marquis or counts of the Breton March, who were drawn in the main from the family of the Widonids, Carolingian armies frequently gained military superiority but were unable to convert this into lasting political control. Final victory remained elusive against an enemy which was hydra-headed but, in self-defence, also began to develop its own political organization. Throughout the period chroniclers offered excuses for the relative failure of the usually all-conquering Carolingian forces: difficulties of the terrain, unusual guerilla and light cavalry tactics employed by the Bretons, their propensity to break treaty obligations and so on. They could not disguise the fact that brute force and burnt earth tactics which worked for the Carolingians in Saxony had failed to break Breton spirits.

It is difficult to analyse reasons for Breton success in any depth. There are no local historical sources of any consequence and knowledge of political conditions has largely to be inferred. Murman (or Morvan), who led the resistance to Louis the Pious in 818, claimed regal authority 'against the usual custom of the Bretons' (Ermold the Black), though his power base seems to have been limited to the region where the Vannetais and Cornouaille meet. Guihomarc'h, who played a similar role in 824, appears simply to have been the leader of a faction, probably in northern Brittany, since the expeditions which gathered to crush him were summoned initially to Rennes. The Carolingians were hampered rather than helped by the traditional fragmentation of Breton aristocratic society. An obvious parallel for the political situation beyond the March is early medieval Wales, dominated by kinglets and local war-leaders rather than by a single powerful ruler. 'Brittany' did not yet exist, only 'Bretons', and when threatened they united in defence of their interests. It was a matter of surprised comment by Abbot Lupus of Ferrières in 845 that during a later crisis they were divided amongst themselves.

Although conditions in the peninsula are not extreme – Montagne Saint-Michel, in the Monts d'Arrée, for example, is only 391 m – the Carolingians certainly found strategy and tactics difficult in a region where communications were not easy once they left the March. The poetic description by Ermold the Black of Murman's encampment in 818 illustrates some of the problems: 'in the middle of the forest, surrounded by a river, and entrenched behind hedges, ditches and marshes, resounding to the sound of arms'. It also finds some slight confirmation in archaeology. At Mohon (M), where Salomon (below p. 157) occasionally resided in the ninth century, the impressive earth banks of Le Camp des Rouëts have recently been dated to the eighth century. More questionably, there are defensive sites, identified by nineteenth-century scholars, like Menez Morvan (Langonnet or Priziac, M) or Castel-Cran-en-Plélauff (C-d'A), which possibly date from this period as may many places including the element Lis or Lez in their names (above p. 137). In other words, although recognition of specific sites frequently 'defeats archaeological identification at present' (Giot), there clearly existed in the Breton countryside numerous fortified positions which when allied to the landscape's natural features, woods, *landes*, precipitous little valleys, rivers, streams and marshes, provided superb cover for guerilla operations as the experience of the Second World War most recently demonstrated. It must be remembered, too, that larger valleys would have presented much greater physical barriers than they do now. Even today the Vilaine, for example, is still prone to massive flooding.

To these natural advantages, the long-standing warlike propensities of the Bretons may also be added. The original Britons were among the few citizens of the Roman Empire who took up arms in its defence. Personal names in Old Breton (some still current) like Marrec (horseman) and Glémarec (brilliant horseman), Guivarch and Guyomarch (worthy to have a horse), testify to early martial values as do accounts of horse races mentioned in several saints' lives. Continuity between the earliest days of Breton settlement and Carolingian times is suggested by accounts of mounted exercises like those held at Worms in 842, where a troop of Bretons displayed their prowess alongside Saxons, Gascons and

Austrasians. Their special expertise lay in quick feints and light-mounted manoeuvres, the delivery of a missile barrage, followed by a speedy withdrawal. In the field the Bretons avoided direct confrontation with opponents more effectively armed and used to heavy cavalry warfare though, as their victories at Ballon (845), Jengland (851) and Brissarthe (866) demonstrate, if brought to battle they gave a good account of themselves (below pp. 154–5). The means by which they raised and organized their forces against Carolingian invasions must remain mysterious. There is, however, no doubt about the outcome: imperial expansion was severely checked.

In the end Louis the Pious, struggling to maintain control in the empire at large, tried the alternative of political *rapprochement*. Following the revolt by Guihomarc'h in 824, the Emperor sent the captured Breton leader home from Aachen loaded with presents. As the Carolingians were dazzled by the sophistication and wealth of Byzantium, their own court similarly impressed peoples like the Bretons who did not yet enjoy the same levels of material culture. They were eager to share its benefits: weapons of Frankish design, for instance, have been found in a seventh-century burial on the Ile Lavret. The economic and social advantages of cooperation in place of conflict were apparent to both sides. Bretons began to enter imperial service as vassals. Guihomarc'h did not long survive his release; he was killed by Count Lambert of Nantes in 826. But a few years later Louis, after the revolt of his sons in 830, abandoning his own plans to invade Brittany again, chose Nomenoë, an imperial *fidelis* and native Breton, to be *missus* in Brittany. This paved the way for its incorporation into the Carolingian polity. It was also formal recognition of Brittany as a single political entity for the first time.

These political developments were paralleled in church affairs where similar moves towards assimilation were afoot. The military imperialism of the Carolingians usually went hand in hand with an expansion of the Frankish church of which the rulers were the particular champions. Charlemagne himself had taken the abbey of Saint-Méen (I-et-V) under his protection; in 816 Louis the Pious confirmed its immunity at the request of Abbot Helogar who was also bishop of Alet. In 818 at Priziac (M) on the western border of the county of Vannes, in the wake of his victory over Murman, Louis issued a diploma in favour of the abbey of Landévennec (F).

This recounts how the Emperor had interrogated Abbot Matmonoc on practices among the Bretons and, discovering that these still reflected Celtic liturgical traditions long abandoned in the Frankish (as in the Anglo-Saxon) church, he ordered the revised monastic rule of Benedict of Aniane to be imposed. The list of witnesses shows it was a decision clearly intended to have general application in all Breton dioceses which were by implication re-attached to the ecclesiastical province of Tours. At the monastery of Saint-Sauveur de Redon (I-et-V), founded by Conwoion in 832, the revised rule (brought by a monk from Saint-Maur de Glanfeuil in Anjou) was implemented from the start. The abbey became a bulwark of imperial and papal influence in a critical zone where Breton and Frank met, and a potent symbol of the way in which Carolingian culture and ideas were moulding developments in ninth-century Brittany.

Nomenoë

The integration of the Bretons into the Carolingian empire – and its limitations – are dramatically highlighted in the career of Nomenoë (d. 851). There is a strong historical tradition that sees him as the creator of the Breton nation. It found its fullest expression in the work of Arthur de la Borderie (d. 1901), though it still finds advocates. But as Hubert Guillotel has recently written, if we accept it, 'we condemn ourselves never to understand the history of Brittany in the ninth century': how the *regnum Britanniae* was painfully formed and what its main characteristics were. Recent scholarship has thus stripped away the romantic view of Nomenoë as the heroic defender of Brittany against the Franks and emphasized the debt he owed to Carolingian example and patronage. With a brilliant application of Occam's razor, Guillotel has suggested a revised chronology of the documents on which a study of his life must rest to reinforce this interpretation. Whilst details may be controversial, other students of the period, too, accept that Nomenoë can only be properly understood in the context of the politics of the Carolingian world where the interests of aristocratic families rather than 'nations' were normally at stake. Although Nomenoë was a native Breton (one of the very few facts about him that can be definitely established), more important than his ethnicity was the manner in which he came to power, the way he maintained it and the legacy he left to his immediate successors.

Virtually nothing is known about him before his appointment as *missus imperatoris* in Brittany around 1 May 831. La Borderie's argument that he was already count of Vannes in 819 and 'governor' of Brittany in 826 must be rejected following a critical re-examination of *acta* in the cartulary of Redon which show Guy, a member of the Widonid family, as count at Vannes until January 830 at least. When appointed Nomenoë was, or certainly became, an imperial vassal (*fidelis*); he was probably first drawn to Louis's attention during the campaigns of the 820s. Through benefices then conferred upon him or as a result of later promotion he came to possess land that once belonged to the imperial fisc as grants to Saint-Sauveur de Redon demonstrate. Of his own patrimony nothing is known though since he was related (probably by marriage) to Rivallon, count of Poher in 844, this may have lain in Cornouaille. As *missus* the main centre of his own power was the Vannetais: two Redon documents of 832 and 834 style him *comes* or *princeps Venetice civitatis*. Other *acta* from the same source show that he exercised his authority both in that county and beyond. As *missus* this was extremely wide-ranging. It included ecclesiastical as well as civil, judicial and military matters, which perhaps explains his high-handed dismissal of all the Breton bishops in 849 (below p. 154). In addition to *missus*, he is some-times styled *dux* or *magister*, and described as 'ruling' (*gubernans, regnans, dominans*). Contrary to normal Carolingian practice, he does not appear to have shared his *missaticum* with an ecclesiastic but he had several subordinate officials, also styled *missi*, to assist him. The novel feature of his *missaticum* was that territorially it included lands which the Carolingians had never succeeded in mastering and a county (Vannes) detached from the former Frankish March. It was thus Louis the Pious himself rather than Nomenoë who first created a union which remained fundamental to the Breton state; during his lifetime Nomenoë did not seriously betray the Emperor's trust.

His loyalty to the Carolingians began to waver in 843 during the civil wars between the sons of Louis the Pious. After first supporting Charles the Bald (840–77), whose share of the empire in the sequence of partitions, culminating in the treaty of Verdun

(843), always included suzerainty over Brittany, Nomenoë became embroiled in quarrels over the county of Nantes. Here a scion of the Widonids, Lambert, was disputing possession with Renaud, count of Herbauge. In May 843 a Breton army led by Nomenoë's son Erispoë and Lambert defeated Renaud at Messac (I-et-V), where the Roman road from Angers to Carhaix crosses the Vilaine. A month later, taking advantage of these divisions among the Neustrian aristocracy, the Vikings sacked Nantes. By the autumn Charles the Bald, hoping to restore order in the west, was at Rennes but his campaign was a failure. In 844 Nomenoë and Lambert continued their feud with the heirs of Count Renaud and raided as far afield as Maine. After a brief truce, military operations began again and on 22 November 845 Charles the Bald was defeated at Ballon, near Redon (I-et-V), when he went to succour those opposing Nomenoë in Brittany. For a few days Lupus of Ferrières feared Charles himself had been killed.

Relations between Nomenoë and Charles were temporarily patched up in 846 when Nomenoë deserted Lambert. By now the Viking presence was making itself felt and there are hints of a challenge to Nomenoë's own authority in Brittany. Around Christmas 846 a Breton army was ravaging the Bessin, contrary to a truce with Charles which Nomenoë seems personally to have kept until 849. In 847 he also suffered three reverses at the hands of the Vikings before bribing them to look elsewhere for booty. Two years later, however, Nomenoë was at the height of his powers. In a synod held at Coitlouh (M?) in May 849 he dismissed the five Breton bishops (Alet, Dol, Quimper, Saint-Pol-de-Léon and Vannes) for simony and replaced them with nominees 'of his own race and language'. A damaging schism with the Frankish church began that was to rumble on during the reigns of his two immediate successors. Then, reconciled with Count Lambert, who had returned from exile hoping to re-establish himself again at Nantes, Nomenoë launched a series of vigorous military assaults on Rennes, Nantes and Le Mans. Lupus of Ferrières, writing on behalf of a synod of Carolingian bishops in August 850, urged Nomenoë to repent and make peace with Charles but to no avail. A raid on Nantes resulted in the destruction of its walls and gates. In the depths of winter Nomenoë pressed on. Then, unexpectedly on 7 March 851, he died deep in Frankish territory at Vendôme. His achievements – the establishment of personal dominance in Breton secular and religious affairs, the beginnings of an administration which united both Frankish and Breton lands – hung in the balance.

Whatever advantages his origins may have conferred (and the silence of the records is total), the career of Nomenoë as it can now be traced demonstrates how much he owed to imperial patronage as a *fidelis* and *missus*. It was this that had elevated his authority above that of other Bretons; it provided the territorial basis for his power. In seeking to extend this he acted within the political framework of the empire by alliances with other families of the *Reichsaristokratie*. Quarrels between the sons of Louis the Pious, local disputes and the havoc caused by the Vikings furnished ideal circumstances for Nomenoë's power to grow as the transition from loyal lieutenant in the 830s to independent leader with expansionist policies after 843 shows. But there were limitations to his ambitions: despite a later tradition that after deposing the Breton bishops Nomenoë had himself crowned at Dol, which he allegedly wished to turn into a metropolitan see, there is no contemporary warrant for this. It was his son Erispoë who first received royal insignia from Charles the Bald and styled himself 'Erispoë, by God's grace, prince of the province of Brittany' or simply 'Erispoë, king'.

The Kingdom of Brittany

The death of Nomenoë raised Charles the Bald's hopes that he might re-impose mastery over the Bretons. In the summer of 851 he launched a major attack on Erispoë only to be defeated at Jengland-Beslé (L-A), a bridging point over the Vilaine, in a battle which lasted over three days. It was an even more humiliating defeat than that at Ballon and Charles fled from the field leaving his camp to be pillaged. The consequences were momentous for the future of Brittany. For reasons about which we can only speculate, shortly after this startling victory, Erispoë agreed peace-terms in a statesmanlike move. In return for the counties of Rennes and Nantes and the *vicaria* of Retz (which the Bretons had already overrun in Nomenoë's last campaigns) and a present of royal insignia, he acknowledged fealty to Charles. For the first time a non-Carolingian was recognized as ruler of a *regnum* within the empire. In 856, as a further mark of esteem, Erispoë's daughter was betrothed to Louis the Stammerer. Until his death in November 857 Erispoë remained loyal to the Emperor.

The acquisition of *Britannia nova*, as the lands conceded in 851 were sometimes called, completely transformed the economic and social as well as the political basis of Erispoë's authority. It also smoothed the way for further significant advances in Carolingian influence. Rennes and Nantes had passed into Frankish hands in the sixth century; for almost four centuries they had been advance outposts of Frankish culture and society, most recently as the core of the March of Brittany. In comparison with land settled by the Bretons in the west of the peninsula these counties had rich agricultural and mineral resources. Although the details largely escape us, there are indications that such factors attracted the Bretons (above p. 141). The eastward and southward expansion of princely control was accompanied by colonization, as place- and proper names found in the cartulary of Redon indicate. Although it may not have been appreciated when the Vikings used it as a point of entry, in retrospect acquisition of all the Loire estuary was the major long-term territorial advantage accruing to Brittany from the treaty of 851.

Very few documents relate to the rule of Erispoë: just seven *acta* survive that were issued in his name, together with one charter delivered jointly with his cousin Salomon. Analysis of the witness lists reveals the presence of Erispoë's close relations (his wife Marmohec, his son Conan, his uncle Rivallon), the bishops whom Nomenoë had promoted in 849 (Courantgen of Vannes, Retwalatr of Alet, Anaweten of Quimper, Clotwoion of Saint-Pol) and a large group of laymen (*nobiles*) who are not otherwise distinguished by rank or office. Reference to counts reflects growing Carolingian administrative influence as does the fact that Salomon, like Erispoë, became an imperial *fidelis*. Possibly in 852 (though much remains mysterious about what happened and when), Charles the Bald granted Salomon 'a third of Brittany', a portion that he may have held under the suzerainty of Erispoë. It may have included the counties of Rennes and Nantes. Whether it was because of this territorial division or some other matter like Erispoë's continuing good relations with Charles the Bald and the marriage treaty of 856, after sharing their authority for some years, the cousins came to blows. Between 2 and 12 November 857 Salomon murdered Erispoë.

The pattern established in the reigns of Nomenoë and Erispoë recurred in that of Salomon (857–74), the most successful and ambitious of all Breton rulers. As a result of his usurpation and complex local political circumstances (including rivalry with Robert the Strong, ancestor of the Capetians, and the continuing presence of the Vikings in Neustria, as well as problems arising from the schism), early in his reign Salomon maintained hostile relations with Charles the Bald. He then recognized more was to be gained by peace and negotiation. In 863 at Entrammes (Mayenne), shortly after abandoning a planned campaign against him, Charles ceded further territory 'between the two rivers' (probably the Sarthe and Mayenne) as well as the lay-abbacy of Saint-Aubin-d'Angers. In the following year at the famous meeting at Pîtres, when Charles issued instructions for defence of the empire against

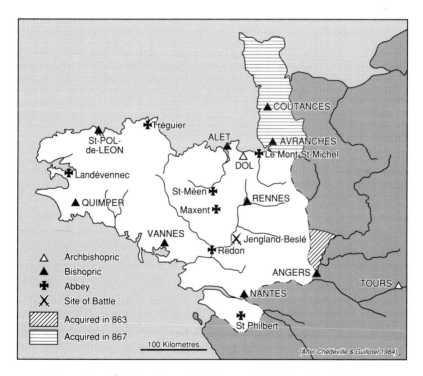

Figure 20   The Kingdom of Brittany under Erispoë and Salomon

the Vikings, Salomon was present and rendered a tribute of 50 pounds of silver. Friendly relations were not yet fully restored: Charles had still to acknowledge openly Salomon's title. But following the defeat and death of Robert the Strong at Brissarthe (15 September 866) at the hands of a joint force of Bretons and Vikings, the way was open for full reconciliation. Pascweten, Salomon's son-in-law, led a delegation to the imperial court and Charles made a further significant territorial concession – the Cotentin – to him. This was the apogee of Breton political dominance. In August 867 Charles symbolically despatched a crown to Salomon who shortly afterwards styled himself 'king'. For the rest of his reign he remained on good terms with Charles.

Salomon's last years saw a number of important developments. Apart from the pretensions which he encouraged in the bishops of Dol to claim archiepiscopal status and hence parity with the archbishop of Tours, metropolitan of Brittany, by 866 Salomon was prepared for a reconciliation between the Breton bishops and their Frankish confrères over the schism. Administratively the pattern already set under his two predecessors continued to develop: further references to counts, the appearance of a constable (*stabularius*), imitation of Carolingian diplomatic style, the decline of the machtiernate (below p. 165), a shift eastwards in the political balance of the *regnum*, the granting of benefices. Nowhere, in the latter half of the ninth century, was Carolingian influence more evident than in ecclesiastical affairs.

Brittany and the Carolingian renaissance

From the early ninth century the Carolingians exerted a growing cultural predominance in Brittany. For political reasons Nomenoë and his successors as rulers of the *regnum Britanniae* controlled episcopal appointments. The first direct contacts with the papacy are recorded, moves which can be interpreted (and all too frequently have been) as a narrow defence of Breton independence against Frankish encroachment. Yet in other respects the Breton *principes* actively encouraged or were powerless to prevent the spread of fashions emanating from Carolingian court circles. The evidence for this may be most clearly traced in ecclesiastical affairs where new vigour was infused into Breton monastic and intellectual life. For instance, on the Crozon peninsula the remote abbey of Landévennec in this period shared many of the concerns that exercised the minds of scholars in more central parts of the Carolingian world, most notably a revived interest in classical literature and Latin style. At the same time Breton hagiography enjoyed a golden age with works like Wrdisten's life of St Guénolé, Wrmonoc's life of St Paul Aurelian (both produced at Landévennec *c*. 890), and lives of St Magloire of Léhon, St Turiau of Dol or of St Malo (this latter written by Bili, a protégé of Bishop Retwaltr). All these display learning that could only have come from a close study of the early church fathers which surviving manuscripts show to have been available locally. In addition, musicologists have recently drawn attention to the precocious development in surviving Breton sources of a distinctive system of notation (*neumes*) which remained in use till the twelfth century.

Analysis of the 125 or so surviving 'Breton' manuscripts from the period 800–1050 – manuscripts with glosses, decoration or other indications of Breton ownership, authorship or usage – reinforces this view of the impact of Carolingian learning. Approximately two-thirds of them were produced in the later ninth century or early tenth. The overwhelming majority are Latin religious works – gospels, antiphonals, service books, saints' lives, writings of the fathers – or didactic ones like three surviving copies of Priscian's Grammar (Paris, BN, MSS. lat. 10289 and 10290; Vatican, MS. lat. 1480). Although there is only one major classical text, a Virgil (Berne, Burgerbibliothek MS. 167), other evidence points to Breton familiarity with the *Aeneid* and other Latin poets. Otherwise the works copied are largely Christian and date from late antiquity: Augustine, Boethius, Eusebius, Orosius. Several works by Bede (relating particularly to computation) were known as was Isidore's *Etymologies*. Collections of canon law, grammatical and medical treatises provide the most technical literature. More obviously connected with Carolingian interests, there are manuscripts with Breton glosses of works by Alcuin, Rabanus Maurus, Sedulius and Smaragdus (a commentary on Donatus).

Most are written in Carolingian minuscule script though some display insular characteristics. In addition to Breton glosses some manuscripts also contain Gaelic ones, while the fashion for Hisperic Latin, a highly ornate, learned and rhetorical style much influenced by Greek, especially associated with both Ireland and

Plate 22　A zoomorphic manuscript: the beginning of St Mark's Gospel from the Evangeliary of Landévennec

Anglo-Saxon England, also found practitioners in Brittany. In illumination, too, certain traits like interlacing and geometric forms suggest insular models although the most extraordinarily exuberant creations of Breton *scriptoria* are largely unparalleled at this stage anywhere in Europe. These are the anthropo-zoomorphic representations of the evangelists in the gospels for which, in a longer perspective, ancient Eygpt might seem the original source. In the case of St Mark, for example, it is obvious that the Old Breton word *marc'h* (horse) inspired the local tradition of depicting him with a horse's head. St John, in an early tenth-century manuscript attributed to Landévennec, has a bird's head; St Luke sometimes has four wings, together with a stylized animal's head; St Matthew alone is usually drawn in recognizably human form.

The latter half of the ninth century thus witnessed in Brittany the flowering of a varied learned culture. Stimulated by both Continental and insular sources, it also developed characteristics specific to the *regnum Britanniae*. It was this rich and syncretic amalgam which from the mid ninth century the Viking invasions threatened. But before examining this theme more may be said about Breton society at large.

The cartulary of Redon and peasant society

The abbey of Saint-Sauveur de Redon has already been mentioned; its cartulary provides a source of unique richness for western France as well as Brittany during the Carolingian period. Compiled in the late eleventh and twelfth centuries, it contains copies of nearly 300 charters relating to the early days of the monastery founded in 832 at the confluence of the Vilaine and Oust rivers. Their value for political history has already been revealed (above p. 153); for the social development of a region finely balanced between Breton and Frankish influences at a critical juncture in its evolution, scholars have long recognized that these charters are of unparalleled importance. Since the mid nineteenth century this evidence has been intensively studied, most recently by Wendy Davies in her *Small Worlds* (1988). Some conclusions may be summarized here.

The picture that emerges is primarily that of a relatively

Plate 23   A page from the eleventh-century cartulary of Redon

homogeneous society of self-regulating and largely self-sufficient small peasant farming communities. These communities, the *plebes* discussed briefly above (p. 136), were scattered thickly across the landscape. Generally some six or seven kilometres apart and covering 40–50 km² in area, the *plebes* were similar to an average English hundred. At their centre lay a nucleated settlement, a *bourg*, normally clustered about a church, served by families of hereditary priests. But agricultural land and dwellings were dispersed throughout the territory of the *plebs*. Although estimations of total population are hazardous, it has been suggested that in an average *plebs* there were approximately 200 adult free male peasant proprietors. The vast majority of these possessed a single holding (Breton *ran*, Latin *pars*), the size of which varied according to natural conditions from very small plots of a few hectares up to 60 ha (150 acres); 10–25 ha seems a usual size. Very similar to a Carolingian *mansus*, such holdings were capable of supporting a single household of three or four working adults.

Around Redon farming was mixed, with arable predominating. The main crops were wheat, rye and oats, though to the east and south of the Vilaine, vines were cultivated. Field size varied. There is evidence for some large open fields, worked communally, but discrete individual holdings were more usual. Livestock was important: cattle are mentioned infrequently, but oxen were used for ploughing and meadows and pasture were to be found in all *plebes*. Sheep and pigs were numerous. *Landes*, open heathland or commons (a source of gorse, broom and fern for litter or heating) and woodland were exploited. A reference to coppicing indicates management of the latter. Banks and ditches delimiting some arable presumably offered protection against the depredations of livestock but the countryside had not yet fully developed proper *bocage*, that characteristic western French pattern of small fields enclosed by banks and hedges, in which some individual trees, frequently pollarded, are allowed to grow. This only became the norm in much of Brittany during the course of the Middle Ages. Although there are few references in the charters to mills or skilled craftsmen like smiths, the landscape was already firmly under human control. Uncultivated waste or primitive forests were comparatively modest in extent. Mention of dams, weirs, tolls and conflict over riparian rights shows that waterways, even the coastline, were also exploited both for fishing and for commerce. Salt was produced by evaporation from saltpans or salines at several sites (cf. p. 209). Explicit mention of markets is, however, rare. Coin, which was certainly minted at Rennes and Nantes, was used both for purchases large and small and for the payment of rents and dues, but was generally scarce in the villages, a fact which finds slightly later confirmation in the excavations at Lann Gouh and Pen-er-Malo (M) (below p. 216).

As for the social organization of the *plebes*, this was dominated by the free male proprietors, the *plebenses*. Women, especially aristocratic ones, could hold property, even exercise public office, but 'they did not have full citizen rights'. Nor did serfs, who lacked freedom of movement and were alienable with their families and the property to which they were tied. Most serfs probably lived as single households on individual *ran*, though several families were required to work larger estates (of which there were not many, mostly east of the Vilaine). Their origins may lie in earlier Gallo-Roman *fundi* or villas which may also account for the apparent persistence of some domestic slavery. In total, the legally unfree element perhaps made up a quarter of the population. Another group consisted of tenants owing dues in money and kind. Over the century their numbers increased to the point where in the 860s they may have formed 10% of the population, as Redon expanded its holdings and formerly free peasants became dependent. Despite this, free peasants, the *plebenses*, continued to form the majority of the population.

About a fifth of them held more than one property, though only a minute proportion held land outside their native *plebs*. Not unnaturally these 'multiple owners' among the peasantry were most likely, along with aristocrats, to own serfs. On the other hand, mere wealth was not apparently the most important factor in determining the part individuals played in certain public activities of the *plebs* like judging disputes, acting as witnesses or as sureties. Preference for more senior members of the community on such occasions is obvious, a sign of how ancient wisdom and custom regulated matters, but any law-worthy, non-servile proprietor might expect to serve in this fashion. He did so generally within his main *plebs* because neither for these purposes nor for others did he travel further afield. Most peasant horizons were thus limited to a few kilometres around their dwellings. This contrasts with the more extensive and frequent movements of the aristocracy or even of the monks and their representatives whose business often took them far from Redon.

A link between these different worlds (because the aristocracy, the Breton *principes* and counts, were in most respects entirely detached from the *plebs*, simply drawing revenues in money or kind from extensive properties which they supervised from a distance) was the machtiern. His powers were a peculiar amalgam of public and private authority quite unlike that of any lord or official in the contemporary Carolingian world. Though no clear analogy has yet been discovered, his origins lie in Brittany's Celtic past as the word's etymology suggests: *mach* signifies surety and *tiern* ruler (cf. Welsh *mechdeyrn*; Cornish *myghtern*, both connected with vice-regal authority). The description appears frequently in the Redon cartulary and occasionally in other Breton sources. From these it is clear machtierns possessed reasonable landed wealth, usually in several *plebes*, and that their status was hereditary. The family of Iarnhitin of Ruffiac (M), for instance, can be traced over four generations whilst the genealogy of his grandson's wife, the *tirannissa* Aourken, the only example of a woman holding the office, extends over nine generations. But although sometimes termed *princeps plebis* machtierns did not automatically succeed to or control individual *plebes*. They exercised their authority *in* a *plebs*, sometimes jointly as in the case of Iarnhitin's sons Portitoë and Guorvili at Carentoir (M) *c.* 830. They might hold up to four or five simultaneously. They were highly esteemed by the *plebenses* from whom on occasion they received various dues. But there were distinct limitations to their powers.

In the legal sphere, for example, though many transactions took place before a machtiern at his *lis* and his intervention is often noted – at Cléguérec (M) in 833 one sat on a three-legged stool in front of the church to record a donation to Redon – actual decisions were delivered by judges chosen among the *plebenses*. The courts over which machtierns presided, sometimes in company with *missi* representing the rulers of Brittany, were thus local not seigneurial ones. The machtierns did not impose punishments nor take fines. Their right to levy taxation was similarly restricted. Their most obvious function was to be present on occasions when some kind of public record was required. Their residences, it has been suggested, often served as a public registry, for sales and other business affecting the *plebs*. As the element *mach* suggests, a key aspect was their role as guarantors for any deals struck. They may have carried out inquiries in the event of a dispute. Finally, it may be emphasized that there is little evidence of their exercising any sort of military authority by virtue of their office.

Enjoying local prestige but with limited responsibilities and powers, machtierns thus seem to reflect an earlier age, one that possibly goes back to the earliest days after the migrations. More certainly, the cartulary of Redon catches them at a critical moment. By the mid ninth century their days were numbered. The creation of the *regnum* and a rudimentary central administration, anxious to extend its authority, challenged their local autonomy. Viking threats added urgency to demands for taxes and other resources which machtierns might raise as representatives of the *principes*. A few, it appears, were drawn towards the courts of the Breton rulers where disputes concerning them were now also heard. The beginnings of commendation and vassalage further worked to undermine their independence. Locally within the Redon region itself the growth of the abbey's lordship had serious adverse effects as the abbot assumed machtiernly powers in several *plebes*. These were immeasurably strengthened when, buttressed by privileges from the *principes*, confirmed by the Emperors, he established a powerful judicial immunity. Unlike machtierns, the abbot 'did not share presidency of the courts with the *missi* of any count or ruler' (Davies). After *c.* 875 references to machtierns thus become extremely rare, whilst the peasant communities in which they had once exercised their unique authority now fell increasingly under the control of agents of the *regnum* and aristocrats – clerical and lay – holding territorial and judicial powers entirely different in kind. A contributory factor in the machtierns' decline may have been the Vikings.

The Vikings and the end of the Breton Kingdom

The first serious Viking raids on England and Francia occurred at the end of the eighth century. In 819 the monks of Noirmoutier (Vendée), just off the Poitevin coast, asked Louis the Pious to provide them with a refuge on the mainland during the campaigning season. By the 830s the monks were living permanently at Déas (Saint-Philbert-de-Grandlieu, L-A), where considerable remains of their cruciform church still survive. But their respite was brief as Viking bands began to winter at the mouth of the Loire. Other rivers, too, like the Vilaine, Rance and Couesnon provided ready access to the centre of Brittany and the March. On 24 June 843, taking advantage of the feud between Nomenoë, his ally Lambert, count of Nantes and Renaud, count of Herbauge, that left the city of Nantes defenceless (p. 154), they slaughtered Bishop Gunhard and his congregation, gathered in the cathedral to celebrate the Nativity of St John. Just upstream the terrified monks of Saint-Martin-de-Vertou (L-A) loaded six boats with their possessions for flight. In the next few years the Loire valley became a major theatre of warfare as Viking bands, Carolingian aristocrats and Breton princes struggled for dominance in a confusing series of alliances since Christian rulers had few qualms about allying with pagan warriors when it suited them. As for the monks of Noirmoutier and Saint-Philbert, in the 850s they were sheltering at Cunauld in Anjou. By 875 they had moved as far inland as Tournus in Burgundy, a pattern of migration in disturbed times which many other houses subsequently followed (below pp. 175–6). But after these first misfortunes, it appears that the main weight of Viking attacks fell on Brittany in the early tenth century rather than in the ninth century.

The relative strength of the *regnum Britanniae*, together with the energetic rule of Charles the Bald and his lieutenants, especially Robert the Strong, who provided stiff military resistance, are the major reasons for this. As a result the Vikings, after their initial inroads along the Loire, turned their attention towards England where the Great Army campaigned from 866. This sequence of alternating periods of attack and remission recurred several times in the next few decades. Whenever the Vikings met determined opposition they turned to softer targets. In the case of Brittany, the death of Salomon (874) and disputes between his successors, paralleling what happened in Francia after the death of Charles the Bald (877), allowed the Vikings to return. Again, however, in the late 880s Alain, count of Vannes, king of the Bretons (d. 907), offered renewed resistance. A Viking band was defeated at Questembert (M) *c.* 888, inaugurating another period of remission. This was brought brutally to an end in 913 as a marginal note in a computus table from Landévennec records: *destructum est monasterium sancti Vuinvaloei a Normannis.*

In the next few years several transitory Viking states, similar to that forming in Normandy, were established in Brittany. Annals from Saint-Sauveur de Redon, under the year 920, furnish a bleak commentary on events: 'The Northmen devastated all of Brittany, defeating, killing or exiling the Bretons. Then the bodies of the saints who were buried there were carried into diverse lands.' Frankish records, notably Flodoard of Reims, and archaeology provide confirmatory detail. The county of Nantes was abandoned to the Vikings in 921 by King Robert I and in the north-east William Longsword, duke of the Normans, advanced through the Cotentin and Avranchin. The powerless King Raoul (922–3) ceded to him *terram Brittonum in ora maritima sitam*. A coin discovered last century at Mont Saint-Michel with the fragmentary legend + VVILEIM DUX BRI seems to refer to his brief period of rule. This was brought to an end by the return (to which William himself assented) of Alain Barbetorte, count of Cornouaille, from England *c.* 936, the same year that Louis IV d'Outremer returned to France and Carolingian rule was restored.

The chronicle of Nantes presents these events in the most dramatic terms: the flight of the secular and religious leaders of

Brittany, its devastation at the hands of the Vikings, followed by an heroic campaign of reconquest by Alain Barbetorte. Modern criticism makes it impossible to accept all this at face value, though it is clear that a political vacuum was created in the *regnum Britanniae* by the flight of counts like Mathuédoi of Cornouaille, together with his son (Alain Barbetorte). They found refuge at the court of the kings of Wessex, Edward the Elder (899–925) and Athelstan (925–39). Only one comital family seems to have withstood the onslaught, that of Berengar of Rennes. He was surrounded by Vikings in northern Brittany (where Le Camp de Péran at Plédran, C-d'A, has recently yielded weapons and other artefacts comparable to those found in the Viking kingdom of York and datable to the early tenth century), Cornouaille, Nantes and Normandy. A first attempt by Alain Barbetorte to take advantage of their internecine feuds and regain his inheritance in 931 failed. Whilst the disruption of regular religious life is also well attested. In 926 Hugh the Great, duke of the Franks, was able to send to England relics which had been carried to the Ile-de-France by refugees from Dol. The surviving distribution of early Breton manuscripts also shows the dispersion of monastic communities in these years (p. 176).

Between 913 and 936 the *regnum Britanniae* thus ceased to exist. The phoenix which eventually rose from its ashes was the future duchy. As for the Vikings, the nature of their threat changed as political circumstances also altered. In the late tenth century coastal raiding did not completely cease as the discovery of a Viking warrior grave on the Ile de Groix (M) shows. As late as 1014 there was an old-fashioned raid in which Dol was burnt; it had previously been destroyed in 944. But with the failure of Viking states other than Normandy to take root and the re-assertion of comital rule in Brittany and neighbouring regions, it seemed that the Carolingian world had escaped remarkably unscathed from its Viking ordeal. The reigns of Alain Barbetorte and his successors would show whether this was truly so in Brittany.

8

The Origins of Ducal Brittany

The dukes and the development of feudalism

The return in 936 of Alain Barbetorte (d. 952) from England marked a first step towards the restoration of central authority after the painful Viking interregnum. In the next century or so many of the structures of Carolingian Brittany surfaced again. The nascent duchy became even more inextricably part of the wider world of Francia, though it was overshadowed by powerful neighbours and its internal development was slow. First Alain Barbetorte, as count of Cornouaille and Nantes, and then Conan I, count of Rennes and his descendants between *c.* 970 and 1066, reigned as *duces Britonum*. In comparison with the rulers of the *regnum Britanniae,* these princes were less imposing figures and exercised an increasingly precarious hegemony. For one thing, the area over which they ruled was now reduced by the loss of those parts of the Cotentin, Avranchin, Maine and Anjou which Salomon received from Charles the Bald, losses only partially balanced by the annexation south of the Loire of Mauges and Tiffauges, ceded in 942 by William, count of Poitiers. And for another, within the duchy, as rival dynasties contended for power (there was from the late tenth century a separate comital family in Cornouaille), and external forces intervened, central control was inexorably weakened.

Around AD 1000 seigneurial families began to flex their muscles to the detriment of both dukes and counts. Some, like Rivallon the Vicar (*vicarius*), ancestor of the lords (*domini*) of Vitré (I-et-V), seized for their own private profit rights which had once been vested in them as representatives of public authority. Similarly, land which had been comital demesne at Tinténiac (I-et-V) *c.* 1024 x 1034 was by *c.* 1060 in the hands of a seigneurial family with a long history before it. Others managed to obtain church lands, by force or otherwise: the lords of Châteaubriant, vassals of the counts of Rennes, occupied properties belonging to the bishop of Nantes and the founders of the closely linked houses of Dol-Combour and Dinan were younger brothers of Archbishop Junguené of Dol (d. *c.* 1037), who plundered his temporalities to endow them. Witnesses at an inquiry in 1181 recalled the tradition that the archbishop had invested his brother Rivallon of Dol with twelve knights' fees. In other cases it is impossible to determine how the lords acquired the castles from which they dominated the surrounding countryside by the mid eleventh century: whether through investment by the duke, a count or bishop or simply through strong-arm tactics. In either case the result was the same: a society dominated by a hierarchy of great castellans holding military, political and economic power – a feudal society owing little to earlier Celtic or Carolingian traditions – formed in Brittany just as it did simultaneously in neighbouring provinces.

Breton feudalism had its own characteristics. In comparison with the Anglo-Norman world customs and services were for long surprisingly imprecise in many respects. The idea of knighthood as a privileged order developed quickly: Auffroy *miles*, father of Main II, lord of Fougères (I-et-V), appears as a witness in ducal charters between 1008 and 1031; Main himself is described as *Maino homo militie seculari deditus* in a charter of William, duke of Normandy, in the mid century. But there was not initially that close connection between knights' fees and specific military obligations which is found in post-Conquest England. It is only in the late twelfth century that real efforts were made to define the nature or length of services closely. The practice of exacting liege homage, for instance, developed slowly. An accord in 1198 between Guillaume, lord of la Guerche, and André II of Vitré, where Guillaume agreed to serve at his own expense when duly summoned with ten knights for three days a year and to do liege homage, is one of the first recorded instances.

Slow as they were to achieve definition, feudal institutions generally developed first in Bretagne Gallo, the region most obviously in contact with other provinces in which comparable changes were most dramatically occurring. From there they spread, especially to Penthièvre, the Trégor and Finistère, within a couple of generations. By the late twelfth century Brittany was divided into some forty major castellanies. Alongside, and not exclusively dependent on them, there also emerged hundreds of smaller centres of seigneurial authority and exploitation.

Over 600 mottes dating in the main from the tenth to thirteenth centuries have already been discovered even though only two of the five modern *départements* of Brittany have been surveyed at all

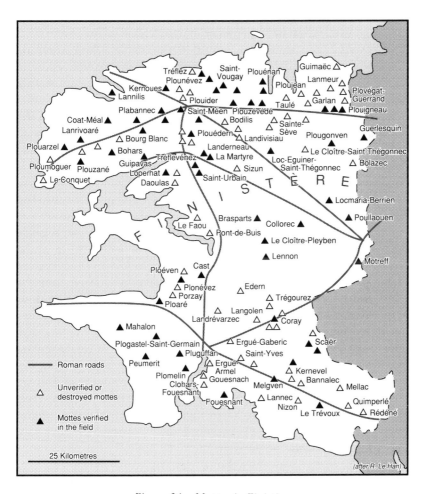

Figure 21   Mottes in Finistère

thoroughly. As Marcel Planiol wrote nearly a century ago, 'when we rediscover Brittany around 1050, its appearance no longer recalls the Brittany of the machtierns and of the cartulary of Redon, such as we knew it at the end of the ninth century. The charters of the eleventh and twelfth centuries reveal to us a fully developed feudal regime. A host of lords, petty and great, dominate the countryside.' The mottes are a visible sign of this development. Archaeological and documentary evidence combines to demonstrate that on many of these sites, where mottes were later succeeded by *manoirs* or *châteaux*, there has been a continuous seigneurial presence from the Middle Ages until today.

From this point Breton political society was dominated by a conservative and tenacious landed aristocracy, whose chivalric values were largely developed outside the province, above all in 'la douce France'. The consequence was to introduce conflicting cultural and social tensions, sometimes fruitfully enriching, sometimes destructive of native traditions, which have determined the course of Brittany's development: the attraction exercised at all social levels by the political and economic forces of royal and metropolitan France against the continuing attachment of Bretons to their own local roots, traditions and institutions.

A handful of medieval Breton nobles possessed great wealth, but the great majority of the *noblesse* (already numbering several thousand families in the twelfth century) were modest country gentlemen: that *plèbe nobiliaire* which was still full of life at the end of the Ancien Regime. For many of the *noblesse* as well as for other ranks in society royal France continually offered over the centuries multiple opportunities for fame and fortune, temptations against which the rulers of the duchy had to strive manfully if they were to preserve their authority. Social and political evolution in Brittany owe much to such powerful external forces washing over the province with tidal regularity.

The way in which viscounts (*vicecomites*), originally appointed to assist the Carolingian count in his duties, gained their independence and became hereditary lords themselves is a good indicator of how Brittany followed more general evolutionary patterns. At Rennes the viscount removed himself from the count's immediate entourage when he set up his castle at Josselin (M) shortly before 1040. It is still owned today by a cadet branch of the founder's family, the viscounts of Rohan. In the county of Nantes it was around 1060 that the viscount established a separate lordship at Donges (L-A). In Alet and Léon other viscounts soon followed suit (Poudouvre, Faou and Léon itself). So although the survival of administrative subdivisions of counties (*pagi* and *vicaria*) suggests continuity from the heyday of Carolingian rule, matters were as different in practice in Brittany as they were in neighbouring Anjou or Poitou.

For two centuries the duke was faced with a continual battle to maintain his predominance. Many lords, notably in Finistère where the duke seldom ventured in the eleventh and twelfth centuries, ignored him with impunity. It required the strenuous efforts of Henry II to bring them to heel (below p. 195). Even in the counties of Rennes and Nantes, where Carolingian traditions were more than a memory, there were those who openly defied the duke from newly erected castles. A good example is Ancenis (L-A). First mentioned *c*. 987 when it still belonged to the count of Nantes, by Conan II's reign it had passed to a certain Guihenoc (*Wihenonis de Castro Anceniso*). A charter which can be dated no more closely than 1054–84 informs us that Count Hoël of Nantes had confirmed a grant by his knight Bernard of Guérande whilst besieging Ancenis. The outcome of that attack is unknown but Guihenoc's descendants still owned the castle when it was finally slighted on Charles VIII's orders in 1488.

As for the duke's standing amongst contemporary princes, whilst Alain Barbetorte was treated as an equal by men of the stature of Hugh the Great, duke of the Franks, Herbert, count of Vermandois, William Longsword, duke of the Normans, and William Towhead, count of Poitiers, his successors fell increasingly under the domination of closer rivals. This theme will be examined more fully later (below pp. 187–93) but it can be noted here that in the tenth century the counts of Anjou became the arbiters of comital power in the county of Nantes, whilst the counts of Blois and then the dukes of Normandy were the principal influence in Rennes.

Nevertheless, despite the weakness of ducal authority, highlighted in the mid eleventh century during the long and disturbed minority of Conan II, who nominally reigned from 1040 to 1066, the period in which, not entirely coincidentally, many castles and their lords are first mentioned, contemporaries continued to treat Brittany as a region with its own peculiar customs. Chroniclers like the

Plate 24   The (?late eleventh-/early twelfth-century) stone-revetted
motte of Lezkellen en Plabennec (F)

Burgundian Raoul Glaber or William of Poitiers write in amaze-
ment about its inhabitants' strange ways, a sure sign that the
Bretons possessed a corporate cultural identity.in addition to their
fragile political structures. The latter, for instance, echoing Sallust,
speaks of each Breton knight fathering fifty children by the ten
wives he shared *more barbaro*. These Rabelaisian figures were, said
William, given to a life of fighting and horsemanship, neglected
agriculture and good manners, lived on abundant milk but scant
bread, and pastured huge herds on wide open tracts of land from
which no other harvest was taken. Hostile Frankish comment on
the Bretons was a regular topos though Classical writers rather
than personal observation are the ultimate source of this exaggerated
description. But when added to more laconic accounts of military
achievements (defeating the Angevins, for example), such literary
flourishes provide eloquent testimony that the Bretons, despite
internal divisions and under-developed political and social institutions, had established a particular place in the harsh world of
French feudal principalities.

Church and society in the central Middle Ages

Among those who most vigorously condemned barbaric conditions in the duchy were churchmen. 'I dwell among scorpions, surrounded by a double wall of bestiality and perfidy', lamented Baudry of Bourgueil, archbishop of Dol (1107–30), whilst the great scholar Peter Abelard (*c.* 1070–1142), who came from Le Pallet (L-A) near Nantes, wrote bitterly of his experiences as abbot of Saint-Gildas de Rhuys (M) in Breton-speaking Brittany whose monks he found not only incomprehensible but uncouth in every respect. But was such comment fair? What were the problems that the church faced in Brittany? How far did it share in the major developments of the western church? What, if anything, remained of earlier Celtic traditions by the central Middle Ages?

The damage inflicted by the Vikings on the Breton church was as severe as in any other region of Europe. Already undermined by Carolingian reforms intended to promote uniformity in monastic observance, few native practices from the early Middle Ages survived this hiatus in spiritual life. Restoration of church buildings, training of new personnel and raising morale once the Viking menace ceased was slow and depended heavily on external stimulation. The dispersion of monastic communities and their treasures dealt a severe blow to the cultural life of the province which had reached a zenith of achievement in the late ninth century. Between the sack of Landévennec in 913 and the early 930s, many of the spiritual leaders of Brittany were exiles.

The monks of Landévennec found safety temporarily at Montreuil-sur-Mer (Pas-de-Calais) under the protection of the count of Ponthieu. Those from Redon, after a prolonged and erratic journey via their Breton forest retreat at Plélan (M), to Angers, Candé and Auxerre, finally took shelter in Poitou for a few years. Those from Saint-Gildas de Rhuys wended their way to Déols in Berry. Monks from Léhon (C-d'A), together with Salvator, bishop of Alet, and other refugees from the ravaged dioceses of Dol, Avranches and Bayeux, bearing the bones of their saints just as the monks of Lindisfarne carried St Cuthbert round northern England, were welcomed by Hugh the Great in the Ile-de-France or found a temporary resting place in the Orléannais. Evidence for these remarkable journeys has been painstakingly pieced together from many diverse sources, most poignantly from still surviving manuscripts from Breton *scriptoria* scattered during the exodus, or from glosses written in Breton in manuscripts which later remained in the houses in which the refugees had sheltered. In all but a few cases, the period of exile came to an end in the early 930s when both regular and secular clergy and their relics began to return to the duchy.

Through the patronage of Alain Barbetorte, for instance, conditions at Landévennec returned to normality with the construction of new buildings in the mid tenth century, currently being revealed by excavation, and new endowments. In other regular communities the re-establishment of a strict monastic regime was more hesitant and hindered by a lack of resources: recruits, manuscripts, lands in working order. It was only at the end of the century that tentative signs of revival can be observed at Redon and this was distinctly limited. When the monks came to compile their famous cartulary in the mid eleventh century it is clear that the copyists no longer understood the Breton terms they found in the Carolingian charters and even their latinity was suspect. Between 992 and 1009 the abbacy was held by Mainard II, abbot of Mont Saint-Michel, an enthusiast for the ideas of Gerard of Brogne. He had reformed houses in Lorraine and the Low Countries, including St Peter's at Ghent at which Mainard's uncle, Mainard I, also abbot of Mont Saint-Michel, once trained.

Another important influence was Abbot Gauzlin from the famous house of Fleury (now Saint-Benoît-sur-Loire, Loiret) to whom Duke Geoffroy I (992–1008) turned for help in promoting reform. He responded by sending the monk Felix. But after a few years, because of difficulties during the troubled minority of Geoffroy's son, Alain III (1008–40), Felix returned home disconsolate, only to be ordered back to Brittany *c.* 1024 when dowager Duchess Havoise once more implored Fleury's aid. Thanks to this initiative regular life was restored at Saint-Gildas de Rhuys and at Saint-Melaine de Rennes. Earlier Geoffroy had also encouraged monks from Saint-Magloire de Paris, founded by exiled Breton monks from Léhon, to repay their debt by re-establishing that priory.

When he came of age, Alain III continued to encourage monastic reform, one of the few areas in which a deliberate ducal policy may be detected. He ordered Hinguethen, abbot of Saint-Jacut-de-la-

Mer (C-d'A), to re-establish the former abbey of Saint-Méen at Gaël which he moved to a new site at Saint-Méen-le-Grand (I-et-V). He also founded the first major house for women in the duchy, Saint-Georges de Rennes, of which his sister Adela became abbess, for nunneries are surprisingly absent from Celtic and Carolingian Brittany. But it was particularly to Marmoutier (Indre-et-Loire) that Alain turned towards the end of his reign. His example was followed by many seigneurial families now coming to the fore. Between *c.* 1030 and 1150 Marmoutier established nearly 30 priories in the diocese of Rennes alone, 20 priories in that of Nantes, and 25 in that of Saint-Malo; by 1200 it possessed more than 100 priories in Brittany. Its only rivals were Saint-Florent de Saumur (Maine-et-Loire), in whose favour over 50 priories were established during the same period, and the three Benedictine houses at Angers, Saint-Aubin, Saint-Nicolas and Saint-Serge, which collectively came to control nearly 40 Breton priories.

The vast majority of these new foundations were in the four dioceses of Bretagne Gallo (Dol, Nantes, Rennes and Saint-Malo, formerly Alet) where their contribution to economic and social development, as well as to spiritual life, cannot be too strongly stressed, reinforcing as they did links with France. Finally, from the mid eleventh century, native Breton houses began to contribute to the movement of renewal by establishing their own priories in regions into which Marmoutier or the Angevin houses had not penetrated. Saint-Melaine de Rennes and Saint-Sauveur de Redon were the main native leaders in extending traditional forms of Benedictine monasticism across the duchy.

At the same time, both inside and outside Brittany, new and exciting forms of monasticism developed around 1100, to which Bretons made a special contribution. There was revived enthusiasm for ascetic and strenuous spiritual exercises, leading to experiments with both eremitical and coenobitic forms of communal living. In the great forests which still marked the frontier districts between Brittany, Maine and Anjou, men and women fleeing the world began to congregate around hermits and teachers of exceptional charismatic power like Robert of Arbrissel, Raoul de la Fustaye and Vital of Savigny. Patronized by local seigneurial families, and held in the highest regard by all ranks in society, they founded abbeys like La Roë (1100), Savigny (1112), Fontevraud (1104) and its Breton daughter, Saint-Sulpice de la Forêt (*c.* 1120). These attracted many postulants and provided a serious challenge to traditional houses, for example, by permitting entry of both sexes. Robert of Arbrissel, in particular, exercised a powerful ministry towards women which scandalized more conservative thinkers.

Shortly afterwards, through the enormous prestige and energy of St Bernard of Clairvaux, the Cistercian order also began to attract many local devotees. Between 1130 and 1143 no fewer than ten major houses were created by the order in Brittany. It then also absorbed the local Savignac order entirely. Another three Breton Cistercian houses were added later in the century by which time there were also ten houses run by Augustinian canons, three further native Benedictine foundations and last, but by no means least, several foundations in favour of the military orders of the Hospital and the Temple. The modest Breton monastic endowment of 1100 was thus completely transformed by developments which opened the province to some of the most dynamic forces at work in twelfth-century society.

If the revival of monasticism can be traced with some confidence, it is more difficult to follow the fortunes of the secular church from the days of Alain Barbetorte. The interruption of episcopal lists in Brittany, as elsewhere, is commentary enough on the confusion caused by the Vikings. After bishop Electran died at Rennes *c.* 871, there is, for example, a gap until the mid tenth century, although the city was the seat of a count throughout that period. At Alet only two bishops are known for the whole tenth century; the same is true for Saint-Pol-de-Léon between 848 and 950. As for Saint-Brieuc and Tréguier, the site of abbeys dating back to the migration period, it is now thought that it was around 950 that they were formed into dioceses at the expense of Alet and Dol, thus completing the list of nine (Nantes, Quimper and Vannes are the others) into which Brittany was divided until the Revolution.

Before the Gregorian reform movement, it was usually in connection with their political rather than their spiritual role that we hear of Breton bishops. The pretensions of the bishops of Dol to exercise metropolitan authority reappeared in the mid tenth century. Wicohen (d. 988), already a leading adviser of Alain Barbetorte, seems to have become the most influential figure in the province after Alain's death. He consorted with the great men of Francia and styled himself 'bishop of the Bretons'. In 990, when all nine bishops were listed as witnesses to a charter of Conan I, Main of Dol was described as *archiepiscopus*. Archbishop Junguené under Alain III, partly through his own talents, partly through the support of his three brothers Haimon, Rivallon and Josselin, played a similar role to Wicohen. In 1076 Pope Gregory VII finally conceded the pallium to the saintly Even, formerly abbot of Saint-Melaine de Rennes. But the other Breton bishops resented his enhanced authority. There was a local schism in the early twelfth century. Eventually the unlikely combination of the Angevin Henry II, the Capetian Philip Augustus and Pope Innocent III effectively squashed the metropolitan ambitions of Dol, though distant echoes might be heard as late as 1300.

Around AD 1000 most Breton dioceses were the personal preserve of seigneurial families. At Quimper in 1008 it was Benedict II, count of Cornouaille, who became bishop. He was succeeded by a son and grandson and the family link with the see was only finally severed in the early twelfth century. This was by no means an isolated example of the nicolaitism which had infected the Breton church to a degree that appears exceptional even in pre-Gregorian France. At Rennes the lords of La Guerche (I-et-V) established a stranglehold on the bishopric. At Nantes in 981, in a more unorthodox move, Bishop Guerech was called to succeed his brother as count, and for much of the eleventh century it was again successive comital families who provided the bishop, often simoniacally. When an Italian, Airard, was promoted by Pope Leo IX in 1049 as a harbinger of reform, he soon had to beat a retreat following the unrepentant chapter's hostile reception. His successor, Quiriac (1059–79), was brother to Hoël, count of Cornouaille, who had recently succeeded to Nantes as well. To his credit, he recognized the new mood abroad and was among the first to promote much-needed clerical reform.

In most other parts of Brittany it was the early twelfth century before Gregorian ideas made significant progress: dynasties of bishops largely disappeared, but those of canons and parish priests (perhaps reflecting deep-rooted Celtic tradition) were not un-common for several further generations. At Saint-Pol-de-Léon it required the murder of Bishop Hamon (by his nephew in a family feud) in 1172 to prise the see from the hands of the viscomital family. The return, often to monasteries rather than secular foundations, of tithes and other ecclesiastical property seized by the laity, continued unabated well into the thirteenth century. As a result monks acquired considerable responsibility for parochial work in later medieval Brittany. This was often discharged through the priories to which reference has already been made.

Much of what is known about Breton parish churches in this period reflects little credit on the majority of priests. Their concern was cultic rather than pastoral; a sense of vocation was often missing. In its absence superstition and magical practices were rife, the darker side of those heightened sensibilities which the new religious currents of the late eleventh and twelfth centuries encouraged. The ascetical excesses of a Robert of Arbrissel (who favoured syneisactism, sleeping with the opposite sex as a means of strengthening chastity) led all too easily to the deviations of heresiarchs like Eon l'Etoile. A fanatical evangelical from Loudéac (C-d'A), Eon provoked orthodox clergy by his self-proclaimed mission to judge all men. He was eventually brought before Pope Eugenius III at a council at Reims in March 1148, when his views were comprehensively condemned. Eon himself escaped with a sentence of perpetual imprisonment, saved briefly by his obvious mental instability, but some followers were not so lucky and were burnt. Among the most serious persecutors of Eon and his like in Brittany was Jean de Châtillon (1144–63), who moved his see from Alet to Saint-Malo. But others, including the bishop of Saint-Brieuc, who in 1129 condemned the habit of burials at crossroads, the chronicler Guillaume le Breton, who describes a case of demonic possession in Brittany in 1198, and Innocent III himself, continued to detect unorthodox opinions flourishing in a region where provision for pastoral care before the coming of the friars was extremely inadequate.

Material evidence does a little to offset this gloomy picture as does the renewed spate of saints' lives which were written or refashioned in this period. Apart from the substantial proto-Romanesque remains of the church of Saint-Philbert-de-Grandlieu (cf. above p. 166), there is now little Carolingian ecclesiastical architecture left standing in Brittany. But subsequent periods are better represented. The recently excavated cathedral at Alet was rebuilt in the tenth century, whilst the reconstruction in stone of earlier wooden churches in the diocese of Rennes in the eleventh century has also been highlighted in a recent study. If there are few Romanesque or Gothic masterpieces to compare with those of Normandy, Anjou, Poitou or more distant Burgundy, the corpus which Roger Grand compiled of Breton churches containing Romanesque features underlines the fact that not only major ecclesiastical sites but a large number of more modest buildings – parish churches, chapels and priories – were built or rebuilt in the central Middle Ages. Among important survivals, those of Saint-Sauveur de Dinan (C-d'A), Brélévenez (C-d'A) and its near homonym Merlévenez (M), Saint-Jean-de-Béré (L-A), Perros-Guirec (C-d'A), Ploërdut (M), and La Trinité-Porhoët (M) present substantial Romanesque features. The so-called Temple at Lanleff (C-d'A) is a circular structure of the early twelfth century obviously influenced, as was Sainte-Croix de Quimperlé (F), by the church of the Holy Sepulchre at Jerusalem. But the most potent stylistic influences, as the spread of monasticism itself would suggest, not surprisingly came from the Loire valley, Poitou and Saintonge. Later that of Normandy came increasingly to be felt, especially when Romanesque works were replaced by those displaying Gothic features like the enlarged and rebuilt cathedrals of northern Brittany: Dol, Saint-Malo, Tréguier and Saint-Pol-de-Léon.

Bretons and the wider world

In a charter of *c.* 1080 Roger II of Montgommery, one of the Conqueror's most ambitious and successful companions, boasted that he was 'a Norman of Norman stock' (*Nortmanni ex Nortmannis*). This is one of the few direct statements by a Norman aristocrat revealing a consciousness of his origins. Anglo-Norman kings frequently addressed writs to all their men 'both English and French' without further distinction. In contrast Bretons in the Anglo-Norman world – in England and in southern Italy – as well as elsewhere in France were frequently identified as such in contemporary charters: *Maino, brito*; *Thomas Brittonus filius et heres domini Iohelis*; *Robbertus britius*. This formula was certainly encouraged by the fact that Bretons were slow to adopt regular surnames preferring, as the example of Thomas son of Juhel shows, an older patronymic naming-style, which was widely used in the duchy itself. This may be seen as a Celtic habit, though it is worth remembering that it was also briefly fashionable elsewhere too, among the Normans themselves, for example. Nevertheless use of *Brito*, which in some cases eventually became a proper surname (Le Breton), may be taken as a pointer, evidence that the Bretons considered themselves sufficiently different from surrounding peoples to assert their 'Breton-ness'.

Bretons may also be recognized, at least at the knightly level, even when the epithet is lacking, thanks to other characteristic names indicative of their ethnic origins. By this means it is possible not merely to trace the movements of individual Bretons in a period which saw much emigration from the duchy, but also to measure the continuing influence of their homeland on them, even after several generations of absence. Indirectly such evidence of sentiment amongst émigrés also casts light on the strength of native feelings about which local Breton records in the twelfth century often remain unhelpful.

Currently most is known about the Bretons who settled in England after the Conquest. Even before 1066, there was never a period at which movement across the Channel in either direction entirely ceased. In Edward the Confessor's reign Ralph the Staller (Raoul I, lord of Gaël) was the most prominent Breton in England. But he was not the only one and they were simply precursors of the great influx with William the Conqueror and his sons. If later land holdings are a fair indication, after the Normans, Bretons provided the most numerous contingent to William's forces. By 1086 up to 20% of England may have been in Breton hands, a figure that would have been higher had it not been for the revolt in 1075 of Raoul II de Gaël, earl of East Anglia, and the subsequent expulsion of many of his followers.

The generation of those who benefited from 1066 was succeeded by one that enjoyed Henry I's patronage. It was not so numerous, but it included some who subsequently possessed wide estates and authority: William d'Aubigny, *brito*, of Belvoir (Leics.), Alain FitzFlaad, hereditary seneschal of Dol (whose descendants included the FitzAlan earls of Arundel and the House of Stewart, ancestors of Elizabeth II), Brian FitzCount (son of Duke Alain Fergent and later a loyal supporter of Empress Matilda), Harscouët of Saint-Hilaire, members of the Dinan family and so on.

The number of Bretons amongst the highest aristocracy in Anglo-Norman England and Scotland was inevitably limited, though the ducal house retained territorial links with England for the rest of the Middle Ages, following William I's grant of the great Honour of Richmond to Alan the Red (Alain le Roux), one of

Count Eudes's many sons. But at the level of baronial and knightly society, Bretons established themselves prolifically. Alan the Red, for example, settled in his new lordship many lesser Bretons with the result that not only in North Yorkshire but in Lincolnshire, especially around Boston, in East Anglia (where Alan succeeded Raoul of Gaël), and in the other counties where the Honour of Richmond held lands, Bretons were numerous. For generations the names Alan and Brian alternated in the family of the lords of Bedale, descendants of Alan's steward of Richmond, Scolland. In the late twelfth century the names of other honorial tenants – Alured, Gurwant, Guihomar, Harscouët, Hervé, Hoël, Roald, Rualent – testify to their Breton ethnic roots. The *Cartae Baronum* of 1166 (returns to Henry II's great inquiry into feudal military services) reveal a similar widespread distribution of Bretons in every other honour or region of England. There was, for instance, a particular concentration in the Welsh border country between Shrewsbury and Monmouth; many, too, were settled in Devon and Cornwall. By the early twelfth century, it has recently been suggested, there is evidence that besides family links, political connections can also be established amongst leading Bretons in England. It may be that they were even polarized by a long-standing division between the two main branches of the ducal family to the extent that it determined loyalties during the civil wars of Stephen and Matilda's day when Bretons can be found fighting on either side. Other scholars have linked the growing enthusiasm for Arthurian tales in Anglo-Norman England, culminating in Geoffrey of Monmouth's *History of the Kings of Britain* (*c.* 1136), with the advent of Breton lords and their patronage of wandering minstrels and story-tellers. Geoffrey himself may have been of recent Breton stock.

Be that as it may, there is no doubt that some Bretons in England, like the Aubigny, Dinan and Zouche families, still retained active links with their relatives in Brittany even after Henry II's accession. It was while staying with his near relative Hugh de Plugenet in Oxfordshire around 1180 that the Breton knight Hamon de Saint-Ciriac, who had vainly visited the shrine of St Thomas of Canterbury in search of a cure, experienced St Frideswide's healing touch. In this and a number of other documented cases – how many it is impossible to say – such links were not finally severed until well into the thirteenth century. They might even be re-activated at a later stage as were those of Aubigny in the fourteenth century, whilst the pattern of inter-marriage between families of known Breton stock in England, established at the Conquest, can still be traced in some instances as late as the fifteenth (though whether those involved were then currently aware of their distant common ancestry is impossible to decide). The general point is this: after 1066 many Bretons moved easily in the wider ambit of the Anglo-Norman and Angevin worlds. This sharpened awareness of their own individuality, indicated by assertions of their Breton origins. But it also laid them open to external influences and encouraged changes, for example in legal practices concerning feudal succession or services, which undermined Breton specificity and brought them into line with neighbouring societies.

In the case of the Bretons who accompanied William the Conqueror or went with Robert Guiscard and Count Roger the Great to southern Italy, rewards were gained largely through military success and exploiting political opportunities. The early twelfth-century chronicler William of Malmesbury cynically but accurately observed that the Bretons were 'a race of people poor at home who sought abroad a toilsome life by foreign service . . . [where] they decline not civil war if they are paid for it'. But there was also a steady stream of individual émigrés from Brittany who gained their livelihood by more peaceful means. Emigration was by no means a novel Breton phenomenon but it seems to have reached a peak between *c.* 1070 and 1100. Then after a trough (probably explained by internal colonization in the twelfth century – above pp. 177–8 and below pp. 211–12), it began to rise again in the later thirteenth century. Since then it has remained a major feature of Breton society till modern times.

Among the principal reasons for this unceasing movement may be numbered the quest for learning as well as for new economic opportunities: at Saintes (Charente-Maritime) in 1072 we find *Johannes Britto, vir litteratus*. Shortly afterwards Peter Abelard (d. 1142) was to make Paris the favoured destination for Breton students. There were notable Breton Parisian academics in every subsequent generation though it was not until the thirteenth century that their numbers increased dramatically. Breton clerks, notaries and illuminators were also permanently present in Paris from the twelfth century onwards; around 1268 Thibaud Breton *venditor librorum* was among the wealthiest tax payers in the city.

The royal capital also attracted many Bretons whose main attribute was their physical strength. There is a considerable medieval satirical literature poking fun at poor Bretons who got all the menial tasks (cutting broom, carrying water or cleaning latrines). Amusement was also derived from their awkward efforts to speak French (in 1234 a royal clerk left a house to the Hôtel-Dieu for a chaplain who could hear confessions in Breton). It was remarked that they were all cousins. Like immigrants or *Gastarbeiter* in all periods, they had responded to a hostile host population by banding together for support and protection. By the time tax records allow more detailed analysis of the Breton community in Paris in the late thirteenth century, they confirm the low social and economic status of the majority of the émigrés. They lacked capital and were condemned to eke out a living as petty officials, small craftsmen and manual labourers. A later petition (1399) from the 'humble purse makers of the Breton nation dwelling in Paris' survives. The documents also confirm the considerable scale of emigration. In 1292, of those whose surnames allow a geographical attribution, the Bretons were the largest 'foreign' element in Paris, rivalled only by the English. It is also clear that the movement was from over-populated parts of the duchy, rather than simply poorer regions. Emigration from Haute Bretagne was most common in the twelfth century, in the thirteenth names from Basse Bretagne increasingly appear.

The attraction which medieval Paris exerted is readily comprehensible. No other town enjoyed a comparable magnetic power. But a number of cities – La Rochelle and the towns of the Loire valley – saw the establishment of important Breton colonies. On the other hand evidence for Breton dealings at the Champagne Fairs is slight. Apart from Paris, the usual direction for peaceful emigration was chiefly towards neighbouring Anjou, Maine and Poitou, to towns rather than the countryside and, for preference, along waterways rather than land routes. Besides testifying to the way in which social and economic factors worked in favour of the assimilation of Brittany into the Capetian world (cf. pp. 196–8), analysis of this pattern of emigration over a long period also shows how differences between the two halves of the province were also gradually being eroded. Symbolically, when in the early fourteenth century several colleges were founded in the university of Paris for Breton students, the majority of places were reserved to those from Bretagne Bretonnante, providing a measure of the assimilation of the duchy and its inhabitants into a wider world. After this brief discussion of the social aspects of integration, it is time to turn to the political consequences.

9

Plantagenet Interlude

Relations with Normandy and Anjou

Direct contact between the rulers of Brittany and the kingdom of France gradually ceased in the course of the tenth century. Alain Barbetorte was on occasion to be found, as at Rouen in 942, in the company of Louis IV d'Outremer and other great men of Francia. After him, although Alain III once visited Henry I at Orléans, no duke of Brittany acknowledged fealty or performed homage directly to the king of France until 1199; no duke, count or lesser Breton lord witnessed a single Capetian charter between 987 and 1106 with one exception when Count Geoffroy Boterel, probably seeking royal aid for the release of his father Count Eudes in 1057, attested an act of Henry I; no royal *acta* were issued by French kings for Brittany between Lothair, who died in 986, and Louis VI in 1123. Following Alain Barbetorte's death in 952, leaving no clear heir, a power vacuum in the duchy was filled by the counts of Rennes. From *c*. 970 Conan I (d. 992) acted as duke of Brittany. His family retained the title, though they also used that of count, until 1066. But they had a hard struggle both internally and externally to maintain their authority. In particular they were faced by the rise of powerful neighbouring principalities, Anjou, Blois–Chartres and Normandy, replacing the distant Capetian influence. This led to frequent intervention by outsiders in Breton affairs, though it also had the ultimately beneficial consequence of promoting – as Carolingian intervention had earlier done – a sense of Breton identity.

It was the counts of Anjou whose ambitions first affected the province. Seizing their opportunity during the minority of Barbe-torte's sons and exploiting the weakness of the counts of Nantes, Fulk I and his successors, especially Fulk Nerra (987–1040), acted as protectors or even exercised control directly at Nantes. It was in defence of these interests that the Angevins twice fought with Conan I at Conquereuil (L-A) not far from the Vilaine on the frontier between the counties of Rennes and Nantes. On the latter occasion in 992, though his forces won the battle, Conan lost his life. Angevin cultural and economic influence grew more evident still in the county of Nantes for a period thereafter. Despite great seasonal variation in flow and a meandering course which still makes navigation difficult, the Loire provided a route to the sea for landlocked Anjou whose abbeys acquired properties in Brittany (cf. pp. 176–7). Besides the spiritual benefits such foundations brought, they also stimulated trade and the economy. Many benefactions to them consisted of estates at the mouth of the Loire where since Carolingian times monks had obtained salt in exchange for wine from their inland estates. Another sign of the dependence of the region on a burgeoning Angevin economy, allied to its precocious military and political expansion, is that the coinage struck at Nantes imitated Angevin patterns. When in the latter half of the twelfth century the ruler of Anjou, Henry II of England, once more directly asserted Plantagenet control over the county of Nantes, he was following a policy which had been a constant element in his dynasty's external policies for two centuries.

At the start of this Angevin ascendancy their immediate rival in Breton affairs was the house of Blois. As the counts of Anjou supported the counts of Nantes, so the counts of Blois supported those of Rennes. The only surviving charter which Conan I witnessed was issued at Chartres in the company of Count Eudes in 978. These semi-permanent comital alliances shaped politics in western France from the mid tenth century until the 1020s at least. But from the 990s, the dukes of Normandy replaced the counts of Blois as the greatest influence on the counts of Rennes. They succeeded in exacting a form of feudal recognition, later interpreted as constituting homage. A double marriage between Conan I's son and successor, Geoffroy (992–1008), and his sister Judith, and Duke Richard II (996–1026), and his sister Havoise, symbolized this new orientation of political influence in Brittany.

sunt :ma
rius dixert·
p apud
sensum
sequeretur
quae saltim
obis uttiiq;
nus iudicare·
a promere ;
ncendia iacta·
eloquuum .
ant qui
it apices.
ite puocabor
et odio

FRONIMI

deernam sui. ecce
u. id zorobabel
is numero quadrin
imilia trecentis

neu templi. ecce
eholocausas sollemp
nas. erreskauratione

INCIPIT LIBER EZ
NANNO P
CYRI REGIS
ut compleretur uerb
ore hieremiae. susci
spm cyri regis per
uocem inuniuerso
pscripturam dicen
rex persarum· O
dedit mihi dns deus
pte mihi utaedifica
inhierusalem quae
q uis est inuobis d
eius. sit deus illius
dat iherusalem qu
et aedificet domum
ipse est deus qui e
E t omnes reliqui
ubicumq; habitant
uiri deloco suo E
et subfrancia. etpeco
quod uoluntariae offerunt
est iniherusalem· E t surrexerunt
deiudea etbeniamin. et sacerdote
cuius suscitauit deus spm. utascend
candum templum domini quod e
uniuersiq; qui erant incircuitu ad

Plate 25   Initial from a late eleventh-century two-volume Bible illuminated at Mont Saint-Michel and owned by the abbey of Saint-Sauveur de Redon in the twelfth century

When Geoffroy departed for Rome on a pilgrimage from which he never returned, he left his sons Alain and Eudes under the protection of Richard II, who also proffered assistance during the last Viking attack on the duchy in 1013–14. Later under Robert I (1027–35), relations between Brittany and Normandy deteriorated. It is not certain who was to blame. Disputes about the frontier along the Couesnon river led to hostilities in which Robert was twice victorious but suffered counter-attack by Alain III. Eventually peace was patched up by Archbishop Robert of Rouen, uncle of the two protagonists, at Mont Saint-Michel, itself a possible bone of contention. For Conan I and Geoffroy had been buried there and it has been plausibly suggested that Alain III was considering turning the abbey, in recent times as much in the Breton as Norman orbit, into a family mausoleum as Saint-Denis and Fécamp already were for the Capetians and Normans, and as Fontevraud was to become for the Plantagenets. In the event Robert I was able to reassert control over Mont Saint-Michel, whilst increasing Norman military strength in this sensitive March district is evident in the building of a castle at Cherrueix (I-et-V) to the west of the Couesnon, though the river generally continued to delimit Brittany from Normandy and Maine. When criminals were banished from the duchy in the later Middle Ages, it was across the Couesnon that they had to go.

The middle decades of the eleventh century were extremely turbulent in all western French principalities. The minorities of William the Conqueror (1035–87) in Normandy and Conan II (1040–66) in Brittany and the aggressive policies of Geoffrey Martel (1040–60) of Anjou, especially in the Touraine, Poitou and Maine, followed by a succession crisis on his death, stirred lesser figures, notably ambitious castellan lords, to assert their independence of central authority. This was seriously weakened in Brittany as elsewhere by civil war, especially that between Conan and his uncle and former guardian, Eudes. Eventually it was the duke of Normandy who emerged least scathed from this testing period for princely rule. Strengthening his domestic hold and gaining a formidable reputation as a soldier, William the Conqueror also attracted into his service Breton lords from the north-east of the duchy. In 1064 he even campaigned in Brittany against Conan II in support of Rivallon of Combour. Conan, who was not without his own military ambitions, was killed in 1066 shortly after successfully besieging the Angevin stronghold of Pouancé (Maine-et-Loire).

1 The ducal family: the descendants of Count Eudes, brother of ALAIN III (1008–40)

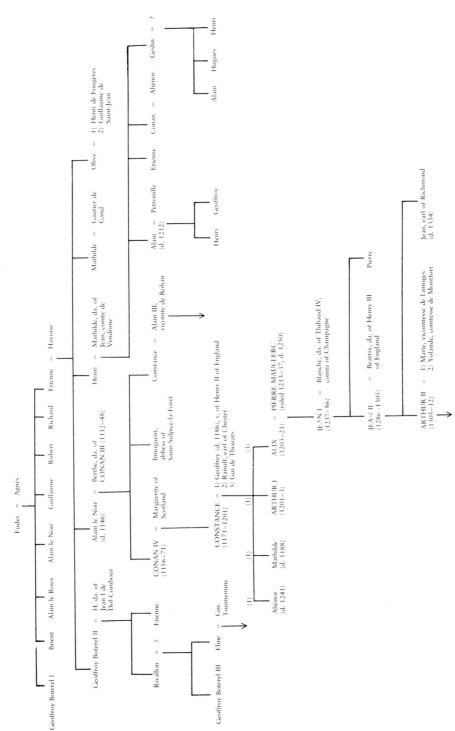

Names in capitals are rulers of the duchy with their regnal dates, unless otherwise stated.

His death created, as was common in such personal states as these principalities then were, a succession problem, since he left no direct heir. The ducal title passed to Hoël, count of Cornouaille and Nantes, who from 1066 to 1084, thanks to his marriage to Conan's sister Havoise, held all the major counties of the duchy. But the victory in England of William the Conqueror in 1066 threatened this hegemony. In particular it promoted the interests of Count Eudes, the late duke's uncle, and his descendants (cf. table 1). Several sons had taken part in the conquest of England. Eventually the family was rewarded with Richmond, one of the greatest of all feudal honours. Linked with their lands in Brittany, conveniently situated in Penthièvre and the Trégor, this allowed them to challenge Hoël and his son Alain IV (Alain Fergant, 1084–1112) for supremacy. During these years the divided Bretons – an illegitimate son of Alain III, Geoffroy Grenonat, who had been given the county of Rennes for life, also joined his cousins in opposing ducal authority – were no match for their more powerful neighbours.

Breton domestic affairs in the late eleventh century were thus enmeshed with those of a wider Anglo-Norman world. When, for instance, in 1075 one of the leading Breton beneficiaries of the Conquest, Raoul of Gaël, earl of East Anglia, revolted and William was able to rid his kingdom of the 'vomit of the Bretons' as Archbishop Lanfranc bluntly put it, congratulating him on the rebels' defeat, there were serious repercussions on the Continent. William was forced to launch a new expedition against Raoul and his allies in Brittany. He suffered a rare reverse at the siege of Dol (1076), when Philip I of France, making the Capetians' first military sally into the duchy, came to the aid of the rebels. Nevertheless Norman political and military might could not usually be denied. Alain IV took Constance, a daughter of the Conqueror, for his first wife. He also dutifully served in the Norman army, whilst on many other occasions William I and his immediate successors recruited troops extensively in Brittany. Norman supremacy was confirmed when Louis VI recognized their suzerainty over Brittany at the treaty of Gisors in 1113.

It was typical of how Brittany, a minor power in comparison with Normandy and Anjou, was pulled first one way and then another, that on the death of Constance, Alain IV married secondly Ermengarde, daughter of Fulk le Réchin (1067/8–1109). Under his rule Anjou more than recovered the influence lost in the years immediately following Geoffroy Martel's death in 1060. Angevin political influence in Brittany was reinforced further by cultural factors. Churchmen of Gregorian persuasion and Angevin training like the puritanical Marbod, bishop of Rennes (1096–1127) and the scholar-poet Baudry, archbishop of Dol, introduced some of the reforms which were so badly needed as we have seen (above p. 179). The strong current of revived Benedictine monasticism flowing from the great Loire abbeys and enthusiasm for eremitical movements which again owed much to Angevin inspiration have already been mentioned (p. 177). Duchess Ermengarde, whose religious patronage was widespread and generous, was to exercise a powerful influence throughout the reign of her son Conan III (1112–48).

These developments also helped to bring the Bretons into contact with the Angevins' traditional ally, the Capetians, who briefly in the 1120s took a direct interest in Brittany. In 1123 Louis VI confirmed the privileges of the cathedral of Nantes first granted by Charles the Bald. Conan III became the first Breton duke to perform military service for the French crown. He not only sent a contingent to serve against Emperor Henry V when he threatened invasion of the realm in 1124, the first occasion that the royal Oriflamme was paraded, but also served personally in campaigns in the Auvergne in 1122 and 1126. However these closer links proved ephemeral and not destined to develop further until the end of the century. Paradoxically the reason for this was the final triumph of the Angevins in their age-old rivalry with the Normans, a struggle which manifested itself at various levels within Brittany but in which the Bretons themselves were often simply puppets or by-standers.

Henry II and his sons

As part of the Anglo-Norman world of the early twelfth century, Brittany was naturally affected by the death of Henry I of England (1135) and the struggle for his crown that developed between his daughter Matilda, wife of Geoffrey, count of Anjou (1131–51), and her cousin, Stephen of Blois. Though Conan III did not possess estates in England (it was the cadet branch of the ducal family who then owned Richmond), Bretons who held lands there may be found fighting on both sides during the anarchy, their choice (as noted above p. 183) possibly determined by feuds within the duchy itself. These were soon to become even more bitter. Among strong partisans of Matilda was Count Alain (d. 1146), earl of Richmond, husband of Conan III's daughter Bertha. On his death, leaving a young son, the future Conan IV (1156–71), his widow married secondly the powerful noble Eudon, viscount of Porhoët. When Conan III died in 1148, after disinheriting his son Hoël for unknown reasons, Eudon claimed the duchy on Bertha's behalf. Civil war quickly followed.

For some years the duchy was effectually partitioned between the acting duke Eudon and Hoël, whose principal base was the county of Nantes. Other great barons like the viscounts of Léon, Count Henri of Tréguier or Henri and Raoul II 'by the grace of God' lords of Fougères, largely pursued their own interests unhampered by superior authority. Eventually (perhaps with Angevin connivance), the citizens of Nantes expelled Hoël in 1156. In the same year Conan IV, certainly with the blessing of Henry II, who confirmed his succession as earl of Richmond, returned to the duchy. He took over from his step-father at Rennes, a move which turned Eudon (d. 1179) into another rebel against ducal authority for the rest of his life. Briefly at Nantes it was Geoffrey, Henry II's younger brother, who established his position before succumbing to an early death on 26 July 1158. Henry II, poised to seize Nantes into his own hands, was foiled by the speedy reaction of Conan who hurried to take possession. Shortly afterwards, however, now ruler of the nominally reunited duchy, Conan felt it expedient to acknowledge Henry II's overlordship. This he did at Avranches at Michaelmas 1158. He was destined never to escape his tutelage to the Angevin king.

During the next few years Conan IV was a familiar figure at the Angevin court – he was present at the council of Clarendon when Henry promulgated the famous constitutions in January 1164. Conan's interests in Richmond brought him across the Channel on several other occasions. In 1160 he married Marguerite, sister of Malcolm IV of Scotland, an alliance which has sometimes been seen as a token of defiance, but which is unlikely to have been arranged without Henry's approval. If it was indeed an attempt to break free of the Angevin yoke, it was shortlived for when a daughter, Constance, was born from the union, Henry quickly arranged in 1166 for her to marry his fourth son, Geoffrey. Conan, whose reign was continually troubled by quarrels with a turbulent nobility by now unaccustomed to close ducal control, agreed to hand over the administration of most of Brittany to Henry to keep for the child-couple. During the last five years of his life, Conan simply held the lordship of Guingamp (C-d'A), wrested from his uncle Count Henri of Tréguier, whilst the Angevins hurried to impress on the duchy the indelible marks of central authority that characterized rule in all their scattered possessions.

From 1171 to 1181 it was directly to Henry II himself that the seneschal and the justiciar of the duchy – both novel offices – answered. Even when Geoffrey was finally allowed to marry Constance in 1181 and go to Brittany, his father kept a close watch on his actions, though the notorious quarrels within the Angevin family, as the king and his sons frequently waged open war on each other, allowed Geoffrey a freedom to intrigue which he was not slow to exploit. Nevertheless, in a few short years between 1166 and 1186, the Angevins succeeded in bringing a degree of governmental organization to Brittany that was of enduring significance.

This was when regional and local seneschals were established. It was also when the system of issuing *brefs de mer* was first regularized. The *brefs* (the name is a significant indicator of Anglo-Angevin origins) were safeconducts issued in ports such as Bordeaux and La Rochelle which guaranteed merchants security against piracy for the hazardous passage around the treacherous coast of the peninsula and the right to salvage what goods they could in the event of shipwreck. *Brefs de mer* remained a financially remunerative ducal prerogative for the rest of the Middle Ages. Among legal reforms introduced by the Angevins, court procedures were overhauled. In 1185 the *Assize* of Count Geoffrey, analogous to similar measures taken elsewhere in the Angevin dominions, sought to minimize the effects of fragmentation of baronial and knightly estates by confirming primogeniture as a principle in noble successions. It was broadly upheld in all subsequent revisions of Breton customary law under the Ancien Regime. Breton feudal military services were light in comparison with those demanded in other regions, but this period also saw efforts to define these and other obligations more closely. The ruthless destruction by Henry II of castles – Bécherel (I-et-V), Léhon, Fougères and Rennes are just four examples – and expropriation of individual families, like that of the viscounts of Léon, revealed the lengths to which the Angevins were prepared to go to impose their rule. Accommodating to this was indeed a painful process. For the first time many Bretons experienced the results of firm central direction.

The consequence of using the Angevin new broom in Brittany was predictable. Angevin *vis et voluntas* stirred up opposition. Some, conscious of literary models, sought comfort by looking back to a remote golden age. The idea that King Arthur still lived was strong in Breton popular imagination as early twelfth-century evidence makes clear. Now, however, the age of Arthur, when Bretons allegedly enjoyed independence and military success, strongly influenced contemporary political thinking as well as literary expression. The naming of Geoffrey Plantagenet's post-humous son as Arthur is, however, ambivalent testimony to the potency of the message. Was the name chosen by Duchess Constance (1171–1201) and her advisers as a deliberate appeal to Breton sentiment, a case frequently argued by those sympathetic to the separatist cause down to our own day? (Certainly there seems to have been little love lost between Constance and her Angevin relatives. Her second marriage to Ranulf, earl of Chester, hereditary viscount of Avranches, arranged like the first by Henry II, was a platonic affair from which both were later happy to escape.) Or was Arthur simply a choice determined by aristocratic and courtly fashion, a name currently made popular by the romance literature which the Angevins themselves had so much encouraged? Whatever the case, the harsh rule of Henry II and Richard I, who was equally unwilling to give Duchess Constance and her precocious son a free rein, caused mounting resentment. After Richard's death in April 1199, it drove Arthur into the arms of Philip Augustus and opened a new chapter for the duchy as a direct fief of the French crown.

Philip Augustus and Brittany

Since the false dawn in Franco-Breton relations in the days of Louis VI, the crown of France, despite the immense success of the

Angevins, had itself registered a number of important advances. Even Henry II had been forced to concede that he owed it fealty. He was reluctant to provide his own tenants-in-chief with an example of a contumacious vassal. In 1158–9 it was with the express permission of Louis VII that Henry had intervened in Brittany in an attempt to bring peace to warring factions. The latter half of the century saw a stricter hierarchy of homages emerge in France at large from which the Capetians were the principal beneficiaries; in 1169 Geoffrey performed homage for Brittany to young Henry, as his father's heir, whilst he in turn performed homage for Normandy to Louis VII. The suzerainty of the king of France over Brittany, nominal for so long, became more of a reality when during the quarrels of the Angevins, Geoffrey turned directly to Philip Augustus, with whom he formed a passionate friendship. On the king's side, this naturally involved political considerations as well as personal emotions. When Geoffrey died from injuries sustained at a tournament held in Paris in August 1186, Philip had to be prevented from throwing himself into Geoffrey's open grave when he was buried in the abbey-church of Saint-Denis, itself a mark of signal favour. Philip then claimed the wardship of Geoffrey's daughter, Aliénor, though Henry II was too shrewd to allow her to escape from his clutches.

His death, the Third Crusade and finally the energetic rule of Richard I, once released from his captivity in Austria, delayed for a few more years further Capetian advances in Brittany. But the ill-feelings generated by Richard I in his relations with Duchess Constance and the frustrated ambitions of Arthur, especially when John succeeded Richard, allowed Philip the opportunity he had been long awaiting. First, in return for his support, including the promise of marriage to his daughter, Marie, the king persuaded Arthur to perform liege homage in 1199, an act pregnant with significance. For although another turn of fortune's wheel in 1200 meant Philip had almost immediately to renounce this homage, he persuaded John in his role as duke of Normandy to admit Arthur as his man for Brittany and pay a relief for his succession. Then when the English king in turn was declared to have forfeited his lands for failure to appear at the royal court in 1202, once again Philip received Arthur as his liegeman. Kings of France were from this point the immediate suzerains of the duchy.

The murder of Arthur by John (around Easter 1203) confirmed

the Bretons in their hatred of the Angevins. Many of them took part in the campaigns to expel John from his Continental possessions. In 1206 Philip Augustus, at the head of an expeditionary force engaged in mopping up operations after the conquest of Normandy, journeyed as far as Nantes where he confirmed Gui de Thouars, third husband of the late Duchess Constance, as guardian of their infant daughter, Alix, half-sister of the dead Arthur. In the absence of Aliénor, an unfortunate pawn in John's hands who died still a captive in England in 1241, Alix was recognized by the leading Breton churchmen and barons as the rightful heiress of the duchy. Her marriage, at first hotly sought by local aspirants, was finally arranged by Philip II in 1212 to a junior member of his own family, Pierre Mauclerc, second son of the count of Dreux. By it the king clearly intended to link the duchy of Brittany more firmly to the crown, following the policy of pacific expansion and indirect rule the Capetians had already used to good effect in many other parts of their kingdom. Whether it would work with regard to the factious Bretons now that Angevin ascendancy had finally been brought to an end with the defeat of John and his allies in 1214 was an open question. With the accession of Pierre Mauclerc some interesting answers were quickly forthcoming.

10

Consolidation and Growth, 1213–1341

Pierre Mauclerc and his successors

It is difficult to know what Philip Augustus expected when he allowed Pierre Mauclerc (1213–37) to marry Alix of Brittany. The remarkable expansion of the royal demesne during his reign, whilst vastly increasing his resources, also imposed an enormous burden on his administration. To share that in a distant and unruly part of the enlarged kingdom with a relative may have seemed a sensible policy. Granting apanages was a traditional Capetian practice for slowly assimilating outlying parts of 'France'. But Pierre proved to be one of the most ambitious of all Capetian princes and resented attempts to trammel him. There was a period after the king's death when Pierre was at the heart of every noble rebellion against the crown. That in the end the Capetians did not regret even more the day marriage gave Pierre the duchy, was largely thanks to the traditional factiousness of the Breton nobility, the limited period during which Pierre legally held the duchy (from the death of Alix in 1221 he was simply its *baillistre* or guardian on behalf of his son Jean) and his own recklessness. It was characteristic that when he finally handed over the duchy in 1237, he embarked on a renewed career as an adventurer and crusader. He had always been a gambler, a figure who could easily have stepped directly out of a *chanson de geste*. It was fitting that he died, whilst returning to France, from wounds sustained at the battle of Mansourah (1250), without doubt one of the most colourful princes the Bretons ever had.

From the beginning Pierre picked up where the Angevins had left off. He tried to impose on his new vassals the restraints which a feudal lord coming from the Ile de France found natural and reasonable – reliefs, wardship, precise military obligations, control of castle-building. He also sought to limit more specifically local customs like the unrestrained use of *lagan* or right to shipwreck, against which the system of *brefs de mer* was also directed. There is the story of one thirteenth-century lord of Léon who claimed that a single jagged rock was worth 100,000 écus a year to him thanks to the wrecks it caused. But the result of Pierre's assault on seigneurial privilege was predictable; he met violent opposition. Nor was this exclusively from lay lords, because he richly won his soubriquet 'Mauclerc' for attacks on the church's temporal possessions. His dispute with the bishop of Nantes, in particular, resulted in considerable mayhem but no bishop was safe from depredation. The viscounts of Léon, whom the Angevins once appeared to have broken, were amongst the most redoubtable lay opponents of Pierre's efforts to enforce his authority, but baronial coalitions attracted wide support throughout Brittany. Neighbouring Angevin lords like Amaury de Craon, whose family had been rewarded in Brittany by Angevin and Capetian alike, also fished in troubled waters. Eventually on 3 March 1223, Amaury was defeated outside the walls of Châteaubriant, a victory that made Pierre Mauclerc undisputed master of the duchy for the next few years. But his own intrigues from 1227, both with other rebellious French princes and with Henry III of England, allowed his domestic enemies new opportunities to unseat him. In 1230 Breton barons opposed to Pierre and his English ally appealed to the crown for help and provided it with a legitimate excuse for intervention.

Mustering a powerful army, Louis IX marched on Brittany in June 1231 and at Saint-Aubin-du-Cormier Pierre was forced to sue for peace since many of his most powerful subjects had already been won over by the king. His ability to cause harm in the future was undermined by their promise to rally to Louis if Pierre violated the agreement. This did not stop him trying; in 1234 he was once more in league with Henry III, who offered the bait of Richmond. But Pierre's rule in the duchy was coming naturally to its end. In 1231, although deserting Pierre, the Breton lords swore to uphold his son's rights to succeed as their natural lord when he came of age. In 1237 he did so and Pierre ceded power to him, though not before a commission sent by Louis IX in 1235 had collected a long and revealing litany of complaint against his arbitrary rule.

Despite this, the new duke did not seriously modify his father's internal policies. He took a similarly hard line with the nobility and church, but proved to be a more skilful politician, gradually reconciling or defeating his enemies. He avoided the full consequences of excommunication and other sanctions taken against him by pope and king. As a result Jean I (1237–86) remained securely on his throne for almost fifty years. This extended reign, the longest enjoyed by any duke, allowed him time to pursue policies which were not spectacular but which gradually extended his rights and resources.

Although there had been an earlier form of inauguration ceremony, in 1237 for the first time there is mention of the duke being invested with a sword and banner as a sign of his authority. It is clear that contemporary Capetian practice provided a model not only in ceremonial but also in developing chancery practice, for instance, or legal reforms like the *Assise des pledeours* (1259). In 1275, Jean and Philip III (1270–85) agreed to remove impediments to the swifter exercise of justice by renouncing reception of *aveux* (avowals) from tenants-in-chief and rear-tenants, a practice which was interfering with the developing system of appeals from lower courts to higher ones. By the end of the century, the duchy was divided into eight *bailliages*, each with a ducal seneschal to receive appeals from seigneurial courts within their circumscription. Those from six of these courts were taken to that of the seneschal of Rennes, whilst appeals from his court and that of the seneschal of Nantes went directly to the Parlement of Brittany, first explicitly mentioned in 1288. From there remedy lay to the Parlement of Paris, arrangements formalized in 1297 when it was stipulated that no cases of first instance but only those concerning false judgement or denial of justice in the duchy should be heard by the king.

Earlier, in issuing an *ordonnance* expelling Jews from Brittany in 1240, Jean I specifically asked the king to confirm this decision. Later he re-enacted in the duchy royal measures against usurers, another sign of the moral authority exercised by Louis IX. The duke was also conscious of his duty to enforce law and order. Dissident lords were, if necessary, brought to heel by force. Jean I's reign was punctuated by several minor wars which surviving records only dimly reveal like one with Hervé de Léon in 1240–1 and a more violent dispute with Olivier de Clisson and Eudo de Pontchâteau between 1254 and 1261. In 1257 the duke sacked Dinan, then held by Alain d'Avaugour. In this case as well as those of the viscounts of Léon and lords of Lanvaux (M), the duke combined military action with an unscrupulous exploitation of the lords' financial difficulties. Each of these families was inveigled into mortgaging estates on impossible terms so that eventually Jean I was either able to endow junior members of his own family with them or add them directly to the ducal demesne.

When a family in difficulty had the temerity to turn to the new Parlement in Paris for help, as Jeanne, lady of La Roche Derrien, did in 1269, the duke refused to be bound by royal decisions and wreaked his vengeance, completing a ruin which Pierre Mauclerc had first threatened. More peaceably, by the *Assise des rachaz* of 1276, which most noble families eventually agreed to observe, the thorny issue of *bail* (wardship), left indeterminate by the *Assise* Count Geoffrey issued in 1185 concerning feudal successions, was resolved. It had been one of the major grievances against Mauclerc that he had ruthlessly exploited estates falling into his hands, especially where the heir was a minor. Now the duke renounced prolonged wardship, conceded greater testamentary freedom to his great vassals and allowed them to recover any portion for which homage had been performed by younger brothers (*jouveigneurs*) dying without heirs. In return he was granted the right to a year's revenue from the estates of a deceased tenant-in-chief (*rachat*), regardless of the heir's age, though an allowance (normally a third of the revenues) was made for dowagers. Such measures stabilized relations between the duke and his nobles, fixed the rules governing noble tenure in Brittany for the rest of the Middle Ages and enabled Jean I and Jean II (1286–1305) to stand head and shoulders above even the greatest Breton nobles in terms of landed wealth.

There were limitations on the duke's autocratic style of rule. Legal procedures were slow. Old habits died hard. Arbitration by interested parties meant that many disputes were settled without coming into the duke's purview. Although from the mid thirteenth century references to the custom of Brittany (*iuxta ritus et usus Britannia, usus et consuetudinis patrie*) become more frequent, this had yet to be written down. When it was (between 1312 and 1325), it was done so unofficially as a manual for practising lawyers. Nor does the *Très ancienne coutume* contain much that is specifically Breton, apart from retaining procedures like *premesse* or *retrait-lignager*, which allowed the wider kin rights to repossess lands alienated by the conjugal family, or *finporter* which similarly permitted relatives of an injured party to be involved in a subsequent prosecution. Such practices may owe something to earlier Celtic traditions in which the role of the kindred (*kenedl*) was paramount. Otherwise, the Breton custom was based almost exclusively on the neighbouring customs of Anjou, Touraine and the Orléannais, a further sign of the French infiltration.

Like the crown, too, the duke faced intractable problems because of the rudimentary administrative means at his disposal. Private warfare posed problems in Brittany as it did in the realm at large, problems which Louis IX began to tackle in an *ordonnance* of 1261 but which were still proving recalcitrant many decades later. The will of Geoffroy Tournemine (d. 1264), lord of La Hunaudaye (C-d'A), in which he sought to make amends for damage caused during the 'war of Plancoët' and several other similar incidents otherwise unrecorded, reveals how violent life could be in one corner of the duchy. The peace of the *pays de Rays*, beyond the Loire, was much disturbed in the 1280s by quarrels among local lords. Nevertheless the reigns of Jean I and Jean II did witness some important advances in administration. Most critically, a proper accounting system was begun.

The first surviving ducal accounts date from 1262. By the end of the century regular sessions of the embryonic *chambre des comptes* were held at fixed times and locations, usually in the Vannetais. At these an increasing number of receivers and other officers from the demesne appeared to undergo examination of their stewardship. Ducal control of coinage (a monopoly since the seigneurial mint at Guingamp had fallen into ducal hands in the late twelfth century) was by the late thirteenth century eagerly exploited. The principal mints were at Rennes and Nantes. In 1274 Philip III delivered an *arrêt* against Jean I for weakening his coinage and royal officials increasingly attempted to regulate ducal issues. Their efforts were not always well rewarded. Royal *ordonnances* in 1311 and 1316 recognized the right of the duke to continue minting. In the course of the fourteenth century he became still more jealous of his rights. Ducal ambitions culminated in the issue of a gold coinage by Charles de Blois (1341–64), an example followed by all his successors down to Duchess Anne (1488–1514). Although never a major currency, Breton money circulated widely in the later Middle Ages. The dukes were conscious of how it promoted both their own image and that of the duchy. It is indicative of Breton touchiness on this subject that when Charles V of France briefly held the duchy between 1373 and 1379, the coinage he issued bore the legend *Moneta Britannie.*

With increasing wealth as Brittany at last began to participate in the trade and commerce of the west, the growth of a more advanced central and local administration and the assertion of authority over other powerful interest groups in the duchy – the nobility and the church – the dukes' prestige was markedly enhanced during the thirteenth century. External recognition of this was provided by Philip IV (1285–1314) who in 1297 promoted Jean II to be a peer of France. Belatedly the royal chancery adopted the ducal rather than the comital title which it had pointedly used since 1206 when referring to Brittany. But the period of laissez-faire which had largely prevailed in Franco-Breton relations since Philip Augustus's brief intervention was not destined to last for much longer.

In the thirteenth century there was an inexorable growth in the power and prestige of the French monarchy. The consequences of this for relations between the king and the leading princes of the kingdom were critical. From around 1250 royal advisers – many deriving ideas from their studies of Roman law in which the sovereign position of the Emperor was emphasized – began to demand for the king a similar position of supremacy within his kingdom. The phrase *rex in regno suo imperator est* was widely cited to justify these claims. Some interventions by the king and his councillors in the affairs of Brittany have already been noted – in justice where the Parlement of Paris now exercised sovereign authority as the final court of appeal and over coinage. When added to the traditional demands a feudal suzerain might make of his vassal (military aid, counsel), this meant that dukes and their servants came increasingly under the scrutiny of royal officials. The results of this in the case of the duke of Guyenne (who also happened to be king of England) are well known. The origins of the Hundred Years War lie in the complex tangle of disputes which arose from interpretation of the treaty of Paris (1259) in which Henry III acknowledged that he was the liegeman of Louis IX for

Guyenne, and in the way in which evolving ideas on sovereignty changed that relationship, posing practical problems of government which ultimately proved insoluble by diplomacy.

In the case of the duke of Brittany, who did not have the resources that an Edward I or Edward III could command, it was more difficult to counter royal pressure. By the beginning of the fourteenth century royal influence was becoming irresistible. The crown started to dispose of Breton benefices for its own civil servants; taxes levied in Brittany for the church in practice passed mainly into the king's hands; the crown became more exigent in demanding military service; it expected the duke to implement the punitive measures it had taken against the Lombards or Templars and so on. In Philip IV's later years, Jean II and Arthur II (1305–12), leading Breton churchmen and nobles were summoned to various national 'assemblies'. Although this pandered to Breton self-esteem, it also demonstrated that the duchy was in danger of absorption into the Capetian kingdom as Normandy and Anjou had once been.

Some of these developments, of course, were welcomed by the duke and his council. Nor should the predatory nature of royal power be over-emphasized. In the matter of justice, for example, the compromise arranged in 1297 over appeals when the duke became a peer of France was beneficial to both sides. There is as much evidence of cooperation as of confrontation between the royal and ducal administrations. Litigants who had not exhausted the judicial resources available locally in matters of first instance but had gone directly to Paris, or those who had failed to follow the appeals procedure through the hierarchy of Breton courts, found their cases returned to Brittany for judgement. But as the ducal administration itself grew, it became more jealous of its master's prerogatives. In the widespread reaction against the authoritarian rule of Philip IV after his death, Jean III (1312–41) obtained a charter confirming a number of these privileges as a guarantee of Breton administrative autonomy. The change of royal dynasty in 1328 was also helpful to the Breton cause. In the same year Jean III fought personally in the French victory at Cassel over the Flemings in revolt. A grateful Philip VI confirmed the concessions made by his Capetian predecessors.

Within a few years of this the first clear statement on ducal 'regalities' is heard. By this was meant the sole exercise of certain sovereign rights by the duke of Brittany, even at the expense of the king of France: in other words, the expression of an explicit Breton political ideology. The combination of practical powers, thanks to administrative advance, with a considered legal position to justify ducal policies, was destined to give Brittany the lineaments of a genuine state for the rest of the Middle Ages. Less predictably, the opportunity to pursue the idea of autonomy arose from a severe crisis which bitterly divided Brittany, the War of Succession which followed the death in 1341 without heirs of John III. But before turning to this critical event, economic and social developments during the twelfth and thirteenth centuries may be sketched.

Developments in trade, towns and rural life

Although Brittany was a human reservoir from which spilled a steady stream of emigrants, before the thirteenth century its inhabitants (a few saints apart) had yet to acquire a reputation for sea-faring. Breton crusaders, of whom there were many, normally hired shipping after leaving the duchy. The commercial development of the western seaboard of France in the twelfth century (La Rochelle was a boom town from the 1170s) and the general growth of international sea routes along which trade flowed from the Mediterranean and Iberia to the Low Countries and the British Isles ineluctably brought the peninsula into contact with one of the main currents of commerce in Europe at large. At first Brittany had little to contribute to this trade. The pathetic remains of recently excavated villages like Pen-er-Malo (Guidel, M), buried under sand-dunes since the twelfth century, and of Lann Gouh en Melrand (M) are testimony to the poverty of the Vannetais (below p. 214). But the mere fact that ships, making the difficult passage around Brittany's rocky and deeply indented 1200 km coastline, were forced to take on food and water or to shelter from storms in its many bays and creeks, encouraged indigenous maritime enterprise. A tangible sign of this is the distribution pattern from the eleventh century of the coarse Breton pottery known as 'céramique onctueuse' manufactured in the neighbourhood of Bodérès-en-Plonéour-Lanvern (F) just west of Quimper. This 'greasy' ware (recognizable to the touch because of its talc content) was exported for the rest of the Middle Ages.

From the early thirteenth century documentary and archaeological evidence for the growth of numerous small northern Breton ports begins to accumulate. It was at Saint-Gildas (now Port-Blanc, C-d'A) in the Bay of Saint-Brieuc that Richard, earl of Cornwall, landed in 1230 on his way to assist Pierre Mauclerc. Less surprisingly, the main body of Henry III's expedition in that year docked at Saint-Malo, recently established on its island site. It was destined to become one of the major ports of the duchy, the home of merchants, pirates and explorers to modern times. Recent finds – ceramics, coins – from medieval Exeter testify to the close ties which once again linked Saint-Malo and the Rance valley with the other side of the Channel by this date.

Already stimulated by its place in the Angevin empire, after 1206 Breton trade with Saintonge and Guyenne as well as across the English Channel grew steadily. This particularly benefited the

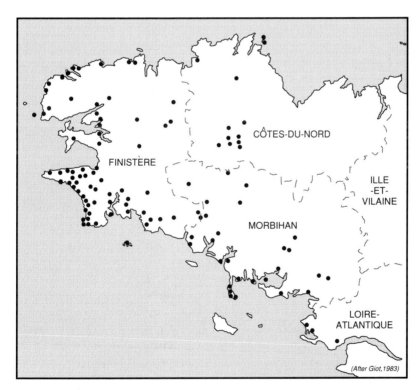

Figure 22   Distribution of Breton 'greasy' ware

south-western coastline from Nantes to Brest. The evidence of
receipts from the *brefs de mer*, a major item in the earliest ducal
accounts, is eloquent testimony to these links. By the late thirteenth
century Breton sailors were a familiar sight on the quays at
Bayonne or Bordeaux, where a fifth to a quarter of the ships loaded
were Breton. They also broke the blockade Philip IV imposed on
trade with England during the Anglo-French war of 1294–7. What
their ships lacked in size (few of them exceeded 100 tons) they
made up for in sheer numbers. Patterns of trading that were to
characterize the Breton fleet for the rest of the Middle Ages were
already in place by 1300.

The principal attraction was wine but raw materials like iron ore
and woad (for dyeing) drew the Bretons to south-west France and
the Basque provinces. In reciprocation, the farming of lucrative
ducal and seigneurial fish-drying installations (*sécheries*) around
the coast of Finistère were eagerly sought by Bayonnais merchants
and Italian financiers. The *sécheries* (whose products were in one
sense the medieval equivalent of *garum*, above p. 95) were destined
to survive until the discovery of the Newfoundland banks in the
sixteenth century drove locally dried fish from the marketplace.

Plate 26   Salines at Guérande (L-A)

Salt, another important product won from the sea, especially at the mouth of the Loire and in the Bay of Bourgneuf, where a coarse grey salt was gathered after evaporation from water sluiced through shallow pools by a method still practised around Guérande and Le Croisic (L-A), only became a major item of Brittany's international commerce in the course of the fourteenth century. But its importance in local trade was clearly established by 1300. In the *pays de Rays* monasteries and lords were already drawing impressive revenues from it when records become available.

The revival of urban life, a feature of the High Middle Ages at large, occurred slowly in Brittany. Its civic inheritance from late antiquity was limited. The classical roots of Nantes, Quimper, Rennes and Vannes have already been described (pp. 84–7); late imperial defences shaped their physical development in a literal sense until medieval population growth forced them to burst out of their Gallo-Roman carapaces. At Nantes this happened in Pierre Mauclerc's reign; at Rennes it was not until the fifteenth century that the earliest defences were finally replaced (below p. 266). Elsewhere former major centres of late antique population failed to survive (Corseul), or quietly vegetated (Carhaix). Breton society in the immediate post-migration period was almost exclusively rural.

A few important religious centres formed the nucleus for later urban development – the abbey-bishoprics of Dol and Saint-Pol-de-Léon, and probably of Tréguier and Saint-Brieuc as well. The Carolingian period saw some modest revival of urban activities. Maritime contacts between Alet and Saintonge are revealed by the translation of the relics of St Malo in the mid ninth century. The counts of the Breton March spent some time at Vannes, Nantes and Rennes which, like Quimper, had resident bishops. But none of them really flourished before the Viking invasions, whilst the Breton princes and aristocracy passed most of their lives in rural palaces (above p. 150). From the eleventh century, however, Brittany witnessed a wave of new urban foundations. By the end of the Middle Ages some sixty Breton towns can be identified.

At Redon the monastery of Saint-Sauveur was the *fons et origo* of the future town (above p. 152). The same is true of Sainte-Croix at Quimperlé. Usually, however, it was through the joint efforts of church and laity that new towns were born. The establishment of a castle was often coupled with the foundation of a neighbouring priory, for example, at Dinan, Donges, Fougères, Josselin or Vitré. Frequently the monks were encouraged to found their own *bourgs*. In any event the spiritual and physical protection offered by this alliance of ecclesiastical and secular authorities attracted population to many hitherto unimportant sites like Châteaubriant, Châteaugiron (I-et-V), Clisson (L-A), Hédé (I-et-V), Jugon (C-d'A), Lannion (C-d'A), Malestroit (M), Moncontour (C-d'A) and many others. Some lay just inland of the coast at the point where rias became bridgeable (Auray, Châteaulin, Dinan, Hennebont, Landerneau, La Roche Bernard, Morlaix). Some clearly owed their importance to natural defensive features or offered protection in disputed frontier regions like the marcher towns of Fougères, Vitré, Ancenis or Clisson. Yet others, especially those of the interior, centres like Montfort, Blain (L-A), Quintin and Châtelaudren (C-d'A), for example, represented the colonization of forest and waste, the development of agriculture, imposition of lordship, growth of population, manufacture and commerce. Only two deliberately planned medieval towns with a gridiron pattern of streets have been recognized in the duchy, Saint-Aubin-du-Cormier and Gavre. Both were established by Pierre Mauclerc. But all lords were interested in fostering urban development. Without their intervention it would certainly have taken a very different form in Brittany.

Once towns were established, lay and ecclesiastical lords kept a tight control because of the fiscal advantages they offered. There was only one attempt in medieval Brittany to form a commune – at Saint-Malo in 1308 – and that was quickly suppressed. Elsewhere, urban self-government came slowly. Only at the end of the Middle Ages did a *procureur* (an embryonic mayor) tentatively make his appearance in even the largest towns. Normally a captain appointed by the town's overlord exercised control, reflecting the fact that the economy was, by comparison with other regions, still very under-developed in 1300. By the time figures can be calculated with some certainty in the fifteenth century, Nantes and Rennes, with 13,000 or 14,000 inhabitants, were the major centres. Dinan, Fougères and Vannes, the next in rank, probably only contained around 5000 people (below pp. 265–7). None of them enjoyed metropolitan status. From the central Middle Ages Brittany had a plethora of small towns. Some to this day retain virtually complete circuits of walls of which the best surviving examples are Guérande, Saint-Malo and Dinan.

Major changes occurred in the medieval countryside although the detail is less well known. Comment on particular crops and productivity will be reserved until later when records are more informative (below pp. 261–2). But it is clear that with regard both to the techniques of agriculture and to patterns of tenure, features were now established or reinforced which survived until recent *remembrements* destroyed the palimpsest of tiny fields, enclosures, commons and waste (*landes*), copses and woods, that formed both the *bocage* of eastern Brittany and the small-scale farming of the west. Already a region of dispersed dwellings, scattered farmsteads and hamlets, engaged in mixed husbandry in Carolingian times, the coming of feudal lordship does not seem to have resulted in any major disturbance of agriculture, no *incastellamento* or re-organization into larger units of settlement.

Some characteristic forms of banal lordship were imposed – peasants were forced to use the seigneurial mill, oven or wine-press. The apparent disappearance of hand-mill querns, present at Lann Gouh en Melrand and Pen-er-Malo en Guidel in eleventh- and twelfth-century contexts, from later Breton rural excavations is a possible index of increasing seigneurialization. Breton manori-alism, however, appears inchoate in comparison with conditions elsewhere. The extent of open-field farming was limited. There were unfree serfs (*mottiers*) on some estates like those of the military orders, for example, or of lords like the viscounts of Rohan in Léon and Cornouaille. But they were very much a minority. Serfdom, if it had ever been general (and the Redon evidence suggests it was not), was already almost entirely absent from the rest of the duchy by the twelfth century as it was from neighbouring Normandy. The most distinctive forms of dependent tenure in Breton-speaking Brittany, *domaine congéable* and the *quévaise*, both appear to be the consequence of colonizing new lands. This occurred particularly under the direction of the Templars, Hospitallers, Cistercians and Premonstratensians. It was by their efforts that much land was brought into cultivation in the poorer upland parts of the province like the Monts d'Arrée, central forested regions including Paimpont, a remnant of the legendary Brocéliande (the scene of many an Arthurian adventure), or in low-lying marshes in the *pays de Rays* or *marais de Dol*. In eastern

Brittany the evidence of place-names shows that those with the characteristic central medieval suffix *-iére* preceded those with *-ais*. Both are used chiefly for individual farmsteads or hamlets, but the first are located on hill-top sites, the latter in valley bottoms.

In the system of *domaine congéable* (also called *convenant*), widely practised in Breton-speaking parts of the duchy, there were two distinct elements, the land (*fons*), and buildings, including the farm-house, walls, hedges, banks, fruit trees, etc. (*édifices* and *superfices*). Whilst the owner retained ultimate possession of the *fons*, for the term of a tenancy (traditionally fixed at seven or nine years) the peasant had free disposal of the *édifices* from which he could not be evicted unless the lord reimbursed him for any improvements (including growing crops). It was a system designed to attract tenants while allowing the landlord to make periodic rent adjustments or change tenants before agreeing to a new *convenant*. The system was unambiguously in place by the mid thirteenth century. It survived the Revolution, only finally dying out in the mid twentieth century, a testimony to its flexibility. In practice, peasant-proprietors, especially in the adverse demographic conditions of the later Middle Ages, enjoyed almost permanent possession of their tenures.

The *quévaise* was similarly devised to attract settlers (*hostes*) to recently colonized lands. Each tenement was offered with a house, garden or *courtil* and some arable, usually about a *journal* (an acre) in size and exempt from tithe. In addition the peasant had the right to assart land in the surrounding waste and pasture animals on common land, paying small additional dues or a part of his harvest. Another distinctive feature of *quévaise* was that it was a form of gavelkind: possession of the tenement eventually passed to the youngest child, although there was division of movables amongst all children. The advantage of this was that older offspring could strike out independently knowing their parents would not be left helpless in old age. Like *domaine congéable*, full reference to *quévaise* only appears in the later Middle Ages (from the records of the Hospitaller commanderies of Pont-Melvez (C-d'A) and La Feuillée (F) in particular), though its origins seem firmly fixed in the central medieval period.

Elsewhere most Breton peasants performed few labour services or *corvées*, since landlords seldom kept much land or *réserves* in their own hand. Like military obligations among the aristocracy, commoners' feudal dues were light though landlords kept meticulous record of these whether they were paid in money (*chef-rentes*) or in kind. Land could be held by different forms of lease – *féage, censie* – or rented (*baux*). Whatever allodial land there had once been disappeared, swallowed up by feudal lords so that the principle *nulle terre sans seigneur* applied. Although by no means unique to the duchy, the practice of share-cropping (*métayage*) was already widespread when charters become abundant in the eleventh century. Especially valuable in regions where the predominant type of farming was mixed arable and livestock (for example, in eastern Brittany), *métayage* was particularly favoured by landowners from the greatest to the most obscure country gentry for providing their immediate household needs.

Few medieval Breton *manoirs* (the word itself only begins to become common in the early thirteenth century though its antecedent, *villa*, is much older) lacked an accompanying *métairie* or home farm. As the name implies (*mediataria, métairie*, cf. Modern French *moitié*, half), in return for the right to farm the land a tenant normally shared the harvest and livestock increases equally with his landlord as surviving contracts show. In the Vannetais the system of *mi-croix* was simply an adaptation for sharing the burden and profits of raising livestock. A similar form of agreement, *bail à complant*, the origins of which are classical, was used in regions like the Nantais where the vine was extensively cultivated. Here the landowner conventionally took a quarter of the *vendange*, the wine produced annually.

In the course of the Middle Ages, thanks to freedom from legal restraints and the fact that possession in Brittany was largely governed by economic considerations, a very active market in small parcels of land, associated rents and feudal dues developed. Fragmentation and morcellization were characteristics of noble and commoner estates of every type as thousands of surviving *aveux*, lists of real estate and legal rights, overwhelmingly testify. Although the greatest landholders may once have held whole parishes, vast and continuous tracts of uncultivated land or forest, by the time their holdings are described in surviving records this fragmentation has already occurred. At Hillion and Pommerit (C-d'A), for example, it is seen in the kaleidoscopic confusion of lands assigned in 1319 to produce a rent of 200 *livres* by Guy, count of Penthièvre, for his former tutor Simon de Montbourchier. It is a pattern that has persisted to modern times. Of 42 *féages* described in a document of 1486, the average extent of those at Plougonvelin (F) was 1.8 ha and at Plouzané (F) 6.8 ha. In a survey of these two parishes in 1958, after generations of modern emigration and rationalization, the average farm was between 5 and 9 ha in size at Plougonvelin and between 10 and 19 ha at Plouzané. The pocket-handkerchief patchwork of small embanked fields and petty-hedged enclosures that predominated in much of the province until recently, whilst having Carolingian or even older antecedents (p. 91), was essentially the creation of the central and later Middle Ages.

Finally, although it is too early to provide a proper synthesis in the absence of sufficient archaeological data, knowledge of the material conditions of the peasantry, especially in the Vannetais, has been transformed in recent years. The excavations at Lann Gouh and Pen-er-Malo have been mentioned. Additional work has been done at Kerlano-en-Plumelec and Pont Callec, Berné (M), and Brennilis (F). It reinforces the picture of small agricultural communities, living extremely simple lives in primitive conditions which has already emerged from the Redon evidence.

At Lann Gouh, within a low dry-stone wall enclosure, at the southern end a group of buildings surrounded a small *place*, whilst in the north-eastern quadrant there was an internal enclosure in which no buildings but several millstones were found, suggesting a work-area. The buildings (nine in all, four with hearths) were generally trapezoid in form. Those with hearths were between 38 m² and 54 m² in size (8 m × 4.70, 8.20 m × 3.60, 9.60 m × 5.60). In one case an earlier building had been remodelled into an oval or elliptical shape similar to that found in the slightly later example of Pen-er-Malo. Stone walls, made of small granite blocks with earth mortar but without foundations, were on average 65 cm wide and stood to a height of 50 cm. Floors had up to 15 cm of beaten earth. The hearths were usually off-centre. Smoke presumably escaped through the single entrance or through the roof. No trace of crucks survive. By analogy with later buildings it can be suggested that roofs rested on the walls and were covered in thatch. Since this projected down to the ground wall-bases were

Figure 23   Plan and reconstruction of a twelfth-century house at Pen-er-Malo, Guidel

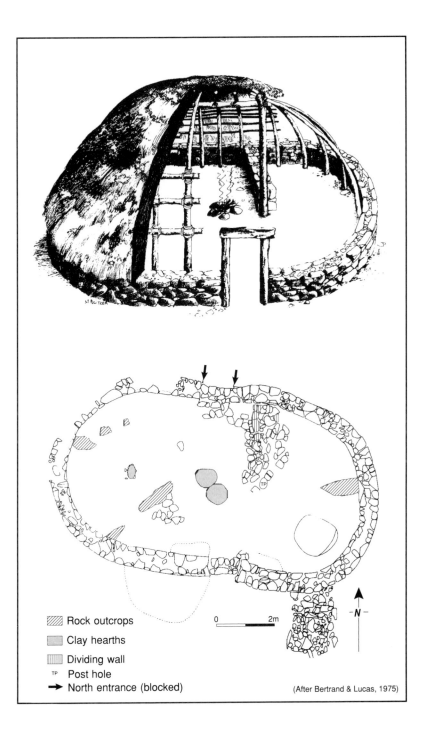

invisible and the overall appearance was of a closely enveloped hut. Two houses showed evidence of an internal division suggesting co-habitation of man and animals, a practice current in Brittany till the mid-twentieth century. Similar houses have been discovered at Pen-er-Malo and Plumelec (M).

As for the community that inhabited Lann Gouh, it was essentially a mixed agricultural one, perhaps six or seven families, 30 persons in all (cf. Pen-er-Malo where seven 'buildings' were found). Hand-mills testify to cereal-growing, whilst distaffs suggest the spinning of wool. No coins were discovered but the presence of 'céramique onctueuse' shows that the community was not entirely cut off from the outside world. As might be expected from its site on the littoral at Pen-er-Malo bone finds not only show cattle, sheep, pigs, rabbits and poultry in the diet but mussels, fish and other crustacea. Although some factors changed, a majority of Bretons lived in similar rural communities for the rest of the Middle Ages and beyond (below p. 259).

11

The Civil War, 1341–65

The succession crisis

A disputed succession in the mid fourteenth century provoked a major crisis in ducal relations with France and led to a bitter civil war. This brought to an end the period of relative calm that had lasted in Brittany since the mid thirteenth century. The political, economic and social consequences of the war were of fundamental importance in shaping the history of the province and its people during the rest of the Middle Ages. In this chapter a brief outline of the reasons for the conflict will be sketched, together with an outline of events. In the next some of the longer-term ideological, political and institutional results of the war will be described following victory for the Montfortist faction.

Jean III was thrice married but had no legitimate children. In 1317 he had endowed his younger full brother Guy (d. 1331) with estates in Penthièvre. He later married Jeanne d'Avaugour, representative of a cadet branch of the ducal family. Their possessions formed a huge apanage in northern Brittany, reminiscent of the eleventh-century division between Alain III and Count Eudes (above p. 192). It was the couple's daughter Jeanne who came to be considered by most interested parties as Jean III's probable successor since precedent allowed female succession in Brittany and she was the duke's closest direct descendant. Not surprisingly Jeanne's hand in marriage was much sought after, among others by Edward III of England for his brother John of Eltham (d. 1336). But it was a nephew of Philip VI of France, Charles, younger son of Guy, count of Blois, who in May 1337 finally carried off the prize.

This match seemed to guarantee that the duchy would be closely attached to Valois France as the new dynasty strove to establish itself. The simultaneous outbreak of hostilities between England and France, the strategic importance of Brittany athwart lines of communication with Gascony, and the fact that there was another (and male) candidate for the ducal throne ensured that the issue of the Breton succession would not be so easily settled.

Jeanne's rival for the succession was her half-uncle Jean de Montfort, son of Arthur II (1305–12), by his second marriage to Yolande, countess of Montfort l'Amaury. Arthur II made provision for Jean and his sisters. But neither Yolande nor Jean himself ever accepted that they had been sufficiently endowed, given the great landed wealth of the dukes of Brittany. Indeed Jean de Montfort became a life-long seeker after land, exploiting to the full whatever rights he possessed thanks to complex ties formed by endogamic marriage patterns among the higher nobility of northern France. These provided multiple opportunities to advance successoral claims. It can also be noted (a significant fact in the light of what happened in 1341) that Montfort did so in strict propriety within the law. His marriage to Jeanne, daughter of Louis, count of Flanders, for example, was followed by a long dispute with his father-in-law over lands in Rethel and Nevers claimed on Jeanne's behalf. It also appeared that since he possessed the county of Montfort (Seine-et-Oise), his main interests would remain centred on Paris where he was *persona grata*. Before 1341, Montfort spent little if any time in Brittany where he had few obvious supporters and his sole territorial interest was the castellany of Guérande conferred on him by Jean III as his share in Arthur II's succession. But the death of Jean III (30 April 1341) and the chance to claim his half-brother's inheritance as his closest male heir was an opportunity that a perpetual litigant like Montfort could not afford to ignore.

In a famous account that has been followed with few reservations by all subsequent historians, the near-contemporary chronicler Jean Froissart recounted how Jean de Montfort, hearing of his half-brother's death, hurried to the duchy and in a lightning campaign seized all the main strongholds. Then he dashed to Limoges, of which he also claimed the viscounty, to take possession of Jean III's treasure there. Returning again quickly to the duchy, Froissart states, Montfort finally also found time to

II The ducal family: the descendants of ARTHUR II (1305–12)

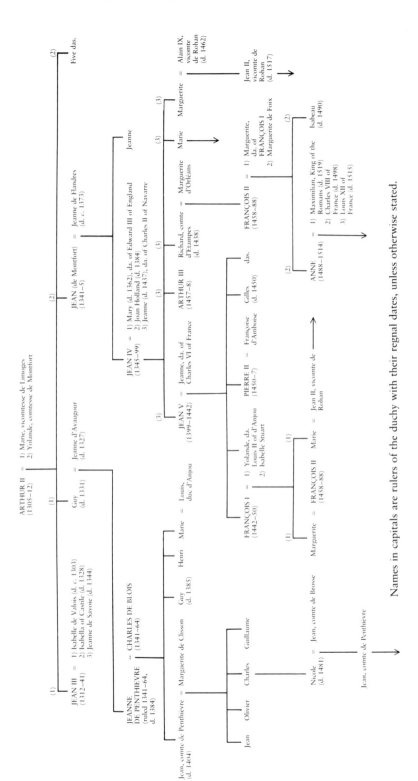

Names in capitals are rulers of the duchy with their regnal dates, unless otherwise stated.

make another flying visit. This was to Edward III in England, whose support of his candidature for the ducal title he obtained before returning once more to Brittany. Disappointingly, it must now be admitted that little of this picturesque narrative stands up to close critical scrutiny, certainly not the *Blitzkrieg* which Montfort allegedly waged in Brittany in the summer of 1341 nor the journey to England.

It is not known where Montfort was when Jean III died, but he was in Brittany shortly afterwards. There he found the late duke's executors peacefully at work. It may be imagined that he tried to consult leading figures but the one great noble whom Froissart mentions as a supporter, Hervé de Léon, can definitely be ruled out: early in 1342 he was captured fighting for Jeanne de Penthièvre. On the other hand Montfort certainly received at Nantes in July 1341 an envoy from Edward III, apparently sent on the king's own initiative, the first evidence of contact with the English. But for much of the summer Montfort, like Charles de Blois and Jeanne de Penthièvre, waited peaceably until summoned to appear in Paris before the commission nominated by Philip VI to examine their conflicting claims. Headed by the bishops of Laon and Noyon, this began its formal hearings on 25 August, completed them on 4 September and issued its decision in the *Arrêt de Conflans* on 7 September. By this Philip VI announced that he would receive Charles de Blois into his homage for the duchy of Brittany. Anticipating this unfavourable outcome, about 1 September, Montfort had secretly fled from Paris. It was on returning to Brittany, fortified in the knowledge that Edward III was prepared to lend support to prevent implementation of the *arrêt*, support marked by a grant to Montfort on 24 September of Richmond, the traditional honour of the ducal family in England, that an appeal to arms rallied a number of Breton partisans to Montfort's side and skirmishing began.

The course of the war

The immediate cause of the civil war was the matter of the Breton succession: whether the half-brother or niece of the late Jean III had the better claim. The custom of Brittany allowed both representation (of a deceased father's rights by his child) and female succession in major fiefs (the case argued on behalf of Jeanne de Penthièvre), but it was also possible to argue (as Jean de Montfort did) that the position of duke was different from that of great barons and that since the duke of Brittany was a peer of France (as he had been since 1297), the rules governing the ducal succession should be those applied to peerages and to the French crown itself where male succession was favoured. Witnesses called in August 1341 provided precedents for both positions; in admitting Charles de Blois to his homage, Philip VI knowingly controverted the legal argument by which he had himself gained the throne of France. Whether, in reaching a conclusion favourable to his nephew, the king and his advisers were swayed by political considerations as blatantly as it appears in retrospect, we cannot say. The result of their decision was, however, to have dramatic consequences since it drove Jean de Montfort (who also had the interests of his own son to defend) into the arms of Edward III, anxiously casting around for another excuse to invade France after the fiasco of his Flemish campaign of 1339–40.

Initially there was little support from any quarter of Breton society for Jean de Montfort. Yet a shrewd observer in 1341 would have seen signs that the closer relationship with France which the marriage of Jeanne de Penthièvre and Charles de Blois symbolized would not be welcomed by all Bretons. In 1334, for example, leading barons opposed Jean III's own plan, in the absence of a direct heir, to make the duchy over to Philip VI. Recognizing their concern to preserve Brittany's freedom from royal interference (which had recently increased in a number of fields), in his last years Jean III, whilst punctilious in the performance of his obligations, also began to insist on his own prerogatives, in monetary matters, for example. The development of a more complex ducal administration and with it the creation of vested interests of officers anxious to extend their influence unimpeded within the duchy as royal officials were doing within the kingdom, together with the formulation of more advanced ideas on ducal rights, emphasized the separation of the duchy and kingdom. It reveals that in Brittany, as in Guyenne or Burgundy, these years on the eve of the Hundred Years War were of critical significance for relations between the crown and the princes. Jean de Montfort could appeal to those who feared the accession of a prince closely identified with the crown at a moment when there was genuine concern about its centralizing policies.

In the event, however, it was not the greater lords who came to Montfort's assistance. By and large, throughout the civil war they supported Charles de Blois. But a group of lesser figures – knights and esquires, many of them from Breton-speaking Brittany – did rally to Montfort's cause. Why they did so remains largely unknown but we may suspect that this was a reaction against increasing French influences, though it also has to be admitted that in supporting Montfort, they were upholding someone who till that moment had displayed little evident enthusiasm for his Breton ancestry. There was also assistance for Montfort from towns and ports whose burgeoning connections with England and Guyenne inclined them to accept Edward III's patronage of Montfort's cause. But his first efforts to succour Montfort were ineffectual. Before a small expeditionary force could be despatched from England in the autumn of 1341, Philip VI had sent his son, John, duke of Normandy, with a large army to help Blois establish his rule in the duchy. Gathering at Angers early in October, it steadily made its way towards the Breton frontier. Champtoceaux (Maine-et-Loire) was successfully besieged and the army arrived before Nantes on 1 November just as naval forces sailed up the Loire to join the blockade of the duchy's leading city where Montfort made a stand.

Around 18 November Nantes capitulated and Montfort was captured. Negotiations continued for some weeks in an effort to get Montfort and Blois to reach a compromise, which would have allowed the former compensation for giving up his claims. But while these discussions were in hand, Montfort's wife, Jeanne de Flandres, whom Froissart characterized as having the heart of a lion and courage of a man, assisted by a small, enthusiastic band of followers sent at least two embassies to England and resisted further Franco-Breton attacks. By February 1342 a formal alliance with Edward III had been arranged and he began to send increasing military help. Sir Walter Manny arrived in March, William Bohun, earl of Northampton, followed in July and Edward himself, with some 5000 men, landed at Brest in late October to restore Montfortist fortunes and to try a different avenue of approach in his duel with Philip VI.

After their initial success in capturing Nantes, the Franco-Breton forces consolidated their hold on Rennes and Vannes in the spring of 1342. But headway elsewhere was slow. Brittany was well supplied with castles and small towns, each of them a potential centre of resistance. Although the Breton landscape was not particularly wild, with its many forests, woods, *landes*, rivers, streams and steep valleys, it was ideal terrain for small-scale guerilla warfare. The Montfortist cause was thus far from lost when Jean de Montfort was captured in November 1341. During 1342 the battle lines were drawn which, with minor modifications, shaped the conflict until the end of the war.

Thanks to Edward III's help, a ring of fortresses around the coast from Morlaix to Guérande at the mouth of the Loire were brought under Montfortist control where for the most part they remained until 1364. The king himself in an otherwise rather uninspired expedition in 1342 besieged Vannes. Philip VI, who had come with an army against Edward's forces, finally refused to fight just as he

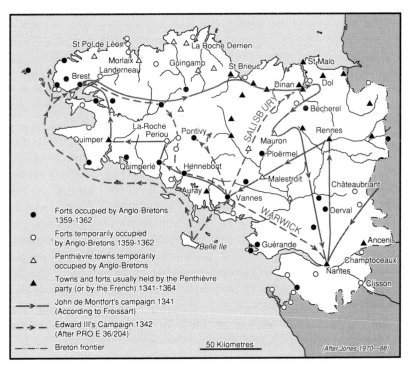

Figure 24   The Breton civil war

had done in similar circumstances in Flanders two years previously. Stalemate threatened. Through the mediation of two cardinals sent by Philip's former tutor, Pope Clement VI, a general Anglo-French truce was sealed at Malestroit (M) on 19 January 1343. This allowed the kings to withdraw their forces, preserved their respective territorial positions and made provision for further negotiations to be held under papal aegis. The local issue of the Breton succession had become part of the general Anglo-French conflict from which it would henceforth be impossible entirely to disentangle it. Only a few of these wider ramifications need be noticed here.

On leaving Brittany Edward III took with him Jeanne de Flandres, who had so staunchly defended her husband's interests even if she had not achieved all the heroic deeds attributed to her by Froissart in a celebrated passage of his *Chroniques*. She was accompanied by her two young children, the future Jean IV (ruled 1364–99) and his sister, Jeanne; and Edward III appointed lieutenants to act jointly in his own name and that of Jean de Montfort in Brittany. Whilst the ill-observed truce was in force – Vannes was delivered to him by traitors to the cause of Charles de Blois and became the centre of the Anglo-Breton administration for the duration of the war, and there was a Franco-Breton siege of Guérande in 1344 – it was usually only necessary to despatch modest financial or military help to individual garrisons under threat. But around Easter 1345, Jean de Montfort, a prisoner since November 1341, finally tired of enforced inactivity, broke parole and made his way clandestinely from Paris to England where he performed homage to Edward as king of France. To counter recent advances by Blois around Quimper, Montfort returned to the attack in June 1345 with the earl of Northampton. Hardly had he set foot in the duchy when on 26 September he died, the victim of disease from an infected wound sustained whilst besieging Hennebont, leaving his five-year-old son as his heir. Once again the main burden of defending the Montfortists fell on Edward III.

Between 1345 and 1362, when the young Jean de Montfort was declared of age, English lieutenants, nominally assisted by individual captains of fortresses, which they often treated as private property, more than preserved the foothold that the Anglo-Bretons had established in 1341–3 but at the expense of a harshly oppressed subject population. The exaction of 'ransoms', regular, forced payments in money and kind, was systematized with several towns or castles forming the centres of 'ransom districts' – Vannes, Ploërmel and Bécherel, for example. Blois tried hard to counter these moves. The cities of Rennes and Nantes remained loyal to him; in 1344 he failed at Guérande but took Quimper. A number of small but hard-fought battles occurred – Morlaix (1342), La Lande de Cadoret (C-d'A, 1345), La Roche Derrien (1346 and 1347) – in the last of which on 20 June 1347 Blois was captured by Sir Thomas Dagworth and sent as a prisoner to England. In his absence, Jeanne de Penthièvre now proved as indomitable in defence of their cause as Jeanne de Flandres had once been for her husband's, hence the popular label for the conflict of 'The War of the two Joans'. The English, now engaged with the French in several theatres of war, were unable to capitalize fully on Dagworth's success. General truces and the scourge of the Black Death in 1348–9 led to a new stalemate.

From the start the Breton war had attracted adventurers eager to exploit the disturbed conditions for personal gain. The years between 1347 and 1356 saw them enjoy remarkable freedom of action: captains like Raoul de Caours, who swapped from English to French allegiance in 1350, Sir Walter Bentley, Robert Knolles, Dagworth himself, and soon the future constable of France, Bertrand du Guesclin, satisfied their passion for war and plunged the Breton countryside into turmoil with a confusing series of small-scale attacks, sieges and battles. In March 1351 there occurred one of the most notable exploits in the annals of chivalry, the Battle òf the Thirty. Two teams of knights, representing the Franco-Bretons (under Jean de Beaumanoir) and the Anglo-Bretons (under Robert Bembro), agreed to fight each other *à outrance* halfway between Josselin and Ploërmel. The result was a victory for Beaumanoir's team. According to Froissart twelve Anglo-Bretons were left dead on the field against three of their enemies, though most survivors bore scars from this savage encounter for the rest of their days, displaying them to the curious like Froissart himself who met one participant, Even Charruel, in Paris some twenty years later. A vivid poetic account of the fight was soon in circulation. But, like other chivalric flourishes such as Du Guesclin's supposed joust with Thomas of Canterbury at Dinan, for instance, this deadly tourney had little impact on the war's fitful course.

In 1352 Bentley, who had succeeded Dagworth as royal lieutenant, achieved a notable victory at Mauron (I-et-V) on 14 August 1352 against Guy de Nesle, marshal of France, and a Franco-Breton force which included many members of the newly formed rival to the Garter, the Order of the Star. On 1 March 1353 Edward III, despite his role as guardian of Jean de Montfort, came to terms with Charles de Blois, whom he recognized as duke. The treaty was not, however, executed for reasons which remain obscure. In 1354–5 there were further sieges, including one of Nantes by the English. In the summer of 1356 Henry, duke of Lancaster, succeeded as royal lieutenant and following a campaign in Normandy, accompanied by Jean de Montfort, he arrived to conduct a siege of Rennes which proved to be one of the longest during the whole Hundred Years War. He only lifted it unwillingly and with bad grace in July 1357 on the express command of Edward III, following a new truce with France. Blois was finally allowed to return to Brittany and ransom himself for the enormous sum of 700,000 écus (£133,333 6s 8d) in August 1356, on condition that he took no further part in the war until his ransom was fully paid. He also had to deliver his two sons, Jean and Guy, as pledges for his good faith. Guy never saw Brittany again, dying in captivity in 1385. Jean was eventually released in 1387 but only after another heavy ransom. The next few years after 1356 did not see any major military action in the duchy, but the chance survival of the accounts of Giles de Wyngreworth, the Anglo-Breton treasurer (1359–62), together with subsidiary documents, provide for the first time during the war detailed information on conditions there, especially in the 'ransom' districts and on the extent of exploitation of the Breton countryside.

The treaty of Brétigny-Calais (1360) stipulated that the Breton succession issue was to be settled by separate negotiations. When these were held at Saint-Omer in 1361 no final agreement could be reached. In 1362 Edward III allowed Jean de Montfort to return permanently to the duchy. The last royal lieutenant, William, lord Latimer, officially handed the administration over to him in July but stayed on in an advisory capacity along with several other Englishmen in ducal service. Further attempts to negotiate a settlement with Blois, including the intervention of Edward the Black Prince in 1363–4, again failed despite several local truces. In September 1364 Anglo-Breton troops, reinforced by contingents sent from Guyenne by the prince of Wales and led by his famous companion-in-arms Sir John Chandos, were besieging Auray when Blois mustered his army under Bertrand du Guesclin, fresh from victory in the previous May over an Anglo-Navarrese force at Cocherel in Normandy. On Michaelmas Day the two armies met. Despite its considerable numerical superiority (the exact figures are disputed), Blois's army was heavily defeated. Charles and many others were killed, whilst of the survivors many were taken prisoner. Few leading families escaped unscathed from the encounter; the Montfortists had finally gained the throne for which they had so long contended.

The first treaty of Guérande

With the death of Charles de Blois at Auray and two of his three sons imprisoned in England, Jeanne de Penthièvre finally conceded defeat. Despite the undoubted personal valour and sanctity of Blois (when his body was prepared for burial it was found clothed in a verminous hair-shirt), his supporters were no longer willing to continue a struggle on which, according to the Montfortists, God had finally pronounced his verdict. Of more immediate importance, Charles V of France, who had reluctantly given Bertrand du Guesclin permission to join Blois before the Auray campaign, also recognized Montfort's victory as decisive. He ordered Jean de Craon, archbishop of Reims, to arrange a settlement that would bring peace after more than twenty years of civil war. On Easter Saturday 1365 in the church of Saint-Aubin at Guérande, the archbishop published the treaty by which the two competing branches of the ducal family were brought to terms. Jeanne de Penthièvre was to retain the title of duchess for her lifetime as well as the lands in Penthièvre held by her father, while rents to the value of 10,000 *l.* were to be assigned to her on lands outside the duchy. Her claims and those of her descendants to the ducal throne were annulled unless the Montfort family failed in the male line, when the Penthièvre family might return to the succession. By the time that this clause became operative, it had also run to females (below p. 248).

In the meantime Jean de Montfort was confirmed at Guérande as the rightful successor to his uncle Jean III. He acknowledged owing fealty and homage for Brittany to the king of France. Practical

Plate 27   The doublet of Charles de Blois

steps were then taken to sort out the administrative, social and legal problems the war had created. The taking of 'ransoms' was to cease at Michaelmas 1365; parishes in arrears or impoverished were to be quit; arrangements were made for the return of confiscated, occupied or church lands to those who had held them when hostilities first began, with a few exceptions (including what the famous English *condottiere* Robert Knolles held at Derval and elsewhere). Criminal offences committed during the war were pardoned. It was a statesmanlike attempt to reconcile the warring factions. In social as well as constitutional terms the treaty provided a framework for the reconstruction of Brittany after a deeply traumatic period. Would Jean IV be able to forge a new unity, and shake himself free of the tutelage which Edward III had long exercised over him, and how would his relations with Charles V develop? These were the major issues that faced the victor of Auray following the conclusion of peace in April 1365.

12

Brittany under the Montfort Dukes, 1365–1491

History and the medieval Breton state

Before answering the questions posed at the end of the last chapter, some preliminary remarks on how Bretons in the late Middle Ages viewed their own past may be helpful. A tradition of local historical writing had not developed in the earlier Middle Ages. The most characteristic native work was hagiography and apart from the *Chronique de Nantes*, surviving medieval annals are too fragmentary or cryptic to be of much assistance in establishing how Bretons then viewed their history. Geoffrey of Monmouth's popular *Historia Regum Britanniae* satisfied those who were interested generally in 'the matter of Brittany'. This work was certainly plundered by later medieval writers concerned with the early history of the duchy. But from shortly after the civil war there were concerted efforts to compose new Breton histories. To a considerable degree these buttressed the practical policies pursued by Jean IV and his successors. Whether deliberately or coincidentally, they provide an important expression of Breton political ideology.

A sequence of works of considerable significance were composed from the late fourteenth century to the early sixteenth. They shared a common point of view. Whilst not official in the strict sense, most of the authors used ducal records to compile their books. Several were ducal servants, closely associated with the chancery, which for diplomatic purposes became increasingly concerned with producing documents that justified in historical as well as legal terms particular policies or claims. Around 1400 Guillaume de Saint-André, secretary of Jean IV, and an anonymous writer (most probably Hervé le Grant, ducal archivist and secretary to Jean IV and Jean V), and later Pierre le Baud (d. 1505) and Alain Bouchart (d. *c.* 1514), during the reigns of François II (1458–88) and Anne (1488–1514), wrote the most important of these new works: Saint-André's verse life of Jean IV and three general histories, the anonymous *Chronicon Briocense*, which breaks off in 1416, Le Baud's *Croniques et ystoires* (first recension 1480, second edition 1505) and Bouchart's *Grandes Croniques* (first published in 1514).

These all reflected their authors' connections with the Montfortist court. Together with Jean de Saint-Paul (d. 1476), of whose work on the kings and dukes of Brittany only fragments now survive, they articulated most extensively contemporary ideas on the nature of the Breton state. In doing so, they wove together various strands spun in previous generations. Most important among them were the notions on ducal 'regalities' noted above (p. 205): the distinctive attributes and privileges enjoyed by the duke as ruler of Brittany. They sharpened perceptions of what made Brittany different from surrounding provinces, defined its customs and territorial extent and, though this may not always have been the intention, their works can be read now as propaganda for the Montfortist state. Drawing on official records, in their turn they shaped the thinking of all who consulted them like other legal records.

There are problems in establishing the extent of their influence. None of the individual works circulated widely in manuscript form. Two (the *Chronicon Briocense* and Bouchart) clearly began as universal histories before they abandoned this form to concentrate on local matters. Three out of four books of Bouchart's work (about half his *oeuvre*) are filled with general material. Overall, however, there was a move to 'bretonize' the writing of history: to concentrate more exclusively on Brittany. This progression culminated in Le Baud who, whilst following many earlier standard authorities (Froissart, for instance), transformed his sources to sustain a narrative that can be considered the first modern history of Brittany. It is true that there is little innovation in much of this writing. History is exemplary and moralizing. It sustains a Christian viewpoint. It is written to provide knowledge that will promote wisdom and modesty in personal behaviour, but it reflects increasing political engagement, an appreciation of the need to provide Brittany with a sound history. This redressed an imbalance in treatment accorded in other (mainly royal) quarters. There is evidence that it both reflected and formed common Breton perceptions of their past. It was the anonymous author of the *Chronicon Briocense* who first openly voiced many of these sentiments, explaining that he was moved to compose his work because little mention appeared in French chronicles of Breton kings and, especially, that Arthur's deeds were ignored. In his view, the *Grandes Chroniques* of the Capetians and Valois suppressed many laudable Breton deeds which he proposed to rescue from oblivion.

All these writers were concerned with authenticity. They cited copiously from actual records (the *Chronicon Briocense* provides texts of thirty-four charters, five papal bulls and a Cardinal's letter). They also recognized limits in the search for truth even for those enjoying ducal favour, which it was imprudent to exceed. Le Baud concluded the first version of his *Croniques* at the death of Arthur III in 1458. As he explains in the fuller version finished in 1505 he was still unwilling to extend his account into the reign of François II: 'I have thus left these events aside until another occasion, since it does not seem appropriate to me to write about the deeds of the living in their own lifetime, because in accounts written in this way, the truth is often suppressed and lies are compounded.'

Not surprisingly by 1514, when the crown held direct power in Brittany, similar scruples affected Bouchart. The first edition of his book ended with the death of François II (1488), obviating the need to recount the painful process whereby Brittany lost its independence. It was only in later editions that continuations to the death of Anne were added but they were written neither by Bouchart nor, very obviously, by a Breton, whilst later histories of the duchy published under the Ancien Regime continued to run the risk of censorship if they expressed views that could be considered derogatory to the crown and too favourable to local privilege and patriotism. The tradition survived 1789: in the mid nineteenth century the Association Bretonne, among whose members was numbered the great regional historian Arthur de la Borderie, was temporarily suspended by government fiat because its scholarly activities touched similar sensitive issues.

Among the themes running through all this historical work, the importance of the writers' attachment to their 'pays natal' can be emphasized. In the case of Saint-André and the Anonymous, writing when the Montfort–Penthièvre feud was still very much alive, this 'nationalism' was expressed in strident terms. The French were lampooned and vilified. Nor did the English, who had helped Jean IV to his throne, escape criticism. Here earlier antipathy between Briton and Anglo-Saxon encapsulated in the works of Gildas and Geoffrey of Monmouth surfaced again. Later, as the terminal dates of Le Baud's and Bouchart's histories clearly show, it was necessary to exercise caution in changed political circumstances, though ways were found of indirectly criticizing France for the hardships that had befallen Brittany. Accounts of oppression in remote periods can be read as commentary on recent events. Above all, the authors were bent on displaying publicly Brittany's equality in historic terms with France.

It was here that Geoffrey of Monmouth proved to be a rich source of inspiration. His account of the Trojan origins of the Bretons put them on the same footing as the Franks and other peoples claiming this distinguished if mythical ancestry. In the same source the argument was discovered that the Breton language was in fact the true Trojan tongue. Other parts of Geoffrey's work 'proved' that the Bretons had a monarchy which was older than that of the Franks and that they were converted to Christianity at an earlier date. Later (and here Carolingian annals were skilfully exploited), the existence of a *regnum Britanniae* was held to be a continuation of the first Breton monarchy. It also legitimated the claims of later dukes as their successors to enjoy regal privileges. History, myth and legend were thus effectively combined to justify the dukes' claims to independence from France.

As Jean Kerhervé has eloquently put it, these writers saw their work as 'a defence of Brittany, an appeal to memory, an appeal to union, to faithfulness, to mobilization against the foreigner'. The ransacking of ducal archives for appropriate material by the historians was paralleled by the activities of chancery officials. If chroniclers and historians were anxious to copy diplomatic and other records, bureaucrats were just as anxious to copy historical materials. For a short and exciting period, history and politics were confidently mixed to promote a coherent Breton ideology. Even today its resonances are still capable of evoking powerful reactions among modern 'nationalists'.

Foreign relations

By the terms of the first treaty of Guérande Jean IV was obliged to perform homage to the king of France. When he did so after some prevarication on 13 December 1366, the formula used was deliberately ambiguous. There was no doubt in Charles V's mind that Jean owed liege homage and traditional forms were observed. Jean knelt, bare-headed, before Charles who took the duke's hands between his own and kissed him. But instead of acknowledging liege status, the chancellor of the duchy, Hugues de Montrelais, bishop of Saint-Brieuc, read out a statement which simply stated that the duke was performing homage 'in the manner and form in which it used to be offered and rendered by his ancestors'. Taken aback by this breach of convention, royal advisers protested and asked for clarification. The bishop simply retorted that they had got what they had asked for and the king, anxious not to drive Jean IV back into the arms of Edward III, allowed matters to rest there.

A precedent had, however, been established which was to affect all subsequent homage ceremonies. These were increasingly played out as political theatre: the French argued that the duke owed liege homage, the duke denied this and after hurried discussions *sotto voce* there would come an offer to perform homage 'as his ancestors had done'. After further debate this would be accepted under protest with both sides congratulating themselves on preserving their respective positions without loss of face. Carefully rehearsed, this ceremony, which had to be performed in the mid fifteenth century on five occasions within less than twenty years, because of a rapid succession of dukes and the death of Charles VII (1461), was invested, especially on the Breton side, with considerable meaning. By this stage, too, and in symbolic support of the Breton view that it was simple homage, the duke now presented himself not meekly on his knees but standing, sword at his side, a posture which writers like Le Baud and Bouchart took as confirmation of the duke's exalted status. He could not formally deny his subservience as a vassal but every effort was made to reduce his dependence and to minimize any residual services that homage entailed. In 1455 Pierre II (1450–7) explicitly rejected the idea that he owed any obligation as a peer of France.

As a result, relations between Brittany and France were seldom easy, even when the duke was personally on good terms with the king as François I (1442–50), Arthur III (1457–8) and François II (1458–88) were with Charles VII. Behind the duke stood officials anxious to protect him against any royal encroachment on what they saw as the duke's prerogatives. They went to homage ceremonies and other meetings with royal advisers armed with *dossiers* replete with documents proving, at least to their satisfaction, the duke's position. Philippe Contamine has demonstrated how, when a dispute broke out between Louis XI and François II over regalian rights in the matter of episcopal vacancies, the Breton chancery was able to respond swiftly since it had prepared its defence in advance whereas the crown had virtually to start from scratch. It even had to ask permission to send investigators to visit archives in the duchy. This was granted but François II made sure that they were accompanied by his own advisers. Surviving records show that they used the opportunity to add further to the evidence available to the duke for the future. A dispute over jurisdiction in the Marches between Brittany, Anjou and Poitou similarly prompted the ducal administration to put together an extensive file over the years. It was by such foresight and constant vigilance in defence of rights that the Montfortist administration defended its external interests so effectively.

The style of Breton foreign policy in the later Middle Ages was set by Jean IV after early difficulties. Owing his throne to English aid, the new duke found it hard at first to assert his own independence though he did go some way towards restoring internal order in government (below pp. 240–1). Divisions created by the civil war and the renewed outbreak of more general Anglo-French hostilities in 1369 drew him back into the fray. One result was that in 1373, following invasion by French forces, he was driven once again into exile in England. However Charles V mishandled a fine opportunity to attach Brittany firmly to the French crown. Having begun proceedings in the Parlement of Paris to confiscate the duchy from Jean IV, the king failed to appease the Penthièvre family whose right to succeed was protected under the treaty of Guérande. A coalition of Breton lords, clerics and townsmen, many of them former supporters of Jeanne de Penthièvre, who lent her own tacit approval, thus banded together. They appealed to Jean IV to return in 1379 to prevent the duchy's absorption into the royal demesne, in one of the most defiant steps ever taken to defend Breton political interests in the Middle Ages. Jean IV eagerly seized this second chance so providentially offered him and finally succeeded in placing Montfortist rule on a sound footing.

Decisive military action by the constable of France, Bertrand du Guesclin, could have thwarted the duke's landing. Instead he remained curiously supine, evidence of the conflicting loyalties many leading Bretons felt as long as the duchy enjoyed a degree of political independence. The death of Charles V and the minority of Charles VI opened the way for new negotiations. On 6 April 1381 a second treaty was ratified at Guérande, which brought warfare to an end and restored legal relations with France. The duke formally renounced his alliance with Richard II of England and Charles II of Navarre, performed homage to Charles VI (September 1381), and came to terms with his domestic enemies, including the new Breton constable of France, Olivier de Clisson (d. 1407). In the next few years he even gave Charles VI military aid and distanced himself from the English, whose retention of Brest castle (officially ceded during Jean's exile in 1378) and continuing unwillingness to return Richmond remained bones of contention.

The main thrust of ducal policy from this point was to establish an independent position by playing off more powerful neighbours. The Anglo-French war in all its various ramifications provided ideal opportunities for this. It was a line of conduct which all subsequent Montfortist dukes followed. A full narrative cannot be provided but it can be emphasized that this led to the establishment of contacts with most western European states. Thanks to marriage alliances, diplomatic and commercial treaties, independent representation at international conferences and church councils, Brittany was placed in the fifteenth century on an equal footing with sovereign states, often materially less powerful than the duchy. Her interests were protected by active diplomacy and international agreements. In 1434 a delegation led by Philippe de Coëtquis, archbishop of Tours, formerly bishop of Saint-Pol-de-Léon, appeared at Basle where the assembled church fathers listened to a disquisition on the duchy's pretensions. In 1441 Jean V reached a specific concordat with the pope concerning the Breton church, which was for all practical purposes entirely separate from the Gallican one. It was with papal support that in 1460 the university of Nantes was founded, providing another important element for a self-respecting late medieval state.

The Hundred Years War, princely coalitions in France and disputes between France and its neighbours thus formed the backdrop for sustained ducal diplomacy. Relations with England, the Low Countries (increasingly the centre of power of Valois Burgundy) and Iberia were for political and commercial reasons especially close if not always amicable. But there were few parts of western Europe where Breton diplomats, merchants, sailors, students or pilgrims did not visit in the fifteenth century. At home the relative merits of particular lines of conduct – support for the English or the Burgundians, how to appease France without sacrificing Breton diplomatic or economic interests – caused frequent and sometimes acrimonious debate. Occasionally it led to damaging divisions within the ducal council itself (below p. 239).

At the beginning of the century the long chancellorship of Jean de Malestroit (1408–43), who made foreign policy a particular concern, provided continuity. He maintained the balancing act started by Jean IV. That duke's third wife, Jeanne de Navarre (d. 1437), married Henry IV of England (1399–1413) in 1403. This did not automatically eliminate friction between Brittany and England, especially in a period of heightened piratical activity in the Channel. From 1403 to 1406 there were retaliatory Breton raids on the Devonshire and Welsh coasts. But during Henry IV's reign and that of Henry V, amicable relations usually prevailed and contacts between the two courts were frequent. Measures were taken mutually to suppress the perennial menace of piracy. At the same time Jean V managed to preserve polite relations with the French court. There his father-in-law, Charles VI, was increasingly subject to bouts of madness and affairs were in the hands of the Armagnac faction. Breton troops fought at Agincourt, where Jean's brother Arthur de Richemont, another future Breton constable of France, was captured, though the duke (like the duke of Burgundy) was just too late to take part personally in the battle, tactically reaching Amiens on 25 October 1415.

After the murder of John the Fearless of Burgundy (10 September 1419), Jean V moved more obviously into the Anglo-Burgundian camp, especially after his traumatic capture and imprisonment by his cousins Olivier, Jean and Charles de Bretagne (13 February – 6 July 1420). Their smouldering resentment against the dominant branch of the ducal family had been fanned over the years by the inveterate hostility of their mother, Marguerite, daughter of Olivier de Clisson. During this testing period the duchess, Jeanne de France, rallied forces in Brittany, many of them formerly sympathetic to the Penthièvre cause. She appealed to Henry V to free Arthur de Richemont to assist her and vigorously sustained the Montfortist cause as Jeanne de Flandres had once done. Physically unharmed but psychologically scarred, Jean V systematically pursued his attackers after his release. They were condemned *in absentia* for treason and *lèse-majesté* by the Breton Parlement in a bold assertion of ducal sovereign rights. By annexing or redistributing their confiscated lands to his own supporters, old and new, the duke effected a major shift of power within Brittany. He created an important vested interest in the maintenance of the Montfortist dynasty amongst beneficiaries. The dispossessed Penthièvre family were only reinstated definitively in the sixteenth century after the annexation of Brittany by the French crown. Abroad, a triple alliance with John, duke of Bedford, regent of France for Henry VI, and Philip, duke of Burgundy, was formed in 1423 against Charles VII, who had certainly approved the coup of 1420 after the event. The alliance was later reinforced when Arthur de Richemont married Marguerite of Burgundy.

True, however, to the way in which Montfortist dukes habitually threaded their way through political minefields, shortly afterwards a new treaty was agreed at Sablé with Charles VII and his Angevin-dominated council. To balance the Burgundian match of the constable, Jean's other surviving brother Richard married Marguerite of Orléans, whilst Jean's own growing family provided further pawns on the diplomatic chessboard. The future François I spent much time at the French court, whilst his younger brother, Gilles, was brought up with Henry VI in England. A sister, Anne, married Jean de Bourbon; the duke of Alençon was already the duke's brother-in-law. In this way Jean V managed to keep at arm's length from much of the bitter fighting that followed Henry V's decision to conquer France.

After the treaty of Arras (1435), with Burgundy and France partially reconciled and England isolated, Jean continued to pursue an independent line though the growing power of the French crown alarmed him. He was thus only half-hearted in support of princely coalitions like the Praguerie (1440), preserving as best he could Brittany's neutrality. This was a progressively more difficult stance as the Anglo-French war approached its denouement. There was damaging division over foreign policy in the ducal family itself between his successor François I and his brother Gilles which reflected their respective youthful ties with the courts of France and England. In these quarrels their other brother, Pierre, and uncle, Constable Richemont, tried to play a pacifying role though their personal interests also came into collision. The imprisonment of Gilles for colluding with the English (1446), and his murder (1450), after a harsh captivity to which François I was largely indifferent, deeply divided the family just when Charles VII reached the zenith of his power.

The reconquest of Normandy and Guyenne (1449–53) and the defeat of England in the long Anglo-French war radically changed the political balance in France. The crown, for the first time since Philip IV's day, was in the ascendant. Princes like the duke of Brittany would have to step warily if they were to preserve the gains which they had undoubtedly made since 1314. They could stand on their dignity and assert privileges as Brittany did in the matter of homage. But if the crown challenged them, careful diplomacy was necessary to fend it off. In the event Charles VII was slow to move onto the offensive; gratitude for the assistance François I, Pierre II and Arthur III rendered in their different ways in defeating the English may explain this reticence. With the accession in July 1461 of Louis XI, eager to show himself the antithesis and enemy of all that his father had stood for, the precarious balance in Franco-Breton relations was dangerously upset. Before discussing that development, however, the achievement of the Montfortist dukes in administration may be considered.

Government and institutions

The creation of a Breton state with its own ideology and foreign policy was sustained by important internal administrative developments. The thirteenth century had seen progress towards more sophisticated rule (pp. 201–4). But on the eve of the civil war, government was still simple in its techniques and ambitions. A proper chancery was only just forming. Accounting methods were limited to exploiting the ducal demesne as a seigneurial estate. There was no regular system of general taxation. The number of officials in central and local administration was small. Parlement, chiefly a judicial occasion, was convened infrequently, and there were often only a few legal experts in attendance. There was no regular meeting of a representative kind. The ducal court and household were modest in size (some 90 members in 1305). Ceremonial was as yet little developed.

All this changed as war forced the rival Anglo-Breton and Franco-Breton administrations to find resources in the mid fourteenth century. Experiments began with general taxation. Charles de Blois levied 5 *sous* per household in the county of Nantes in 1344, an early form of the *fouage*. From 1356 efforts to pay his huge ransom led, as it did in the case of his exact contemporary, John II of France, to money being raised by a whole variety of means. Towns were also authorized to impose sales taxes on foodstuffs, drink and other items. The proceeds were chiefly spent on fortifications and defence, a pattern which continued after 1365. The *billot*, as the levy on beverages was usually termed, became the major regular item in most late medieval urban budgets. To paraphrase Jean-Pierre Leguay, the impressive walls that most Breton towns then raised are eloquent testimony to their inhabitants' capacity for drink. They were also the chief reason for developing more complex municipal administrations, formed to supervise the raising and spending of this taxation. It was Edward III's demand in 1352 that a treaty with Charles de Blois and Jeanne de Penthièvre should be guaranteed by a cross-section of their supporters that led to the summons of the first meeting of the Breton Estates at which town representatives were present. Thereafter, with increasing regularity until in the fifteenth century annual meetings became customary, the Etats became a forum for political debate as well as for authorizing taxation. A decision in 1486 to back the succession of François II's daughters was its last major act before the duchy lost its independence.

A century earlier, once peace had been nominally restored and 'ransoms', the most arbitrary form of exaction, ceased (above p. 208), Jean IV found it hard to turn the clock back. The *fouage* was regularized. It became the main form of taxation in late medieval Brittany. From 1420 it was levied annually. When, in the early 1480s, a 'budget' can be established, the *fouage* contributed around 65% of ducal income. In the interim, some thirty leading towns had purchased exemption from it by paying *aides*, a lighter burden than the *fouage*. To regulate collection of these direct levies and indirect ones like customs dues (which provided 15% of ducal income in the 1480s), and to supervise ducal demesne revenues (5%), the *chambre des comptes* was now given definitive form.

Its origins may be traced back to the thirteenth century but it was only after 1380 that the full hierarchy of officials appears: treasurer and receiver-general, *présidents*, *clercs*, *auditeurs* and others in the central offices of receipt and audit down to minor clerks in the local accounting circumscriptions which, as in France, were mainly based on earlier ecclesiastical administrative divisions. English Exchequer procedures as well as the French *chambre des comptes* provided models for these developments. As a result of more effective exploitation of Breton financial resources, Jean IV may have enjoyed an income of about 100,000 *livres tournois* a year, a sum equivalent or superior to the revenues of the dukes of Anjou, Berry and Bourbon. It was, however, considerably less than that of the dukes of Burgundy or Orléans, who had an income three or four times as large. This financial disparity remained a weakness throughout the fifteenth century despite continuing endeavours to increase revenues. By the early 1480s some 450,000 *l.t.* passed annually through the Breton treasurer's hands. Louis XI's resources were ten times that figure.

Despite this, after 1365 dynasties of experts formed in Brittany to handle the duke's income. Admission to the upper echelons of the financial administration depended on family links and clientage in a world recently analysed in brilliant detail by Jean Kerhervé. He has shown how the private interests of *gens de finances* as well as the public ones of the state were for long served by them sustaining the Montfortist dukes. The analogy with the *légistes* and members of the sovereign courts who supported the Capetian and Valois kings of France and were often more royalist than the king himself is close. At the same time other areas of government also expanded to meet the demands made upon it by the duke, his family, court, household, council and state.

The linchpin was the chancellor, who coordinated every kind of governmental activity, under the watchful eye of the council, which he also chaired. His staff grew modestly throughout the fifteenth century. There were, for example, six or eight chancery clerks *c.* 1400 and twenty-four in 1488. The same is true of the *chambre des comptes*, which also spawned more specialized financial offices, notably the *trésor de l'épargne* (first set up in 1407). This provided the duke with reserve funds under his own close control. There was also a *trésorier des guerres* (first nominated in 1420, regularly appointed from 1449) who oversaw the financing of Breton armed forces. By the late fifteenth century there were more than 400 officials regularly employed administering the duchy's finances. After 1491, many of them were able to make, thanks to their indispensable expertise, private resources and connections, the transition to royal service.

The biggest drain on ducal finances in the late Middle Ages was military expenditure. Traditionally feudal forces had provided services freely. Details of a muster held at Ploërmel in 1294 have survived in the *Livre des Ostz*, which shows a meagre *servitium debitum* of 166 knights and 17 esquires. In the late fifteenth century the duke still depended heavily on the nobility for cavalry and he summoned them fairly regularly. Surviving muster lists, following a series of *ordonnances* from 1451 which specified arms and equipment appropriate to different levels of income, provide much fascinating detail on noble wealth. Those who appeared inadequately mounted or armed were instructed to purchase new armour or horses for the next muster. But already in the fourteenth century the duke had to pay for additional service and continuing military needs led to further developments.

In 1425 Jean V raised a militia of *francs archers* from every parish, an experiment repeated in the kingdom at large in the 1440s (in both cases the hand of Constable Richemont can be detected). Conversely, reforms of Breton cavalry forces followed swiftly after royal ones. In the early 1450s small but permanent lance companies were formed. Generally numbering between 200 and 400 lances (some 800–1600 men), they remained in existence till 1491. These companies, besides offering an opportunity which many nobles gladly seized to pursue proper professional careers in the service of the Montfortist state, also provided the solid core around which the feudal forces that traditionally constituted ducal armies could be assembled. As a result up to 12,000 or 15,000 reasonably well-equipped men might be mobilized in an emergency. As a last resort the duke could also call out a *levée en masse* of all able-bodied men.

The other increasingly specialized field was artillery where technical developments enhanced the importance of the *maître de l'artillerie*. He came to command a corps of gunners, cannon

Plate 28   Adaptation to gunpowder: the gatehouse, Brest Castle (F)
(rebuilt *c.* 1460)

founders and pioneers, whose labour in moving *matériel* and preparing batteries was vital. Among the experts employed at first were a number of Germans but new skills were quickly learnt; Breton artillers served in the campaigns in the 1480s which led to the reconquest of Granada from the Moors (1492). By then the duchy was spending proportionately as much as or more than France on its artillery (some 10% of the military budget), the major purpose of which was increasingly to protect Brittany from its powerful royal neighbour. There was also considerable expenditure on fortifications (cf. further below p. 266).

The duke and his court

The administrative and institutional innovations just outlined mirror developments occurring more widely in the late Middle Ages. In the same way changes at the ducal court can be linked to the ways in which, largely for political reasons, late medieval rulers enhanced their image. To a degree princes had always behaved in this fashion. Since the twelfth century their thinking was also largely shaped by chivalric considerations. Recent archaeological finds at Suscinio on the Rhuys peninsula, where the dukes converted a primitive tower house into a sumptuous and imposing princely residence, show how such ideals permeated Breton thinking together with a growing concern for material comfort. Literary evidence points in the same direction: both Pierre Mauclerc and Jean I have been credited with writing courtly poetry whilst local interest in Arthur and 'la matière de Bretagne' was naturally strong from the late twelfth century. Once again, however, after the hiatus of the civil war, these characteristics were reinforced by the Montfort dukes, especially as broader cultural interests were combined closely with political ones.

A rich and impressive court in which the duke could display his majesty became a necessity. It also clearly appealed to Jean IV's temperament. Among his models there were the splendidly ostentatious courts of Edward III and the Black Prince at which he had spent considerable time. Another contemporary prince, Gaston Fébus of Foix, was renowned, among other things, for his knowledge of the art of hunting. If Charles V of France encouraged more intellectual endeavours amongst his courtiers, his successor reverted fully to these traditional patterns of court life. It is thus hardly surprising that as soon as he could Jean IV threw off the asceticism which marked Charles de Blois's reign. He encouraged all the latest fashions, gaining, for example, a reputation as a breeder of fine hunting dogs, which were sometimes given as presents as a mark of ducal esteem.

His most visible surviving achievement, however, has proved to be the major programme of castle-building which he initiated. In work at Suscinio, Vannes, Dinan and Nantes, in particular, the domestic needs of the ducal family as well as military considerations are clearly evident (after two childless marriages, he and Jeanne de Navarre had seven children). Expensive materials, sophisticated design, high standards of execution and comfort as well as an awareness of the latest developments in fortification demonstrate a desire to impress. His success in doing so is evidenced by the way in which leading seigneurial families imitated the duke in building powerful tower residences like Oudon (L-A), Fougeray (L-A) and

Plate 29   Excavation of the medieval pavement at the ducal castle of
Suscinio (M)

Largoët en Elven (M) or in adapting earlier works to new conditions.

What little is known about life in these various castles as the court journeyed from one to another confirms the picture of a duke who enjoyed courtly entertainments, music and ceremonial. One aspect of this was Jean IV's foundation of the Order of the Ermine shortly after his return from exile in 1379, by which he conformed to contemporary expectations that a sovereign prince should have his own knightly order. The Ermine commemorated those who fell at Auray (29 September 1364). It also served to reward current courtiers. In the absence of surviving records, much of its history and membership remains obscure. It never gained the international reputation of the Garter (1348) or Golden Fleece (1430) but for its sovereign it had the same ceremonial and political purpose and value as they did and Jean V continued to promote it. His itinerary after 1420 shows that he was normally at or near Auray around Michaelmas where it may be presumed he attended an anniversary mass in the chapel of Saint-Michel du Champ which his father had so richly endowed. Later there were two further ducal '*devises*' – the Epi of François I (in all probability an augmented form of the

Ermine) and the Cordelière of François II. All three reveal strong Breton enthusiasm for chivalric display.

In a similar way, Pierre II sanctioned another secular cult which had begun to attract support amongst leading courtiers, that of the Nine Barons of Brittany. In May 1451 he promoted the lords of Derval, Malestroit and Quintin to fill vacancies in what was claimed as the traditional list of nine lordships to which the honour was attached. François II continued the practice. By this date, too, although a full study is lacking, Brittany constituted an heraldic March and the duke had his own kings of arms, heralds and poursuivants. Amongst the late medieval gentry of the duchy, heraldry and genealogy were consuming passions.

By these means the duke became the leader of polite society. Places at court, where many nobles served in a variety of capacities, not all honorific, were much sought after. The panoply of ceremonial became more conspicuous; every opportunity was taken to impress. The coronation ritual was revised in 1402 for the crowning of Jean V. At the same time Philip, duke of Burgundy, acting as guardian of the young duke, also reformed his household. This grew in size and complexity as the century progressed and its dignity was enhanced. Membership increased from about 250 in

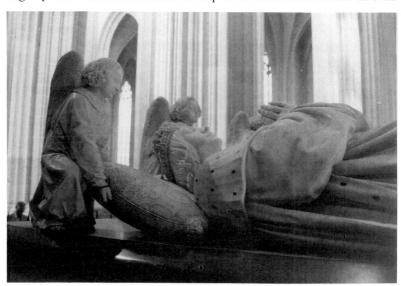

Plate 30   Detail from the tomb of François II and Marguerite de Foix
by Michel Colombe, Nantes Cathedral

1400 to more than 500 by Anne's reign. When Jean V died in 1442 his body was put on public display 'en son habit royal'. The funeral (*béguin*) of François II in 1488 was another occasion for sombre ritual. All the courtiers and major officials were decked in mourning clothes at public expense while the late duke's own royal habit was made of scarlet cloth and ermine. The deaths of duchesses were similarly marked.

More cheerfully, the practice of *joyeuses entrées* was adopted for the duke's (or even duchess's) first visit to important towns. He sat in full regalia, wearing a ducal *cercle*, often decorated with fleurons, a sign of sovereignty which deeply offended Louis XI, at the opening of the Etats, where the order of precedence amongst the nobility in particular was hotly debated. Ecclesiastical patronage provided further opportunities for visual display of the symbolism associated with the Montfort dukes as the statues of Jean V at Locronan, Notre-Dame de Folgoët (F) and Saint-Fiacre de Faouët (M) show. The Ermine had its own collegiate chapel at Auray. When in 1505 Anne, by then queen of France, made a famous pilgrimage to Folgoët, live ermines were presented to her. Their heraldic representation, the arms of Brittany since *c.* 1317, besides marking ducal property, was adopted widely by servants of the dynasty in their own arms, notarial *signa* or devices as a token of their loyalty to the Montfortist state, of which it remains even today a potent and widely disseminated reminder.

The end of independence

Late medieval Brittany was no exception to the general rule that beneath the polished surface of formalized court ritual, there seethed powerful passions. As the soldier-poet Jean Meschinot (d. 1491) wrote from a wealth of experience:

> La cour est une mer, dont sourt
> Vagues d'orgueil, d'envie, orages . . .
> Ire esmeut debats et outrages,
> Qui les nefs jettent souvent bas;
> Nage aultre part pour tes ebats . . .[1]

[1] 'The court is a sea on which arise waves of pride, envy and storms . . . Anger provokes disputes and insults which often wreck ships . . . Swim elsewhere for your pleasures . . .'

During the reign of François II the duchy faced a series of crises in which domestic and external factors were inextricably mixed. The major threat was Louis XI (1461–83), who from the start seized every opportunity to interfere in Breton affairs. He questioned the duke's exercise of his 'regalities' and trammelled his freedom of action as an independent prince. When it became clear François II would leave only heiresses, Louis prepared to claim his rights under ţhe terms of the first treaty of Guérande. He bought for 50,000 *l.* from Nicole de Bretagne any remaining Penthièvre claim; he cultivated connections with the most powerful nobles at the Breton court on whom he conferred lavish pensions.

The classic portrait of the king was sketched in his *Mémoires* by the renegade Burgundian courtier Philippe de Commynes, who joined Louis in 1472. In recent years serious criticisms have undermined the authority of this source. It nevertheless remains true that Commynes caught to perfection the atmosphere of intrigue and suspicion that characterized politics in late medieval France, an atmosphere which Louis himself did so much to create. Amoral behaviour in pursuit of political ends was not new when it was described in another contemporary work of even greater renown: Machiavelli's *Il Principe*. In François II, a man of irresolute will, and his advisers, often at odds amongst themselves, Louis XI found ready material for his special talents to work on.

The twists and turns of everyday politics during the reign of François II cannot be described in detail. But a few general points can be made to underline the complexity of affairs. In 1461, for instance, on his accession, Louis XI dismissed his father's most important advisers, including some native Bretons who took refuge from the king's wrath at the duke's court. They subsequently persuaded François II to join a princely coalition for the Public Weal, though the only important battle of the ensuing campaign (Montlhéry, 16 July 1465) was fought before the Breton army joined the Burgundian one. At the same time, other Bretons previously in Louis's service when he was dauphin like the admiral Jean de Montauban (d. 1466) were now quickly promoted and enjoyed considerable influence in shaping royal policies.

This pattern of contrasting fortunes and clashing allegiances continued throughout the period. At any one moment each court harboured men whose personal interests and ambitions might lead them to sacrifice principles for expediency. Everyone was aware of this, but Louis XI above all others was prepared to cajole, bribe or browbeat those whom he considered essential pawns in the execution of his policies. Because his pocket was deeper than that of the duke, perhaps also because he took an intense personal interest, unlike François II who left much to his advisers, in the end the king's relentless pressure usually succeeded in winning over all but the most obdurate opponents.

It was the combination of inadequate resources and divided counsels that finally undermined Breton resistance to royal attacks. The disparity between Breton and French financial and military means has been mentioned (p. 241). The growth of factions in Brittany can also be traced with some confidence. The Breton victims of Louis's purge of 1461, for example, stiffened ducal resolve to oppose royal demands, but the rewards they received caused jealousy among the duke's indigenous councillors. Suspicions that personal interests counted above those of the Montfortist state were sharpened when Tanguy du Chastel (d. 1477), formerly steward of Charles VII's household, returned to Louis's service in 1468 and redoubled his efforts thereafter to get other leading Bretons to defect. His major success was in persuading the young and ambitious Jean, vicomte de Rohan, to desert in 1470. But others were suspected of wavering in their allegiance to François II like André de Laval, lord of Lohéac, marshal of France, and Péan Gaudin, master of the duke's artillery, though he hotly denied it. Royal blandishment in the form of pensions, offices and advantageous marriages worked surreptitiously to weaken private resolution, whilst xenophobic sentiments were frequently expressed against the non-Breton advisers with whom the duke surrounded himself – Dunois *père et fils*, Odet d'Aydie, Simon d'Anglure, Guillaume de Souplainville, even the duke's nephew, Jean de Chalon, prince of Orange. But the native Breton advisers of the duke were also disunited.

Guillaume Chauvin, chancellor of Brittany (1459–81), was the principal executant of ducal policies by virtue of his office. It is likely that for much of the time he was also a major influence in shaping them, as the only surviving minutes of the ducal council (31 March 1459 to 6 April 1463) suggest. But increasingly the treasurer Pierre Landais (1460–85) rivalled him in authority and influence. In particular, they disagreed over the best way to deal with Louis XI. Chauvin favoured a diplomatic approach, relying on a defence of the traditional rights of the duke to stave off further royal advances. The danger of this was brought home to him personally when he was arrested during an embassy in 1477 because Louis XI had heard rumours of a Breton alliance with the English. More realistically, recognizing that the king was unwilling to acquiesce for long in any diminution of his own perceived rights, except as a stratagem for gaining a new advantage, Landais advocated a bolder policy of foreign alliance to protect the duchy's interests. Economic as well as strategic reasons dictated close contact with England and Burgundy. Landais was also more unscrupulous (and hence more successful) than Chauvin in promoting his own clients to positions of power in the Breton church and state. His pre-eminence was finally confirmed in 1481 when the chancellor was arrested on charges of malversation. Imprisoned in harsh conditions, Chauvin died before his case was resolved (April 1484), the most illustrious but by no means the only victim of a reign of terror which, according to his opponents, Landais inspired. His own downfall was equally dramatic.

Both Chauvin and Landais were self-made men whose talents had enabled them to rise spectacularly, but fifteenth-century Brittany was still very much dominated by great aristocratic families. As uncertainties over the succession increased – the duke's only legitimate son died young and by his second marriage to Marguerite de Foix François II had only two daughters – many leading nobles began to look to the future. In October 1484 a group of rebels led by the prince of Orange and the lord of Rieux, tired of Landais's dominance in ducal affairs, acknowledged at Montargis the French king's right to succeed to Brittany in the absence of a male heir. In June 1485 they staged a coup in which Landais was seized in the duke's presence. A trial followed of which the outcome was never in doubt. Acknowledging that he was responsible for the death of Chauvin but claiming that his concern had always been to maintain the duke's rights, Landais was condemned to death and executed on 19 July before François could intervene.

The last years of the reign were no less free from dissension. Local quarrels amongst the Breton nobility merged with more general unrest in the kingdom at large following the death of Louis XI. A leading role was taken by Marshal Rieux. His dislike of the 'foreigners' who currently held sway over the duke led to a renewal of his alliance with the regents for Charles VIII. French troops invaded the duchy and Nantes was besieged (19 June – 6 August 1487). In the following year Rieux was reconciled with François II and helped to rid the duchy of French troops, before another French attack was launched. This culminated in comprehensive defeat of the Breton army at Saint-Aubin-du-Cormier on 28 July, despite reinforcement by German, Spanish and English troops. The capitulation of Saint-Malo swiftly followed and peace terms were hurriedly arranged at Verger (Maine-et-Loire) on 19 August. All foreign mercenaries in Brittany were dismissed; the duke's daughters were only to be married with the king's consent; various towns and fortresses were handed over as pledges and Charles VIII's rights to the succession were to be examined afresh. Three weeks later François II was dead.

The marriage of his elder daughter Anne, aged eleven, now became a dominant issue among the states of western Europe anxious to prevent Brittany falling into French hands. It also had divisive effects locally, especially after Anne herself precociously and vehemently rejected the elderly candidate (Alain, lord of Albret) favoured by the regent Rieux and escaped from his control with the connivance of Philippe de Montauban, chancellor of Brittany (1487–1514). Jean, vicomte de Rohan, advanced claims to the throne by virtue of his marriage to Marie, younger daughter of François I. Like Rieux before him, he turned to the French, who once more invaded in 1489 before the treaty of Frankfurt brought a general European truce. In 1490 Anne was once again reconciled with Rieux and Maximilian, king of the Romans, sent ambassadors to the duchy. On 19 December 1490 Wolfgang von Polheim, symbolically placing his bare leg in the duchess's bed, confirmed their proxy marriage. Unfortunately the material aid which Maximilian and Anne's other foreign well-wishers, including Henry Tudor, sent proved inadequate to sustain her cause. In March 1491 her former suitor Alain, lord of Albret, delivered Nantes to the French and in the summer Rennes was besieged. By the autumn Breton resistance was finally broken. On 15 November a treaty was sealed at Rennes which allowed Anne to join her husband, Maximilian. But since he had shown so little eagerness to come to Brittany, she displayed a similar unwillingness to leave. Negotiations with the French were re-opened. Most of her advisers were convinced that the only way to establish a firm and lasting peace, after five years of destructive warfare and bitter political division, was for the duchess to marry the king. Whatever theological scruples the couple may have had because of Anne's marriage to Maximilian and the king's own betrothal to Maximilian's daughter, Marguerite of Flanders, were swiftly overcome. On 6 December 1491 at Langeais (Maine-et-Loire) Charles VIII and Anne were married. Although the final act of union was not pronounced until 1532 and measures were taken to preserve local administrative autonomy, with the French marriage Brittany ceased to exist as an independent and essentially sovereign state.

13

Breton Society at the End of the Middle Ages

Population

After high politics we may turn to some general features of Breton society at the end of the Middle Ages, beginning with the population at large. Before the fifteenth century, evidence for its size, distribution and social make-up is indirect. Fiscal records, the earliest parish registers in France and other documents transform the picture after 1426 and allow serious calculations to be made. The most important new sources are the registers compiled between 1426 and 1443 for most rural parishes by commissioners carrying out a general revision of the lists of households (*feux*) liable to taxation. Fortuitously surviving (like the famous Florentine *catasto* of 1427–30), these registers give details of 45,015 *feux*. They also provide information on those exempt because of either their status (nobles, *métayers*, officers or clerics) or poverty, thus allowing differentiation between social groups. Disagreements have arisen over interpretation of the figures revealed. There is the well-known problem of the multiplier necessary to convert fiscal units into real households and variability in average single family size. But, following recent investigation of these questions, some broad conclusions may be stated and the figures of 1426–43 placed in a longer perspective.

To start with what can be reasonably established: the 45,015 *feux* probably represent a total population around 1430 of some 150,000 families, or 750,000–800,000 Bretons. Allowance has to be made for exemptions (20%) and omissions. Returns for a small number of parishes are missing and 80,000–100,000 townsmen

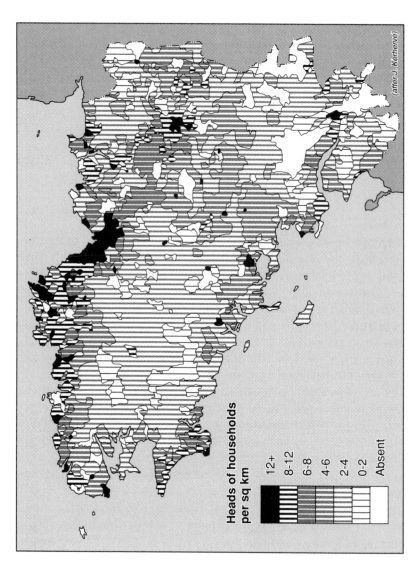

Figure 25   *Density of population c. 1426–43*

Heads of households
per sq km

12+
8-12
6-8
4-6
2-4
0-2
Absent

(after J. Kerhervé)

were not included. It is also clear from the registers and subsequent local inquiries (there was no further general revision in the ducal period) that a considerable decline in population was in train and that this continued for several decades after 1430: at Plouigneau (F) in 1427, for instance, of the 339 real households registered, 136 had no children and 23 contained widows or widowers living alone; elsewhere mention is made of peasant families with as many as ten or twelve children, none of whom subsequently reached adulthood. Likewise it is evident that the 1430 figure also marks a decline (which may be as much as 20–30%) from late fourteenth-century figures though calculations based on the 98,447 *feux* cited in a document of 1392, from which a total population of 1.25 million Bretons has been deduced, now seem too generous.

Breton demographic trends in the later Middle Ages may thus be fitted into a general pattern established for regions where documentation is much richer. After a population peak achieved, without exception, before the first visitation of the Black Death (1347–51), natural and man-made calamities – disease, famine, war – conspired to reduce it dramatically. Unfortunately it is impossible to say with any precision either when the peak was reached or what the extent of decline was in medieval Brittany. References to the Black Death are few. From this it has been deduced that Brittany was initially spared. But a cluster of legacies to Quimper cathedral between November 1348 and February 1349 suggest the disease's passage and memories of the 'first plague' and 'second mortality' (1361) were still vivid at Vannes in 1400 indicating that the province was not completely immune. It certainly suffered from later recurrences. Accounts presented in 1383 refer to the 'mortality' then raging at Rennes and the houses listed as vacant (*frostz*) in the *rentiers* of 1385 and 1398 are an index of its ravages. In some streets as many as a third of the houses were empty.

In the fifteenth century evidence becomes more plentiful. For instance, plague spread widely through the dioceses of Nantes, Vannes and Quimper in 1412–13. In March 1414 business concerning the estate of the late lord of Maure (I-et-V) could not be completed because of the 'mortality in the country'. From 1430 surviving town records show that 'plague' and other infectious diseases recurred with monotonous regularity in most major centres of population. General epidemics were experienced, for example, in 1441–2, 1452–3, 1462–3 and 1473. Witnesses at the inquiry into the sanctity of Vincent Ferrer at Vannes in 1455 described the classic swellings of the bubonic form of plague; pilgrimage to his tomb was later considered a preventative, whilst numerous chapels were dedicated to St Roch and St Sebastian, also considered efficacious heavenly intercessors against the disease. By François II's reign it was routine to prorogue musters, sessions of Parlement or the Etats and to grant remissions of *fouages* or *billot*, when plague threatened or struck. The chancellor, Guillaume Chauvin, left Nantes quickly in August 1471 when plague broke out.

On the other hand there were also signs of recovered demographic vitality in the latter half of the fifteenth century. In some parishes the proportion of children now exceeded 50% of the total population, a stark contrast with the period 1426–43. Higher prices for cereals, for the farming out of mills and increased demand for new tenures also testify to a growing population. Although it remains difficult to measure, the late fifteenth century saw a general recovery to near pre-Black Death levels of population. The main exceptions seem to be along the coast, perennially affected by piracy and loss of sailors, and in the eastern Marches where the war of 1487–91 administered another severe check. It was claimed in 1457 that more than 120 contributors to the *fouage* at Perros-Guirec (C-d'A) had died in shipwrecks in six years, whilst a high proportion of widows has been noted in coastal parishes in Léon.

Within Brittany this population was distributed very unevenly. Despite maritime disasters, it was densest along the north coast and in a band running south-east from the Bay of Saint-Brieuc, via Rennes, to the eastern Marches between Vitré and La Guerche. Other concentrations included the Crozon and Penmarc'h peninsulas of southern Finistère, the Golfe du Morbihan, Guérande and along the Loire valley. But the rest of Brittany's south-western coastline was more sparsely settled, whilst the contrast between the northern littoral and inland parishes was also strongly marked. In the Trégor in parishes less than 10 km from the sea the number of families per hamlet in 1426 exceeded fifteen, for those between 10 and 20 km the figure was between seven and thirteen and beyond 20 km less than seven. The use of seaweed (*goémon*) as a fertilizer, a more varied diet in which fish and crustacea had an important part and access to trade routes may account for these disparities. If the sea is a constant in Breton history, exploitation of it in the late medieval period became more purposeful. Every creek and inlet sheltered communities of fishermen, though many continued to combine fishing with agriculture. Several small new ports sprang to prominence like Audierne, Concarneau, Le Conquet, Morlaix, Pont-Croix and Roscoff in Finistère.

Among regions naturally disadvantaged the upland zones of the interior parts of the western Vannetais and marshy areas of the Nantais were only lightly populated. If we accept Kerhervé's calculations that around 1400 Brittany contained some 65,000 *feux* or 180,000 families contributing to the *fouage*, this gives an overall density of 5.7 *feux* (or 30–36 people) per km². This is high by medieval standards. With minor modifications (for example in Léon where population grew considerably during the sixteenth century), it was a distribution that remained largely unaltered until the great rural exodus of modern times. The pattern of dispersed habitations, already noted in earlier periods (p. 162), was now universal. Carnac in 1475 furnishes an extreme example with the *bourg* itself barely distinguishable from surrounding hamlets. The parish contained 204 dwellings in all (around 600 people) distributed in 70 *villages* or *frairies*, each made up of one to eleven *tenues*. The nuclear family of parents and children was the norm at all levels of society, though extended family groups also existed amongst both the peasantry (for example, in some *frairies*) and the aristocracy. At Garlan (F) in 1482, 6.6% of households contained more than ten members, 11.6% between eight and ten and 16.6% six or seven. Large families – six or more sons, not to mention daughters – were not uncommon among the medieval Breton *noblesse*. One of the province's main exports continued to be its surplus population.

As for the social composition of the late medieval population, attention can be drawn to two characteristic features. First, the high proportion of nobles and their dependants – their immediate families and the *métayers* who worked the home farms attached to most Breton *manoirs*. The predominance of the nobility has been a constant refrain. The registers of the *réformation de la noblesse* – a major revision of tax registers – provide statistical proof: nearly 10,000 families (almost 5% of the population) enjoyed noble status in the mid fifteenth century. This was an aristocratic presence equalled in few other areas of France (where less than 2% appears the norm) and exceeded in western Europe only by the *hidalgos* who may have constituted 10% of medieval Castile's population. The number of great families, those enjoying revenues substantially in excess of 1000 *l.* a year, was naturally limited: Coëtmen, Derval, Laval, Malestroit, Quintin, Rohan, Rieux, Rays, Tournemine and a few others in this period. The vast majority of the *noblesse* existed on more modest incomes, typically less than 100 *l.* a year. These were the owners of small estates dubbed *sieuries* by Jean Gallet, who discovered some 350 of them in the Vannetais alone. Cases of nobles acknowledging incomes of a few *sous* or confessing that they 'daily followed the plough' are not unknown. Though there is some evidence that access to the nobility became more difficult during the century, François II on average granted a dozen letters of franchise or ennoblement annually; the vast majority went to ducal officers.

Petty nobles (*hobereaux*) were particularly thick on the ground in the Penthièvre, Trégor and Léon, where parishes with 25 families claiming noble privileges were common; at Plounévez-Lochrist (F)

Plate 31   The rewards of ducal service: the late fifteenth-century castle of Kerouzéré-en-Sibiril (F), built after licences issued by Pierre II and François II

there were 54, at Maroué (C-d'A) 57 and at Planguenoual (C-d'A) 61! The physical evidence of their presence is the huge number of manor houses still scattered throughout the province. On some sites a primitive motte was followed by a tower house, replaced in turn at the end of the Middle Ages by a *manoir*, with minimal defensive features. Elsewhere timber-framed seigneurial halls (*salles*) were rebuilt in stone as Guyon du Quéleneuc did at Bien Assis, Erquy (C-d'A), after 1412. Some of these buildings, erected by courtiers, were of elegant design like Hac, Le Quiou (C-d'A), or L'Etier, Béganne (M); others were more robust and workmanlike (La Roche Jagu, Ploézal, or Coadélan, Prat, both C-d'A), or provided with a fortified enclosing wall as at Le Plessis-Josso, Theix (M). At Kerouzéré-en-Sibiril (F), in 1453 Pierre II licensed the building of 'a tower twenty-four feet square'. Other *manoirs* might contain a seigneurial minimum of a hall, chamber and cellar, differentiating them from the one-cell dwellings in which most peasants lived, often with their animals.

At this opposite end of the social scale, a considerable number of families were classified as paupers by the commissioners in 1426–43. They are mentioned in 800 out of 1200 parishes. By extrapolation, it appears that one in twelve of all Breton peasants were deemed too poor to contribute, even when the tax was levied on fractions as small as one-twentieth of a *feu*. Gallet's analysis of the Carnac evidence in 1475 points to even higher local incidences of rural poverty: 10% were apparently living in relative comfort, 40% experienced little difficulty in normal seasons, 30% lived on the edge of subsistence, whilst 20% can be classified as poor. Jean le Corroer, for example, held 4 hectares of arable from which he might expect to grow crops worth 20–23 *l.* in a normal year. Setting aside a third for seed, from the remaining 16 *l.* he had to pay 5 *l.* 4 *s.* (34%) in dues, rent, *fouage* and tithe. Even if, as is likely, he had a garden for vegetables and had access to commons, the beach or the sea to supplement his foodstocks, the remaining 10 *l.*, equivalent to 2500 kg of barley, was an exiguous sum from which to feed and clothe the eight members of his family for a year when historians consider 20–25 *l.* the minimum to sustain life for an individual craftsman or friar! The material conditions in which many late medieval Breton peasants lived would have differed scarcely at all from the penury revealed by the excavations at Lann Gouh en Melrand and Pen-er-Malo (p. 214). The tradition of building windowless temporary shacks, sunken-floored huts or simple single-cell buildings for the poorest members of Breton society continued down to the mid twentieth century.

Other evidence shows that misery was widespread. In the mid fifteenth century a quarter of all rural holdings in the Vannetais or Trégor stood vacant and a third of the population was exempt from taxation because of poverty. Life in the towns was little different: nearly 20% of the inhabitants of Jugon were unable to pay tax, whilst at Lesneven and Châteaugiron the figure rose to over 40%. Even in large centres like Nantes and Rennes between 5% and 10% of the inhabitants lived in permanent and extreme poverty. Cases of leprosy were common; documentary and place-name evidence has revealed almost 300 lazar houses in medieval Brittany. *Cacous*, the children of lepers, were particularly employed producing canvas. Other evidence suggests widespread inadequacies in diet and hygiene. Not surprisingly crime, prostitution and alcoholic abuse were common. At Dol 51 taverns supplied the needs of 3000 residents and visitors to the tomb of St Samson in 1416; the modest *bourg* of Antrain (I-et-V) with fewer than 1000 inhabitants required 15 in 1438. But the record is held by Morlaix where 197 hostelries served a population equivalent to that of Dol!

General conditions of life for most late medieval Bretons were thus often difficult. A small percentage of nobles, clerics, officers and townsmen enjoyed a high standard of living: after Silvestre de la Feuillée ransacked the *manoir* of L'Hermitage (Allineuc, C-d'A) in 1468 the lady of Quintin had to borrow wooden platters from her métayer to replace the silverware off which she normally ate. An important sector of free peasantry and urban craftsmen lived easily enough in normal times: the average annual per capita consumption of wine in the Nantais was 120 litres, whilst cider was becoming a popular beverage. But 50% of the population lived permanently at bare subsistence level. Among them there was always a high proportion of really indigent: cripples, chronically ill, those unemployed following accidents at work, the old, widowed or rootless and other victims of the many economic and natural misfortunes that so frequently shook their world.

'Ung droit paradis terrestre'?

Recalling in 1514 the reign of Jean V (1399–1442), Alain Bouchart described a golden age: 'he left his country in peace, rich and opulent in every kind of wealth . . . Brittany in those days was a veritable earthly paradise.' Jean de Saint-Paul had already attributed this state of affairs to the duke's skilfully conducted policy of neutrality: 'he kept his country in high prosperity and riches during the great war that afflicted the kingdom of France, drawing all its wealth into the duchy because of the peace and security maintained there.' Modern investigators have qualified these appreciations. Some structural problems posed by grave demographic difficulties have just been briefly outlined. The small scale of commercial enterprises and low levels of capital investment (in shipping, for example) are also clear when comparisons are made with the Burgundian Low Countries, England or more dynamic regions of France like Normandy. Breton financial techniques and accounting practices were backward and under-developed; no leading European bank had a branch in Brittany. The Italians, who had been briefly interested in the late thirteenth century, returned only after the mid fifteenth when credit also became more readily available. The success of native financiers was closely linked to the growth of the ducal administration (p. 241). The Mauléon and Thomas families of Nantes, Julien Thierry of Rennes and Pierre Landais from Vitré grew rich through their ability to raise and manipulate ducal funds. As the example of the Coëtanlem family of Morlaix, chiefly renowned as pirates, shows, it was office, farming taxes and the acquisition of land, rather than commerce, legitimate or otherwise, that brought lasting economic success in medieval Brittany.

Land was acquired for status rather than profit. Although there were some great estates, individual units of exploitation were small and scattered: the lordship of Largoët en Elven, for example, covered 40,000 ha but apart from a bloc of land around the castle, the rest was spread in 18 parishes, some over 40 km from Largoët like Carnac, where there were ten holdings. The count of Laval as lord of Vitré held lands and other rights in no fewer than 71 parishes. Farming was always hazardous, subject to the vagaries of the weather, crop and animal diseases, political or social unrest.

Ergot poisoning afflicted the poor unfortunates around Fougères who were driven by famine in 1436–7 to eat infected cereals while others grubbed up roots to make a thin soup. A *jacquerie* broke out in the Goëllo in 1425, a time of shortages and high prices which Jean V tried to combat by wage legislation and restrictions on the movement of labour. Another *jacquerie* threatened Quimper in 1490 after several years of steeply mounting taxation.

Even at the best of times yields in much of Brittany were low in comparison with the most advanced regions in late medieval Europe: with cereal crops a return of three or four times the seed sown. Primitive techniques of slash and burn or other temporary modes of cultivation were widely used on the *landes* which the English agronomist Arthur Young still found ubiquitous three centuries later. Climate and geological factors ensured that rye, oats or buck-wheat (*sarrasin*) predominated on most holdings. Higher-yielding wheat was often grown simply to provide seigneurial rent. Accounts for the *métairie* of La Motte, belonging to the lord of Saint-Brice-en-Coglès (I-et-V), between 1423 and 1505 reveal that 13.4 *mines* of rye and 10.4 *mines* of oats were harvested on average but seasonal variations ranged between 3 and 20 *mines*. Crops capable of fixing nitrogen in the soil like peas and beans were generally cultivated only in small quantities as were vegetables and herbs, cabbage, garlic, leeks, mustard, onions, saffron, turnips. The amount of arable per farm was usually between 2 and 6 ha, whilst livestock numbers were small. A rich proprietor at Carnac in 1475, Pierre le Goulaczec, who held 7 ha of arable as well as meadowland, possessed three horses, twenty cattle, seven sheep and two porkers; his most lightly taxed neighbour Jean le Boczec had nine cattle and two goats but these were held by *mi-croix* (p. 213). A tendency for stock-breeding to increase in eastern Brittany during the fifteenth century has been noted. Butter and cheese were important items in domestic trade.

For landlords the upkeep of mills was costly, but most continued to maintain them, though it was as much for their symbolic value as for the profit they brought. The same is true of many of the small dues that they exacted, *chef-rentes*, *champarts*, *gelines*, all meticulously listed in *aveux* and rentals, as were fines and other minor judicial revenues. More profitable were forest resources. Woods were a normal feature of even the most lowly seigneurial estate. Pannage rights were widely exploited. At La Guerche in 1385 it

was paid on 3485 pigs, and on 1497 pigs and 1409 cattle fattened
in Brocéliande in 1419. In the forest of Quénécan (M) the viscounts
of Rohan had raised wild horses since the thirteenth century. The
number Jeanne de Navarre, widow of Jean I de Rohan (d. 1396),
gained during their marriage was a matter of dispute in 1409. The
dukes of Brittany similarly had studs in their parks at Châteaulin
and Suscinio. Wood sales were carefully controlled. At Les
Huguetières near Machecoul (L-A) the count of Laval sold 518
oaks in 1451.

An early act of Charles VIII after acquiring Brittany was to
forbid further cutting in the forest of Suscinio 'where our
predecessors the dukes and princes of Brittany often made their
residence especially for the delights of the chase'. Hunting had
always been a jealously guarded aristocratic pastime. The count of
Penthièvre's tenants living near his warren at Erquy were obliged
to amputate one of their dogs' back legs and crop the ears of their
cats. On the other hand in 1457 the viscount of Rohan and the lord
of Malestroit agreed where spectators might stand to watch their
sport. In 1467 traps (*pièges*) and other 'engines' were condemned
as illegal on the Penhoët estates and the poachers who killed a great
stag with twenty tines were summoned before the ducal council.
François II forbade the use of nets and crossbows in ducal forests in
1473; whilst the most comprehensive account of Breton forest
rights during this period is incidentally provided as a result of the
dispute between Rohan and Laval over their *Usements* in
Brocéliande in 1479. The main animals hunted were deer and boar
though in the twelfth century the monks of Saint-Gildas de Rhuys,
much to Abelard's disgust, had killed bears whose paws they nailed
to a door, whilst wolves survived in a few places till the nineteenth
century.

Forests were also exploited for their industrial resources. Recent
work has highlighted the importance of metalworking, glass-
founding and pottery manufacture in the woods of many major
estates like those of the lords of Châteaubriant or Vitré and the
count of Penthièvre. It was from his own workers that the lord
of Quintin obtained the glass needed to repair windows at
L'Hermitage in 1468; he also had quarries, where in 1347 English
war victims were buried. The slate quarry of the viscount of Rohan
at Hengoet, Sizun (F), was farmed for 20*s*. in 1475 when his
pannage in Ploeanaz forest (F) was worth 18*l*. 15*s*. 9*d*. The

distinctive high-quality granite, kersanton, and millstones were quarried around Daoulas. The forges of Teillay, Juigné and La Poitevinière (L-A), first mentioned in the thirteenth century, only ceased manufacture in the nineteenth. Ploërmel, Pontivy and Loudéac all had late medieval forges. Mineral working at Saffré, Sion and Abbaretz dates back to Antiquity (cf. above p. 101). Other mines were located in the forests of Gavre and Huelgoat, where there were deposits of lead and tin. Small amounts of gold and silver were occasionally found but efforts by German engineers, licensed to prospect by Jean V, had little success; as had their successors around Quimper in 1506. Breton demand for iron ore, copper and precious metals, especially for weapons and coinage, could only be satisfied by major imports as was the need for sulphur and saltpetre, essential ingredients of gunpowder.

From the late fourteenth century until the end of the fifteenth Bretons did reap some commercial and industrial benefits from the crises which affected their neighbours. Following Henry V's invasion of Normandy, for example, many refugees including the future historian Thomas Basin (d. 1491), found safety in Brittany. Some brought skills with them like the leather- and cloth-workers who settled permanently at Fougères and Rennes. In comparison with the Ile de France or Picardy, Brittany escaped the worst horrors of the Anglo-French wars for much of the period. Though as René Cintré's study of the Marches has shown warfare and adverse economic conditions caused havoc in north-eastern Brittany. Here rival garrisons of English and French soldiers from Normandy, Maine and Anjou in the 1420s and 1430s posed a continuous threat to the Bretons, forcing the duke to devote much energy to the fortification of towns like Dinan, Fougères, Vitré, Saint-Aubin-du-Cormier and La Guerche. The soldiery also had a dramatic impact on regular trade in agricultural produce and livestock which was such an important aspect of relations with these neighbouring provinces in peaceful times. The supply of Angevin wine in Brittany, for example, often dried up, whilst in the reverse direction the export of cattle and sheep, which depended heavily on the security of roads, was much affected. Few details relating to *traites*, the taxes levied on merchandise transported overland, are known but such indications that do exist suggest that this was indeed extensive. Likewise, although the best evidence comes from customs accounts for Champtoceaux in 1355–6, the importance of the Loire as a commercial artery between Brittany and the *pays de la Loire* is not in doubt. Michel Le Mené has calculated that at the end of the fifteenth century an annual traffic of 1500–2000 vessels, chiefly transporting salt and wine weighing around 20,000 tons, may be a fair estimation of this trade.

Besides internal French trade, Breton merchants and sailors acted as middlemen in international commerce, extending their activities both in markets which they had traditionally frequented and into new regions (Portugal and the Atlantic islands, Zeeland). There were, however, limits to this growth: the Hanseatic League and the Dutch maintained a firm grip on Baltic trade, the Mediterranean was also largely closed to Bretons, whilst closer to home London, the ports of eastern England and Scotland only rarely witnessed the arrival of Breton ships. Even in areas where Bretons had long traded – the southern and western ports of England, the Low Countries, Normandy, Gascony, northern Spain – there was much competition from native merchants like those of Bristol who restricted direct Breton trade with Ireland or Iceland. If certain products like salt were traded in larger quantities after 1350, despite demographic decline, other staples like wine and cereals were subject to greater seasonal and secular fluctuations.

Of local Breton manufactures only cloth, especially in the form of linen and canvas goods, was able to compete successfully in the major European markets. Fulling mills are mentioned at Châtelaudren in 1198 and become a normal feature of most large seigneurial estates. The majority of towns in northern Brittany made cloth; notable centres included Dinan, Fougères, Rennes and Vitré. In 1434 at Lamballe 53 textile workers were listed in the Faubourg Saint-Martin alone. Further west in Léon and Cornouaille the fine linen that was to enrich a whole region in the sixteenth century – the *pouldavys* or *olonnes* of Pouldavid, Locronan and Merdrignac and other rural parishes around Brest, Saint-Renan, Landerneau, Lesneven and Plougastel-Daoulas – was already gaining an international reputation. Lace-working became an important domestic industry. It is now most obviously revealed in the many local varieties of female head-dress (*coiffes*) still worn (cf. below pp. 286–8).

Brittany's late medieval commercial success was accompanied by some physical expansion of towns, despite demographic problems. The most spectacular example is Rennes. Here the Gallo-Roman

Plate 32   Urban defences: the late fifteenth-century town gate,
Saint-Malo (I-et-V)

defences, protecting 9 ha, which had served the town until around
1400, were first refurbished and then extended by a series of
enceintes. Between 1421 and 1427 work was concentrated on the
old walls, from 1430 to 1448 on a new circuit and then from 1453
to 1476 on a second one south of the Vilaine. By the time it was
finished 62 ha were enclosed. New castles were added to the urban
fortifications of Vannes, Dinan and Nantes in this period, whilst
other major works were undertaken at Clisson, Fougères, Vitré,
Guérande, Guingamp and Saint-Malo, to mention the most
obvious cases. The whole eastern frontier zone bristled with urban
defences as did the coastline. Saint-Malo, Brest, Concarneau,
Hennebont, Vannes and Guérande were especially well defended.

Whilst the necessity for urban fortification may be explained by
the policy of autonomy which the Montfortist dukes pursued,
there was also much civil construction during this period.
Following several fires and earthquakes (1386, 1387, 1401, 1428)
Nantes, it has been said, resembled a gigantic *chantier* in the
fifteenth century as work progressed on the new cathedral (the
foundation stone of which was laid by Jean V in 1434), several
other major ecclesiastical monuments, numerous chapels and
mendicant convents, the town belfry, separate fish and corn market

halls, hospitals and many new multi-storeyed houses and *hôtels*. These latter were often occupied by leading ducal officials or powerful noble families. Demand increased to such an extent that one house sold for 25 *l.* in 1482 was resold a year later for 140 *l.* The same phenomenon occurred in other major centres. At Rennes the suburban *manoir* of Le Puy Mauger was valued at 1103 *l.* after its demolition in 1487 because of a threatened French attack; many other householders also received compensation running into several hundred *livres* on that occasion. At Nantes the bridges needed to span the Loire's many branches were a constant drain on resources. In 1466 the Bohemian traveller Leo von Rozmital, for one, was much impressed by them.

Nantes and Rennes were the leading cities of medieval Brittany with 13,000 or 14,000 inhabitants, far outstripping any rivals. Their development owed much to the stimulation of the ducal court and administration. A reflection of this is the establishment in them of luxury crafts. Eberhard König has recently revealed the presence of an important school of illuminators, refugees perhaps from war-torn Paris, producing high-quality Books of Hours and other manuscripts for a discriminating clientele in the mid century. In 1486 Pierre de la Chasse was instituted as ducal illuminator 'at the usual wages'. Goldsmiths, jewellers, tapestry makers and armourers also flourished. In 1420 as a thank-offering for his release from his Penthièvre cousins, Jean V gave his weight in gold and jewels to the Carmelites of Nantes: 190 lb 7 oz or 380 marks of silver, thanks to the armour, including his helm, worn for the weigh-in.

Religion and everyday beliefs

Although Christianity first appeared in the Gallo-Roman cities of Armorica, it adapted early to a rural context following the migrations. In both Roman and Celtic forms early monasticism was also at home in the countryside. The religious revival that accompanied the Gregorian reform movement, whilst incidentally stimulating urban growth, depended heavily on great landowners, the dukes and nobility. The role of the Cistercians, Premonstratensians, Augustinians and the military orders in opening up Brittany economically as well as spiritually has been stressed (p. 211).

Provision was made for a growing population. Small new urban parishes were carved out of larger rural ones. Many new churches and priories were constructed, deaneries and archdeaconries were created, bishops began to issue synodal instructions, regulating all aspects of the lives of the clergy and laity. There was some resistance, especially to the exaction of fees for marriage-feasts (*past*) or burial (*tierçage*, a third of the value of the movable goods of those dying intestate, a ninth on those leaving heirs). In 1221 Pope Honorius III allowed the newly elected bishop of Tréguier to absolve priests previously excommunicated for concubinage or wearing inappropriate dress. In Breton sources as elsewhere it is the usual story of medieval clerical misdeeds leaving far more obvious traces than virtuous behaviour. There is also the problem of the survival of earlier pagan, magical or Celtic practices and beliefs.

A major advance in pastoral care was, however, registered with the arrival of the mendicant orders. At first their impact was limited. As a region with few major urban centres Brittany was not

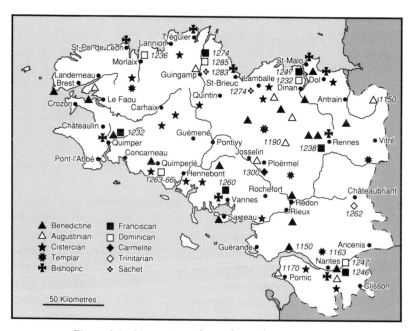

Figure 26   Monastic and mendicant houses c. 1300

immediately attractive. Vowed to voluntary poverty reminiscent of apostolic times, the friars lived on alms not rents. They were thus careful to carry out feasibility studies to establish whether a particular community could sustain a friary. Then they approached those most able to assist them. In Brittany, where seigneurial control over towns was strong, this meant the duke, bishops or high nobility. As a result, despite unpropitious conditions, between 1232 and 1300 fifteen convents were established; from 1300 to 1400 fourteen; then from 1400 to 1520 another twenty, an astonishing expansion, contrasting sharply with experience elsewhere in that late period.

The Dominicans were first in the field with convents at Dinan (1232), Morlaix (1236) and Nantes (1246) but the Franciscans soon followed: Quimper (1232–3), Rennes (1238), Nantes (1247), Dinan (1247), Vannes (*c.* 1260) and Guingamp (1285). Other orders also arrived, notably the Carmelites (Ploërmel, 1300; Nantes, 1318; Saint-Pol-de-Léon, 1353; Pont-l'Abbé, 1383; Hennebont, 1386). Around 1400 there were about 470 mendicants in the duchy (160 Dominicans, 150 Franciscans, 85 Carmelites, 50 Augustinians, 25 Trinitarians). The fifteenth century belonged to the Franciscans: 16 new houses of which 15 adhered to the Observant wing of the movement. There were also three new Carmelite houses but only a single Dominican foundation. On the eve of the Reformation there were 900 Breton friars, nearly half of them Franciscans.

From the start their fervour and learning were harnessed particularly to a teaching ministry amongst the laity. Preaching tours were conducted in the countryside. Each convent had a district within which it collected alms: parishes up to 100 km away, for example, were regularly visited from Quimper. But it was especially in the towns that the mendicants made their mark. Their sermons were artfully shaped according to the needs of each congregation. The use of the vernacular was critical if they were to reach ordinary people though a star-performer like the Catalan St Vincent Ferrer could always draw curious audiences (cf. p. 270). The friars used a vast repertoire of popular and learned traditions. Visual aids and topical allusions enlivened the performance. The friars' prayers and services for the dead were considered very efficacious. Laypeople were eager to be buried in their churches or to obtain a place in their necrologies. The place of the friars at many a deathbed is revealed by the number who acted as executors.

The Lateran Council of 1215 had decreed annual confession and the mendicants were particularly effective in this role as spiritual fathers. The aristocracy had private confessors, friars without exception. Their schools not only catered for novices, but provided much-needed training for secular priests. Those of the Dominicans of Dinan and Morlaix had a high reputation. St Yves Helori (d. 1303) went to lectures at the Franciscan convent of Rennes prior to attending the university of Orléans. It was a pattern followed by many of his fellow countrymen, though Paris was the favourite destination. Hervé Nédélec became doctor of theology there in 1308 before going on to become Provincial of France and Master General of the Dominicans in 1318. For mortification of the flesh, the career of the Blessed Jean Discalcéat (1280–1349), who adopted the strictest possible interpretation of the Franciscan rule, wandered the Breton countryside shoeless and dispensed charity until death surprised him helping plague victims, recalls the austerities of the Desert Fathers.

Admiration for such behaviour and ideals helps to explain the enduring hold which the mendicants established in Breton society. This increased in the fifteenth century. The preaching tour of the great Catalan Dominican Vincent Ferrer in 1418–19 left a powerful local legacy after his death at Vannes. More than ever friars were at the heart of every initiative to improve religious life; local recruitment was high. The Observant Dominicans Alain de la Roche and Paien Dollo were extremely active in spreading the cult of the Rosary not simply in Brittany but in the Low Countries and Germany as well. Others like the Franciscan Olivier Maillard imitated St Vincent; he performed prodigies of preaching on an international scale, returning occasionally to scourge his country-men as at Nantes during Lent 1470 and 1480. The Observant Franciscans even founded three or four convents in remote coastal sites as Celtic saints had once done, a reaction against the materialism of late medieval Brittany with its burgeoning towns and commerce.

Intense external religiosity may also be demonstrated from the enthusiastic support for particular practices or fashions. Whilst local Breton saints always had their devotees, the cult of the Virgin and other major figures like St John spread rapidly during the

Plate 33   Popular piety: the pilgrim church of Saint-Jean-du-Doigt,
Plougasnou (F)

central Middle Ages. Around 1418 the discovery of a bone from his index finger at Plougasnou (F) ensured the fortunes of the flamboyant Gothic church of St Yann-ar-Biz, Saint-Jean-du-Doigt, which once possessed a gold chalice given by Queen Anne after her visit in 1505 seeking a cure for an eye infection. But the most famous local pilgrimage was the Tro-Breizh in which seven cathedrals had to be visited: Dol (St Samson), Saint-Malo, Saint-Brieuc, Tréguier (St Tugdual), Saint-Pol-de-Léon, Quimper (St Corentin) and Vannes (St Patern). The founders' relics were displayed at the major feasts – Christmas, Easter, Whitsun and Michaelmas – and the circuit of about 520 km could be completed in either direction in about a month. Whether or not more ancient links with the legend of the seven sleepers of Ephesus should be sought, it is in the thirteenth century that the cult of the Seven Saints first emerges clearly. After 1347 Tréguier had the added attraction of the tomb of St Yves, whose skull could be touched for 5s. At its height *c.* 1380–1400 perhaps as many as 30,000 or 35,000 people made the journey annually and the Tro-Breizh was still popular in the sixteenth century.

The quasi-Breton monastery of Mont Saint-Michel was another perennially popular shrine. Bretons were cured at Sainte-Catherine-de-Fierbois in Poitou in the fifteenth century and journeyed to Rocamadour (Lot). In 1487 at the height of the Franco-Breton war René de Montbourcher obtained permission to visit Saint-René d'Angers; in 1470 Jean II de Rohan used the pardon of St Philibert to escape from ducal surveillance. Such local patronal festivals and processions, some of which have retained their vigour to the present, were stimulated by papal indulgences to those visiting the shrines on special occasions. Some were conceded partly to raise money for the restoration of buildings damaged during the wars of the late Middle Ages. In some instances – like the Grand Troménie at Locronan, the six-yearly perambulation of the bounds of the immunity of St Ronan – this reinforced earlier practices, themselves a Christianization of older pagan fertility cults (above p. 106).

For Bretons who wanted to see the world, Rome, Santiago de Compostela and Jerusalem remained the most frequented major shrines as they had been in the twelfth century. Canterbury, Cologne (for the Three Kings), Maastricht (St Servais), Padua (St Anthony), Bari (St Nicholas, the patron of sailors) were also occasionally visited. The hospital of St Thomas at Acre was established especially for Breton pilgrims and crusaders in 1254. Debts incurred by Jean I and his men fighting in Tunis in 1270 were still outstanding in 1312 when Arthur II also left a huge legacy for a future crusade. Bretons fell fighting the Ottomans at Nicopolis in 1396 whilst Rhodes was the final resting place of several fifteenth-century knights. Nearer home, the church of St Yves at Paris was a favoured burial place for exiled Bretons, whilst a confraternity dedicated to the same saint flourished at Rome.

Holy relics were eagerly sought, borne home triumphantly and jealously guarded. The head of St Matthew inspired Hervé de Léon to give an annual rent of three measures (*perrées*) of wheat in perpetuity to the abbey of that name in 1206. In 1332 Jean III paid for a wall to protect it; despite suffering at the hands of the English in the fourteenth century, an impressive fifteenth-century list of relics then in the monks' possession survives as do similar ones for Quimper cathedral in 1274 and Dol in 1440. The viscount of Rohan left his collection in 1306 to his successor; in 1409 Alain VIII de Rohan and his brother Charles were disputing ownership of those acquired by their mother. Olivier IV de Clisson left his 'best cross with the relics in it' to Notre-Dame de Josselin in 1407. In 1469 Tanguy du Chastel and his wife Jeanne de Malestroit handed over to the church of Saint-Gilles de Malestroit relics of the saint (previously authenticated by the abbot of Saint-Gilles) 'which we have had encased in a silver-gilt hand' in the hope that his intercession would bring an end to Jeanne's infertility. At Saint-Gildas de Rhuys, whose governance Peter Abelard had found so taxing, the saint's arm and other relics are still preserved at the former monastic church in the gilded containers which the Montfort dukes gave.

Miraculous events in a world beset by fears of poverty, hunger, disease and other dire calamities were daily occurrences. When the body of Vital of Savigny (Mayenne) was translated from the chapel of St Catherine to the main abbey church in 1243, a crowd of 100,000 were allegedly present, among them many Bretons who testified to the cures that the saint had effected. Those accomplished at Louannec (C-d'A) by Yves Helori, the only parish priest canonized in the Middle Ages, were revealed at the inquiry into his sanctity held at Tréguier in 1330. Although he was not officially canonized until 1920, Charles de Blois was venerated in his own lifetime. A popular cult quickly sprang up after his death in 1364.

Healing sometimes followed a vigil at his tomb in the Franciscans' convent at Guingamp. An appeal to his name was even more effective – 180 of the 192 miracles recorded at the inquiry at Angers in 1371 occurred away from Guingamp. They included the release of Breton knights from harsh imprisonment at Valladolid in Spain and victory in a trial by battle between a Breton and a Gascon, besides a vast range of healing miracles. A Breton St Januarius, blood liquefied from a statue of Blois in the Franciscan church at Dinan in 1368 and sceptics were violently chastised. Belief in *revenants*, spirits of the dead returned to their earthly haunts, which is still widely accepted in modern Brittany as a recent study by the Canadian anthropologist Ellen Badone has shown, is also evidenced in medieval sources.

An index of how Brittany was 'sacralized' is potentially provided by images of Christian symbolism. Many hundreds of free-standing stone crosses survive. Unfortunately attempts to date them typologically have not been very successful; widely differing dates have been assigned to individual monuments. Some may date back to the earliest migration period, especially those engraved on menhirs like one mentioned in a Landévennec charter of *c.* 955, and represent an open attack on paganism like those placed on fountains whose origins are also pre-Christian. But it is clear from documentary as well as archaeological evidence that crosses have been erected in every period since at least the ninth century to the present with a consequent variety of religious and secular functions. An early purpose was clearly to ward off the Devil: for travellers at crossroads or on bridges, for example. Many were used to delimit sacred ground (cemeteries or the many immunities, known in Breton as *minihy*, which proliferated during the Middle Ages) or secular boundaries. Others were erected as reparation, for example, by murderers.

A few can be ascribed with some certainty to a particular epoch: one at Bourg-Blanc (F), erected as a memorial to Maurice son of Guy, appears to date from the twelfth century, those at Plogonnec (F) and Plozévet (F) from 1305–6. If they become commonplace in the countryside after 1200, this is not an exclusively Breton phenomenon since it has also been observed in Normandy and Burgundy. Their density, however, especially in Léon where one investigator has found over 700 allegedly medieval crosses, is notable. At the same time, as seventeenth-century missionaries discovered, the existence of crosses, or the erection of Christian chapels over fountains as at Saint-Melar de Lanmeur, by no means signified the elimination of many superstitions that are older than Christianity.

At the end of the Middle Ages, in addition to simple crosses, more elaborate calvaries began to appear. The most impressive still surviving early example is at Tronoën in the parish of Saint-Jean-Trolimon, dated on stylistic grounds *c.* 1450–70, though earlier ones are known either from record sources or surviving fragments, including Scaër (1400), Luzivilly (1422) and Rumengol (1433–57) (all F). There was a renaissance of ecclesiastical architecture, especially but not exclusively in Breton-speaking Brittany. Notre-Dame de Guingamp and Notre-Dame de Kreisker at Saint-Pol-de-Léon were important fourteenth-century precursors, but from around 1420 a series of richly decorated flamboyant Gothic churches and chapels of great beauty and originality were erected. In the diocese of Tréguier alone 16 parish churches and 36 chapels were entirely reconstructed in the fifteenth century. Other major local pilgrimage centres like Locronan and Notre-Dame de Folgoët were built with ducal aid. Among seigneurial

Plate 34   The calvary (*c.* 1450–70) at Tronoën, Saint-Jean-Trolimon (F)

Plate 35   Flamboyant Gothic exuberance: the painted wooden rood
screen by Olivier le Loergan (1480) in the chapel of Saint-Fiacre at Faouët (F)

chapels special mention may be made because of their architectural or decorative splendour of Kernascléden (M), rebuilt by
Alain IX de Rohan (d. 1462), Champeaux (I-et-V), mausoleum
of the Espinay family, and Sainte-Barbe du Faouët (F), erected
between 1489 and 1512 by Jean, sire de Toulbodou. The finest
surviving painted wooden Breton rood screen was built by
Olivier le Loergan in the neighbouring chapel of Saint Fiacre in
1480. The carving and painting of friezes and beam ends was
infused with new vigour. In addition to Danses macabres (below
p. 277), a wealth of other late medieval mural paintings is now
coming to light, adding to those already well known at Saint-

Gonéry de Plougescrant (C-d'A) and Notre-Dame du Tertre at Châtelaudren. On the other hand the characteristically ornate Breton *enclos paroissiaux* containing within a single retaining wall, entered through a monumental gateway, a church, ossuary, calvary and other monuments, found at Saint-Thégonnec, Guimiliau, Pleyben (all F) and many other locations in Breton-speaking Brittany, is a Renaissance development occurring beyond the scope of this account.

Finally, in this all-too-brief survey of a rich subject, the close, matter of fact, community of the living and the dead in medieval Brittany may be demonstrated from the wide range of functions that cemeteries performed besides their obvious one. Hubert Guillotel has made a case for thinking that the spiritual and legal protection they conferred when secular justice was still ineffectual in the eleventh and twelfth centuries was instrumental in reviving urban life. Besides the dead, cemeteries then often contained a living community. Houses were constructed in them, on which tithe and other dues might be levied. Markets were held there. Even when the community expanded, the cemetery usually continued to lie at its physical and spiritual heart. Its removal to a location on the edge of the village in the twentieth century is indicative in every sense of the distance modern man, unlike his medieval predecessors, places between the dead and the living.

The attested historical significance of mortuary rituals and the cult of the dead (in Breton *Anaon*) amongst Celtic peoples at large, and the abundant evidence for their particular intensity in Brittany between the late sixteenth century and the Second World War, has led scholars to project back into the Middle Ages similar characteristics though direct evidence is slight. The specific Breton personification of Death, the Ankou, usually depicted as a skeleton carrying a scythe and threatening the observer, is possibly referred to in a gloss on a ninth-century text. But it was naturally in the post-Black Death period that in Brittany as elsewhere in western Europe iconography emphasized the transitoriness of life and the inevitability of death. A number of Danses macabres, like those at Kermaria-an-Isquit, Plouha (C-d'A), and Kernascléden of about 1460–70, follow the fashion set by the famous murals in the cemetery of the Holy Innocents, Paris, dated to 1424, or at La Chaise Dieu in the county of Forez.

Plate 36   The late fifteenth-century Danse macabre (north face) at
Kermaria-an-Isquit, Plouha (C-d'A)

In the later Middle Ages the religious beliefs and practices of
the Bretons can be examined in some detail for the first time
from both material and written evidence. There is a danger of
attributing novelty to the features then revealed or, conversely, a
temptation to see ill-documented continuity with much more
remote epochs. The fact that many distinctive characteristics are
most evident where Breton was (and is) spoken leads inevitably
towards such a conclusion. It should be remembered, however,
that elements like the Ankou only achieved classic form in more
recent centuries. Some developments represent a reaction to the
powerful cultural influence of 'France'. Papal legislation on the
need to appoint clerics able to speak the language of their
congregation (*De idiomate*, 11 July 1373 and frequently repeated)
was particularly helpful for the conservation of local habits,
where five bishoprics out of nine contained a majority of Breton-
speakers.

All the main spiritual currents that affected the medieval
world washed over the province. In doing so they inevitably
took on strong local colour in a region where syncretism was

habitual. Despite all that has been said about late medieval urbanization, Brittany was still a proud, intensely conservative and predominantly rural society. Though superstition and magic were still present (and the popularity of Arthurian legends about magical stones and fountains may have helped to preserve such ideas), by 1500 Christianity was the major cultural determinant in the lives of ordinary Bretons. In bringing this brief survey of Breton beliefs and practices to a conclusion its main characteristics can be stressed. They were: the predominance of the mendicants, especially the Franciscans; the vigour and animation of parochial life, revealed in architecture, decoration (including external pulpits, statuary, paintings); confraternities; the beginnings of religious drama and mystery plays; enthusiasm for local cults, vivid awareness of death and a continuing admiration for ascetic ideals.

14

Brittany and the Bretons since 1491

A local Savonarola, Brother Pierre Morin of Guignen (I-et-V), whilst castigating his fellow Bretons at the height of the 1487–91 war for their moral failings, including a love of luxury which he said would one day lead them to wear on their heads what they ought to use for footwear and vice versa, more presciently predicted that before long 'the king of France and the duke of Brittany would sit in the same saddle and ride the same horse'. The first half of the sixteenth century saw political union between Brittany and France gradually become the reality which it has been ever since. Whilst Queen Anne as duchess of Brittany recovered some freedom of action after the death of Charles VIII (7 April 1498), thanks to the acquiescence of her second royal French husband Louis XII (1498–1515), who allowed the queen's Breton council to run government on a daily basis, the marriage of their eldest daughter, Claude, to the French heir presumptive, François, count of Angoulême, tightened royal control. Claude made over her rights to her husband who as Francis I (1515–47) nominated officers from the governor downwards. It was the royal court which dispensed patronage and set fashions. Many ambitious Bretons were inexorably drawn to it though, as the works of Noël du Fail (c. 1520–91) show, a separate provincial society existed with its own diversions and rustic charm. Its artistic and spiritual vigour is revealed, as briefly hinted above (p. 277), in the wealth of ecclesiastical and civil architecture that Renaissance and Counter-Reformation Brittany bequeathed to later generations. This was also the period in which Breton first seriously flourished as a literary language, providing particularly for the needs of ordinary

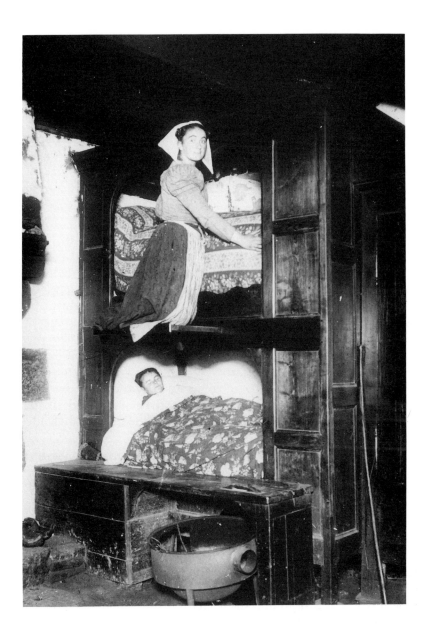

Plate 37   A prized possession: a two-tier box-bed (*lit clos*)

people through religious and secular poetry, drama, dictionaries and instructional manuals.

Politically, a sop to Breton pride was the appointment of the dauphin as duke of Brittany. In August 1532 François III (d. 1536) was crowned in an impressive ceremony at Rennes and the privileges of the duchy were confirmed by a formal act of union, clauses of which are still accepted today as valid in French courts. In 1547 Morin's prophecy was finally fulfilled when Henry II, who on the death of his brother succeeded as dauphin and duke of Brittany, ascended the royal throne. Apart from formalizing existing judicial arrangements, kings of France until the Revolution sensibly left the province's administration and institutions largely to run on the lines already confirmed by the treaties of 1491 and 1532. In 1552 the *présidiaux* courts took over the functions of the council and in 1554 a reformed Parlement de Bretagne assumed responsibility for registering public acts in place of the chancery. There were occasional crises. Indicative of the watchful if usually distant royal control of the province, for example, are the events of 1583 when Bertrand d'Argentré, the great jurist who had just coordinated a definitive revision of the Breton custom (1580), was forced on the eve of publication to withdraw the *Histoire de Bretagne* which the Etats had commissioned him to write because it allegedly contained material deemed to be prejudicial to the crown. It was only published in 1588 after cosmetic amendment to make it acceptable to the government.

More obviously, Brittany was also deeply scarred in the late sixteenth century by the Wars of Religion, when once again foreign powers (England and Spain) intervened and fought on Breton soil, individual leaders like the duc de Mercoeur pursued their own devious ends under the cloak of religion and much physical destruction occurred. The general conflict was eventually concluded by the Edict issued at Nantes on 13 April 1598 which granted toleration to Protestant and Catholic alike. But during the seventeenth century Protestantism locally lost its appeal. Thanks to effective Jesuit missionary work, the hold of Catholicism was re-imposed, a grip only seriously loosened in our own century. By the time the Edict was revoked in 1685, Louis XIV's government had also re-established its authority following the 'Révolte du papier timbré', sparked by harsh economic exploitation, which violently shook Brittany in 1675. This event presents a very different side of

Plate 38   A pardon in progress at Sainte-Anne-la-Palud (F)

provincial life from that so delightfully and snobbishly sketched in the letters of that Breton by marriage, Madame de Sévigné (d. 1690).

From 1687 the crown supervised more closely the financial activities of the Etats though this assembly continued to meet, often in chaotic fashion, till 1789. Indeed in its last years it enjoyed a hitherto unprecedented authority in administering the royal demesne and other fiscal assets in the province. After 1689 the Intendancy was definitively established in Brittany. Parlement, housed permanently in Salomon de Brosse's great Renaissance *palais* at Rennes, continued to function as a sovereign court, its members constituting the province's social and political elite during the last century of the Ancien Régime. This alliance between royal, aristocratic and ecclesiastical authorities and the incessant manoeuvring of various clienteles usually sufficed to keep Brittany politically quiescent despite grumbling discontent over fiscal exactions. An attempt by the mentally unbalanced *hobereau*, the marquis de Pontcallec, to raise a revolt in defence of local privileges in 1720 was easily quashed. At the same time the maritime expansion of France and military rivalry with England transformed the commercial fortunes of the merchants, privateers, *armateurs* and *bourgeoisie* of the great ports – Nantes, Brest, Saint-Malo and Port Louis (now Lorient, M). This created wealth that is still visible in the architecture of Nantes and in many *châteaux* and *malouinières*, large country houses, though the urban patrimony of the other three towns was irreparably damaged during the Second World War. At Rennes a great fire in 1720 led to the remodelling of the town centre in an impressive and spacious neo-classical style that may still be appreciated.

The Revolutionary period was particularly marked in Brittany by royalist and Counter-Revolutionary movements. The peasant rising of the Chouannerie, which had its origins in the Vendée to the south of the Loire, spilled over into the province in an uncoordinated and violent fashion and the Nantais, Vannetais and parts of Côtes-du-Nord (renamed on the occasion of the Bicentenary, Côtes-d'Armor) were all affected. It was put down only with great savagery, leaving a sullen hostility against central governments of whatever complexion that can still be felt in some rural areas. In the nineteenth century, new means of communication, especially railways, and industrial and commercial developments strengthened links between the major urban centres and Paris. Trade with the Antilles continued to benefit Nantes, whilst naval construction and subsequently the refinement of petrol accounts for the growth of Saint-Nazaire as a major industrial centre. Agriculture, however, remained backward and the continuing fecundity of the Breton population, reaching a peak of over three million inhabitants (1881), fuelled massive emigration from the countryside where the Revolution had brought little alleviation in the lot of the average peasant. Many Bretons continued to be drawn to Paris where there was a huge concentration of exiles. The armed forces, especially the navy with major bases at Brest and Lorient, also recruited Bretons in large numbers. Whilst the province produced some great military figures like the generals La Tour d'Auvergne, Moreau and Cambronne and Admiral Surcouf during the Revolutionary and Napoleonic wars, it also suffered disproportionately grievous losses, culminating in the First World War when a quarter of a million Bretons were killed.

A reaction against the traditional exploitation (or neglect) of Brittany by central government both before and after the Revolution manifested itself in different ways in the course of the nineteenth century. Eventually it took political shape with the formation of the Union Régionaliste Bretonne in 1898 and a whole series of successor, rival or splinter movements. To date none has played an effective role in national affairs. A plan promoted by the Parti National Breton (created in 1932) to establish an independent government by negotiation with the Nazis, following the defeat of France in 1940, is the closest radical autonomist views have come to fruition in modern times. Internal disputes among the party leadership, the loyalty (ambivalent as it often was) which ordinary Bretons have since the sixteenth century normally shown towards France, and bitter fighting between collaborators and *résistants*, finally destroyed this distorted vision of an independent Brittany and indelibly tarnished the reputation of its advocates.

Since 1945 separatist groups have continued to proliferate but without the electoral success which other modern political parties like the socialists and communists have enjoyed, whilst central government and latterly the EEC have proved much more responsive to provincial needs and demands. By this means the modern French state has largely undermined or outflanked political arguments for local independence by providing economic and social aid on a huge scale. As a result Bretons now enjoy a high standard of living, comprehensive health, education and social services, good communications and most benefits of modern society. There has even been national recognition of local cultural aspirations. Gone are the not-so-distant days when children heard speaking Breton in the school playground were severely punished. Funds have been made available through 'La Charte culturelle' to

Plate 39   A Pan-Celtic Festival: dancing to the music of Breton
bagpipes (*biniou*) and pipes (*bombardes*)

Plate 40   Old ladies wearing *coiffes* and costumes in the style of
Plougastel (F)

promote the work of university teachers and learned societies on
the history, language and traditions of Brittany. Popular interest is
also sustained by radio and television, whilst the present century
has seen a rich and vigorous modern literature in Breton.

The result is that a society which, at least in rural areas like the
pays Bigouden, the Monts d'Arrée or the Trégor, was until the
immediate post-1945 period still a remarkably traditional, little
mechanized one, has been transformed in a couple of generations,
starting with the landscape itself where the great *remembrements*
have destroyed the traditional *bocage*. Most modern manifestations

of Breton 'nationalism' now take on folkloric rather than political form, seen most obviously in the continuing popularity of religious *pardons*, secular entertainment, especially musical (*fest nozou*) or the wearing of the *coiffe* and Breton costume, often specifically for tourists. *Le Cheval d'orgueil* (first published in 1975) recounts these twentieth-century changes through the eyes of one gifted Bigouden story-teller, Pierre-Jakez Hélias; their political and social dimensions are more clinically dissected in Edgar Morin's study of Plodémet (F) – *Commune en France. La métamorphose de Plodémet* (1967); whilst Ellen Badone's recent account, *The Appointed Hour. Death, Worldview and Social Change in Brittany* (1989), looks at how modern circumstances have modified beliefs and attitudes in an area fundamental to Breton cultural history over many centuries. All three works reveal Brittany standing 'at the crossroads of space and time' (Morin). But that after all is where Bretons have always stood, as this book has tried to demonstrate.

Bibliography

The following titles are divided into general works, sources (often of relevance to more than one chapter), and specific works for individual chapters.

General

La Borderie, A. de *Histoire de Bretagne*, continued by Pocquet, B. (Paris–Rennes, 6 vols 1896–1914) is the classic narrative but needs revision in the light of recent work. This is best approached through the *Histoire de la Bretagne* published by Ouest France with full bibliographies:

Giot, P-R., L'Helgouach, J. and Monnier, J-L. *Préhistoire de la Bretagne* (Rennes, 1979)

Giot, P-R., Briard, J. and Pape, L. *Protohistoire de la Bretagne* (Rennes, 1979)

Chédeville, A. and Guillotel, H. *La Bretagne des saints et des rois, Ve-Xe siècle* (Rennes, 1984)

Chédeville, A. and Tonnerre, N-Y. *La Bretagne féodale, XIe–XIIIe siècle* (Rennes, 1987)

Leguay, J-P. and Martin, H. *Fastes et malheurs de la Bretagne ducale 1213–1532* (Rennes, 1982)

The *Histoire de la Bretagne et des pays celtiques* published by Skol Vreizh is a textbook treatment, with good illustrations and copious extracts from documents. The two relevant volumes are:

Des mégalithes aux cathédrales (Morlaix, revised edn 1983)

L'Etat breton (1341–1532) (Morlaix, 1987)

Balcou, J. and Le Gallo, Y. eds. *Histoire littéraire et culturelle de la Bretagne* (Paris–Geneva, 3 vols 1987) is a magnificent but uneven survey, of which the first volume *Heritage celtique et captation française*, ed. Fleuriot, L. and Segalen, A. P. is of most immediate relevance

Planiol, M. *Histoire des institutions de la Bretagne*, ed. Brejon de Lavergnée, J. (Mayenne, 5 vols 1981–4), although written in the 1890s, has worn much better than La Borderie

Main secondary literature

Actes du 107e Congrès national des sociétés savantes, Brest 1982, Section de philologie et d'histoire jusqu'à 1610, ii. Questions d'histoire de Bretagne (Paris, 1984) [cited as *Questions*]

Barral i Altet, X. ed. *Artistes, artisans et production artistique en Bretagne au Moyen Age* (Rennes, 1983)

Bates, David *Normandy before 1066* (London, 1982)

Bender, B. *The Archaeology of Brittany, Normandy and the Channel Islands* (London, 1986)

Bois, P. ed. *Histoire de Nantes* (Toulouse, 1977)

Burl, A. *Megalithic Brittany* (London, 1985)

Chadwick, N. K. *Early Brittany* (Cardiff, 1969)

Copy, J-Y. *Art, société et politique au temps des ducs de Bretagne. Les gisants haut-bretons* (Paris, 1986)

Davies, W. *Small Worlds. The Village Community in Early Medieval Brittany* (London, 1988)

Dilasser, M. ed. *Un pays de Cornouaille. Locronan et sa région* (Paris, 1979)

Drinkwater, J. *Roman Gaul* (London, 1983)

Fleuriot, L. *Les Origines de la Bretagne* (Paris, 1980)

Gallet, J. *La seigneurie bretonne (1450–1680). L'exemple du Vannetais* (Paris, 1983)

Galliou, P. *L'Armorique romaine* (Brasparts, 1983) [with comprehensive bibliography]

Galliou, P. *Carte archéologique de la Gaule: Le Finistère* (Paris, 1989)

Giot, P-R., Bernier, G. and Fleuriot, L. *Les premiers Bretons. La Bretagne du Ve siècle à l'an mil* (Châteaulin, 1982)

Grand, R. *L'Art roman en Bretagne* (Paris, 1958)

Jackson, K. H. *A Historical Phonology of Breton* (Dublin, 1967)

Jones, M. *Ducal Brittany, 1364–1399* (Oxford, 1970)

Jones, M. 'The Defence of Medieval Brittany: A survey of the establishment of fortified towns, castles and frontiers from the Gallo-Roman period to the end of the Middle Ages', *Archae-*

ological Journal 138 (1981), 149–204 [reprinted in *The Creation of Brittany*, pp. 13–68]

Jones, M. *The Creation of Brittany* (London, 1988) [collection of sixteen articles]

Kerhervé, J. *L'Etat breton aux 14e et 15e siècles. Les ducs, l'argent et les hommes* (Paris, 2 vols 1987)

Langouet, L. *Les fouilles archéologiques du bastion de Solidor, Saint-Malo* (Saint-Malo, 1983)

Laurent, J. *Un monde rural en Bretagne au XVe siècle, La Quévaise* (Paris, 1972)

Le Bihan, J-P. *Aux origines de Quimper* (Quimper, 1986)

Le Gallo, Y. ed. *Histoire de Brest* (Toulouse, 1976)

Leguay, J-P. *Un réseau urbain au moyen âge: les villes du duché de Bretagne aux XIVème et XVème siècles* (Paris, 1981)

Leguay, J-P. *Histoire de Vannes et de sa région* (Toulouse, 1988)

Le Patourel, J. *The Norman Empire* (Oxford, 1976)

Lewis, P. S. *Later Medieval France: the polity* (London, 1968)

Martin, H. *Les ordres mendiants en Bretagne (vers 1230 – vers 1530)* (Paris, 1975)

Meirion-Jones, G. I. *The Vernacular Architecture of Brittany. An Essay in Historical Geography* (Edinburgh, 1982)

Meirion-Jones, G. I. ed. *The Seigneurial Domestic Buildings of Brittany, First Interim Report 1983–85* (London: City of London Polytechnic, 1986)

Meyer, J. ed. *Histoire de Rennes* (Toulouse, 1972)

Mussat, A. *Arts et culture en Bretagne – Un millénaire* (Paris, 1979)

Nash, D. *Coinage in the Celtic World* (London, 1987)

Pape, L. *La civitas des Osismes à l'époque gallo-romaine* (Paris, 1978)

Pocquet du Haut-Jussé, B-A. *Les papes et les ducs de Bretagne* (Paris and Rome, 2 vols 1928)

Pocquet du Haut-Jussé, B-A. *François II, duc de Bretagne et l'Angleterre (1458–1488)* (Paris, 1929)

Provost, M. *Carte archéologique de la Gaule: la Loire-Atlantique* (Paris, 1988)

Simon, M. ed. *Landévennec et le monachisme breton dans le Haut Moyen Age. Actes du Colloque du 15ème centenaire de l'abbaye de Landévennec, 25–26–27 avril 1985* (Landévennec, 1986)

Touchard, H. *Le commerce maritime breton à la fin du moyen âge* (Paris, 1967)

Vilbert, L-R. ed. *Dinan au Moyen Age* (Dinan, 1986)

Selected Sources

Morice, Dom P-H. *Mémoires pour servir de preuves à l'histoire ecclésiastique et civile de Bretagne* (Paris, 3 vols 1742–6) is still of fundamental importance. It contains both narrative and record sources, although many of its contents have been re-edited

Early Medieval Narratives

Brett, C. *The Monks of Redon. Gesta Sanctorum Rotonensium and Vita Conuuoionis* (Woodbridge, 1989)

De Smedt, C. 'Vita sancti Winwaloei primi abbatis Landevenecensis auctore Wurdestino nunc primum integre edita', *Analecta Bollandiana* 7 (1888), 167–261

Fawtier, R. *La vie de saint Samson. Essai de critique hagiographique* (Paris, 1912) must be read in the light of modern critical debate summarized most recently in Dolbeau, F., Heinzelmann, M. and Poulin, J. C. 'Les sources hagiographiques narratives composées en Gaule avant l'an Mil', *Francia* 15 (1987), 701–33, esp. pp. 715–31

Gildas, *The Ruin of Britain and other Documents*, ed. Winterbottom, M. (London and Chichester, 1978)

Gregory of Tours, *The History of the Franks*, ed. Thorpe, L. (Harmondsworth, 1974)

Le Duc, G. *Vie de saint Malo, évêque d'Alet – Version écrite par le diacre Bili (fin du IXe siècle), texte latin et anglo-saxon avec traduction française* (DCRAA, 1979)

Merlet, René *La Chronique de Nantes (570 environ – 1049)* (Paris, 1896) needs careful handling

Plaine, F. 'Vita Sancti Pauli episcopi Leonensis in Britannia Minori auctore Wormonoco', *Analecta Bollandiana* 1 (1882), 208–58

Poupardin, René *Monuments de l'histoire des abbayes de Saint-Philibert (Noirmoutier, Grandlieu, Tournus)* (Paris, 1905)

The most important Frankish narratives concerning Brittany are

Ermold le Noir *Poème sur Louis le Pieux et épître au roi Pépin*, ed. Faral, E. (Paris, 1932)

Flodoard *Annales*, ed. Lauer, P. (Paris, 1906)

Grat, F., Vieillard, J. and Clémencet, S. *Annales de Saint-Bertin* (Paris, 1964)

Loup de Ferrières *Correspondance*, ed. Levillain, L. (Paris, 2 vols 1927–35)
Nithard *Histoire des fils de Louis le Pieux*, ed. Lauer, P. (Paris, 1926)
Regino de Prum *Chronicon*, ed. Kurze, F. (Hanover, 1890)
Richer *Histoire de France*, ed. Latouche, R. (Paris, 2 vols 1930–7)
Wallace-Hadrill, J. M. *The Fourth Book of the Chronicle of Fredegar (and continuations)* (London, 1960)

Among Anglo-Norman writers

Chronicles of the Reigns of Stephen, Henry II and Richard I, iv. The Chronicle of Robert of Torigni, ed. Howlett, R. (London, 1899)
Geoffrey of Monmouth *History of the Kings of Britain*, ed. Thorpe, L. (Harmondsworth, 1966)
Gerald of Wales *The Journey through Wales and The Description of Wales*, ed. Thorpe, L. (Harmondsworth, 1978)
Guillaume de Jumièges *Gesta Normannorum Ducum*, ed. Marx, J. (Rouen and Paris, 1914)
Guillaume de Poitiers *Histoire de Guillaume le Conquérant*, ed. Foreville, R. (Paris, 1952)
The Ecclesiastical History of Orderic Vitalis, ed. Chibnall, M. (Oxford, 6 vols 1969–80)

Later French chroniclers include

De Commynes, Philippe *Mémoires*, ed. Calmette, J. and Durville, G. (Paris, 3 vols 1924–5)
Delaborde, Henri-François *Oeuvres de Rigord et de Guillaume le Breton, historiens de Philippe-Auguste* (Paris, 2 vols 1882–5)
Froissart, Jean *Chroniques*, ed. Luce, S. et al. (Paris, 15 vols 1869–continuing)
Glaber, Raoul *Les cinq livres de ses histoires (900–1044)*, ed. Prou, M. (Paris, 1886)
Les Grandes Chroniques de France, ed. Viard, J. (Paris, 10 vols 1920–53)
Suger *Vie de Louis VI le Gros*, ed. Waquet, H. (Paris, 1929)

Later Medieval Breton narratives

Bouchart, Alain *Grandes Croniques de Bretaigne*, ed. Auger, M-L. and Jeanneau, G. (Paris, 2 vols 1986)

Bush, H. R. 'La bataille de trente Anglais et trente Bretons', *Modern Philology* ix (1911–12), 511-44; x (1912–13), 82–136

Gruel, Guillaume *Chronique d'Arthur de Richemont*, ed. Le Vavasseur, A. (Paris, 1890)

La Borderie, A. de *La Chronique de Bretagne de Jean de Saint-Paul* (Nantes, 1881)

Le Baud, Pierre *Histoire de Bretagne*, ed. d'Hozier, Charles, (Paris, 1638), for the 1505 version; for an incomplete edition (to 1305) of the first recension (1480) see *Croniques et ystoires des Bretons*, ed. De la Lande de Calan, C. (Nantes, 4 vols 1907–22)

Le Duc, G. and Sterckx, C. *Chronicon Briocense, Chronique de Saint-Brieuc* (Rennes, 1972) contains only the first 109 chapters (to AD 640) of a work that ends in 1416

St-André, Guillaume de 'C'est le libvre du bon Jehan, duc de Bretaigne', in Jean Cuvelier, *Chronique de Bertrand du Guesclin*, ed. Charrière, E. (Paris, 2 vols 1839), ii. 421–560 [See also Lecoy, F. 'Guillaume de Saint-André et son *Jeu des échecs moralisés*', *Romania* lxvii (1942–3), 491–503]

Breton charters and record sources

Anciens évêchés de Bretagne, ed. Geslin de Bourgogne, J. and de Barthélemy, A. (Paris and Saint-Brieuc, 6 vols 1855–79)

Bieler, Ludwig *The Irish Penitentials* (Dublin, 1963), pp. 136–59 for a translation of the incorrectly styled *Canones Wallici*, now recognized as 'Breton'. On the nature and dating of these 'laws' see Fleuriot, L. 'Un fragment en Latin de très anciennes lois bretonnes armoricaines du VIe siècle', *AB* 78 (1971), 601–60; idem, 'Les très anciennes lois bretonnes. Leur date. Leur texte', in Simon, M. ed. *Landévennec et le monachisme breton* (Landévennec, 1986), pp. 65–84; Dumville, David N. 'On the dating of the Early Breton Lawcodes', *Etudes Celtiques* 21 (1987), 207–21

Blanchard, René *Lettres et mandements de Jean V, duc de Bretagne* (Nantes, 5 vols 1889–95)

Courson, Aurélien de *Cartulaire de l'abbaye de Redon en Bretagne* (Paris, 1863) is of critical significance, but needs a modern revision

Duchesne, L. 'Lettre écrite à Lovocat et Catihern, prêtres bretons', *Revue de Bretagne* 57 (1885), 3–16

Guillotel, H. 'Recueil des actes des ducs de Bretagne 944–1148', Paris, Université de Droit, d'Economie et des Sciences Sociales, thèse, 1973 [to be published by the Académie des Inscriptions et Belles Lettres]

Jones, M. *Recueil des actes de Jean IV, duc de Bretagne, 1357–1399* (Paris, 2 vols 1980–3)

Jones, M. 'Some Documents relating to the disputed succession to the duchy of Brittany, 1341', *Camden Miscellany* xxiv (1972), 1–78

Kerhervé, J., Pérès, A-F. and Tanguy, B. *Les biens de la couronne dans la sénéchaussée de Brest et St-Renan d'après le rentier de 1544* (Rennes, 1984)

La Bigne Villeneuve, P. de *Cartulaire de l'abbaye de Saint-Georges de Rennes* (Rennes, 1875)

La Borderie, A. de *Monuments originaux de l'histoire de S. Yves* (Saint-Brieuc, 1887)

La Borderie, A. de *Cartulaire de l'abbaye de Landévennec* (Rennes, 1888)

La Borderie, A. de *Recueil d'actes inédits des ducs et princes de Bretagne (XIe, XIIe, XIIIe siècles)* (Rennes, 1888)

La Borderie, A. de 'Recueil de documents relatifs aux monuments de l'architecture militaire du moyen âge en Bretagne, 1222–1497', *Bulletin archéologique de l'Association bretonne*, 3ème sér., 12 (1894), 135–205

La Borderie, A. de *Choix des documents inédits sur le règne de la duchesse Anne* (Paris, 1902)

La Borderie, A. de *Nouveau recueil d'actes inédits . . . (XIIIe et XIVe siècles)* (Rennes, 1902) [includes the 1235 inquiries into complaints against Pierre Mauclerc]

Lejeune, Anne 'Le Conseil ducal de Bretagne au début du principat de François II, 1459–1463', Ecole nationale des Chartes, Paris, thèse 1989 [critical edition of the sole surviving council register]

Maître, L. and Berthou, P. de *Cartulaire de l'abbaye de Sainte-Croix de Quimperlé* (Paris–Rennes, 2nd edn 1904)

Plaine, Dom F. and Sérent, P. de *Monuments du procès de canonisation du bienheureux Charles de Blois, duc de Bretagne, 1320–1364* (Saint-Brieuc, 1921)

Planiol, M. *La très ancienne coutume de Bretagne* (Rennes, 1896; reprint 1984), which also provides sound texts of other ducal *ordonnances* and legal documents, is of fundamental importance

Pocquet du Haut-Jussé, B-A. 'Les comptes du duché de Bretagne en 1435–1436', *BEC* 77 (1916), 88–110

Pocquet du Haut-Jussé, B-A. 'Le plus ancien rôle des comptes du duché, 1262', *MSHAB* 26 (1946), 49–68

Rosenzweig, L. *Cartulaire du Morbihan* (Vannes, 1895) [continued to 1454 by P. Thomas-Lacroix in *Bulletin de la société polymathique du Morbihan*, années 1934–8]

Exhibition catalogues

Archéologie et grands travaux routiers: une ferme gauloise sur la déviation de Dinan (Rennes, n.d.)
Celtes et Armorique (Rennes, 1971)
Au temps des Celtes (Daoulas, 1986)
Aux origines de Carhaix (Carhaix, 1987)
Trésors des bibliothèques de Bretagne (Pontivy, 1989)

Additional bibliography

Chapter 1

Briard, J. *Les dépôts bretons et l'âge du bronze atlantique* (Rennes, 1965)
Briard, J. *L'âge du bronze en Europe barbare, des mégalithes aux Celtes* (Toulouse, 1976)
Briard, J. *Les tumulus d'Armorique* (Paris, 1984)
Briard, J. *Mégalithes en Bretagne* (Rennes, 1987)
L'Helgouac'h, J. *Les sépultures mégalithes en Armorique* (Rennes, 1965)
Monnier, J-L. *Le Paléolithique de la Bretagne dans son cadre géologique* (Rennes, 1980)

Chapter 2

Thom, A. and Thom, A. S. *La géométrie des alignements de Carnac* (Rennes, 1977)

Chapter 3

Gouletquer, P. *Les briquetages armoricains. Technologie proto-historique du sel en Armorique* (Rennes, 1970)
Gruel, K. *Le trésor de Trébry (Côtes-du-Nord)* (Paris, 1981)
Hawkes, C. F. C. '*Ictis* disentangled, and the British tin trade', *Oxford Journal of Archaeology* 3 (1984), 211–33
Le Bihan, J-P. *Villages gaulois et parcellaires antiques au Braden en Quimper* (Quimper, 1984)
McGrail, S. 'Cross-channel seamanship and navigation in the late

first millennium BC', *Oxford Journal of Archaeology* 2 (1983), 299–337

McReady, S., and Thompson, F. H. eds *Cross-Channel trade between Gaul and Britain in the pre-Roman Iron Age* (London, 1984)

Rouanet-Liesenfelt, A-M., Chastagnol, A., Galliou, P., Langouet, L. and Aumasson, P. *La civilisation des Riedones* (Brest, 1980)

Chapters 4 and 5

Cunliffe, B. 'Britain, the *Veneti* and beyond', *Oxford Journal of Archaeology* 1 (1982), 39–68

Etienne, R. 'A propos du *garum sociorum*', *Latomus*, xxix, 2 (1970), 297–313

Galliou, P. *Corpus des amphores découvertes dans l'Ouest de la France, i. Les amphores tardo-républicaines* (Brest, 1982)

Galliou, P. *Les tombes romaines d'Armorique* (Paris, 1989)

Giard, J-B. 'La monnaie locale en Gaule à la fin du IIIe siècle, reflet de la vie économique', *Journal des Savants*, Janvier–Mars 1969, 5–34

Guennou, G. *La cité des Coriosolites* (Saint-Malo, 1981)

Hopkins, K. 'Economic growth and towns in Classical Antiquity', *Towns in Societies*, ed. Abrams, P. and Wrigley, E. A. (Cambridge, 1978)

Langouet, L. *Les Coriosolites, un peuple armoricain, de la période gauloise à l'époque gallo-romaine* (Saint-Malo, 1988)

Langouet, L. *Un village coriosolite sur l'île des Ebihens (Saint-Jacut-de-la-Mer)* (Saint-Malo, 1989)

Langouet, L. and Daire, M-Y. *La civitas gallo-romaine des Coriosolites: le milieu rural* (Rennes, 1989)

Merlat, P., Giot, P-R. and André, P. *Les Vénètes d'Armorique* (Brest, 1982)

Rivet, A. L. F. ed. *The Roman Villa in Britain* (London, 1969)

Chapter 6

Bernier, G. *Les chrétientés bretonnes continentales depuis les origines jusqu'au IXème siècle* (DCRAA, 1982)

Bowen, E. G. *Saints, Seaways and Settlements in the Celtic Lands* (Cardiff, revised edn 1977)

Chadwick, N. K. 'Colonization of Brittany from Celtic Britain', *Proceedings of the British Academy* 51 (1965), 235–99

Davies, W. 'Priests and rural communities in east Brittany in the ninth century', *Etudes celtiques* 20 (1983), 177–99

Duhamel, M. 'Les harpes celtiques', *Mélanges bretons et celtiques offerts à M. Joseph Loth* (Paris–Rennes, 1927), pp. 178–85

Falc'hun, F. *Perspectives nouvelles sur l'histoire de la langue bretonne* (Paris, 1981)

Giot, P-R. 'Saint Budoc on the Isle of Lavret, Brittany', in Pearce, S. ed. *The Early Church in Western Britain and Ireland* (British Archaeological Reports, British Series 102, 1982), pp. 197–210

Giot, P-R. '*Insula quae Laurea appelatur*: fouilles archéologiques sur l'île Lavret', in Simon, M. ed. *Landévennec et le monachisme breton*, pp. 219–36

Giot, P-R. and Fleuriot, L. 'Early Brittany', *Antiquity* 51 (1977), 106–16

Giot, P-R. and Monnier, J. L. 'Le cimetière des anciens bretons de Saint-Urnel ou Saint-Saturnin en Plomeur (Finistère)', *Gallia* 35 (1977), 141–71

Giot, P-R. and Monnier, J. L. 'Les oratoires des anciens bretons de Saint-Urnel ou Saint-Saturnin en Plomeur (Finistère)', *Archéologie médiévale* 8 (1978), 55–93

Guigon, Ph. and Bardel, J. P. 'Les nécropoles mérovingiennes de Bais et Visseiche (Ille-et-Vilaine)', *MSHAB* 66 (1989), 299–353

Guillotel, H. 'Les origines du ressort de l'évêché de Dol', *MSHAB* 54 (1977), 31–68

Jackson, K. H. *Language and History in Early Britain* (Edinburgh, 1953)

James, E. *The Franks* (Oxford, 1988)

Largillière, R. *Les saints et l'organisation chrétienne primitive dans l'Armorique bretonne* (Rennes, 1925)

Loth, J. *L'émigration bretonne du 5e au 7e siècle de notre ère* (Rennes, 1883)

McDermott, W. C. 'Felix of Nantes: a Merovingian Bishop', *Traditio* 21 (1975), 1–24

Matthews J. F. 'Macsen, Maximus, and Constantine', *Welsh History Review* 11 (1983), 431–48

Merdrignac, B. *Recherches sur l'hagiographie armoricaine du VIIème au XVème siècle* (DCRAA, 2 vols 1985–6)

Tanguy, B. 'La limite linguistique dans la péninsule armoricaine à l'époque de l'émigration bretonne (IVe–Ve siècle) d'après les données toponymiques', *AB* 87 (1980), 429–62

Thompson, E. A. 'Procopius on Brittia and Britannia', *Classical Quarterly* 30 (1980), 498–507

Tonnerre, N-Y. 'Le commerce nantais à l'époque mérovingienne', *MSHAB* 61 (1984), 5–27

Chapter 7

Alexander, J. J. G. 'La résistance à la domination culturelle carolingienne dans l'art breton du IXe siècle: le témoignage des manuscrits enluminés', in Simon, M. ed. *Landévennec et le monachisme breton*, pp. 269–80

Barral i Altet, X. ed. *Le paysage monumental de la France autour de l'an Mil* (Paris, 1987)

Brunterc'h, J-P. 'Géographie historique et hagiographie: la vie de saint Mervé', *Mélanges de l'école française de Rome, Moyen âge et temps modernes* 95 (1983), 7–63

Brunterc'h, J-P. 'Le duché de Maine et la Marche de Bretagne', *La Neustrie, les pays au nord de la Loire de 650 à 850*, ed. Atsma, Hartmut (Sigmaringen, 2 vols 1989), i. 29–127

Cassard, J-C. 'La guerre des Bretons armoricains au haut moyen âge', *Revue historique*, cclxxv (1986), 3–27

Davies, W. 'On the distribution of political power in Brittany in the mid-ninth century', in Gibson, M., Nelson, J. and Ganz, D. eds *Charles the Bald: Court and Kingdom* (British Archaeological Reports, International Series 101, 1981), pp. 87–107

Davies, W. 'Les chartes du Cartulaire de Landévennec', in Simon, M. ed. *Landévennec et le monachisme breton*, pp. 85–95

Deuffic, J-L. 'La production manuscrite des scriptoria bretons (VIIIe–XIe siècle)', in Simon, M. ed. *Landévennec et le monachisme breton*, pp. 289–321

Dolley, M. and Yvon, J. 'A group of tenth-century coins found at Mont-Saint-Michel', *British Numismatic Journal* 40 (1971), 1–16

Flatrès, P. 'Les anciennes structures rurales de Bretagne d'après le cartulaire de Redon', *Etudes rurales* 41 (1971), 87–93

Fleuriot, L. with Evans, C. *A Dictionary of Old Breton; Dictionnaire du Vieux Breton* (Toronto, 2nd edn, 2 vols 1985)

Guillotel, H. 'L'action de Charles le Chauve vis à vis de la Bretagne de 843 à 851', *MSHAB* 53 (1975–6), 5–32

Guillotel, H. 'L'exode du clergé breton devant les invasions scandinaves', *MSHAB* 59 (1982), 269–315

Guillotel, H. 'Recherches sur l'activité des *scriptoria* bretons au IXe siècle', *MSHAB* 62 (1985), 9–36

Guillotel, H. 'Les cartulaires de l'abbaye de Redon', *MSHAB* 63 (1986), 27–48

Huglo, M. *Le domaine de la notation bretonne* (Brest: Britannia Christiana, Bibliothèque liturgique bretonne, fasc. 1, Printemps 1981)

Inventaire général de Bretagne, *Camp des Rouëts (Morbihan–Bretagne)* (Rennes, 1985)

McKitterick, R. *The Frankish Kingdoms under the Carolingians 751–987* (London, 1983)

Riché, P. 'Les hagiographes bretons et la renaissance carolingienne', *Bulletin philologique et historique (jusqu'à 1610) du Comité des travaux historiques et scientifiques*, 1966, ii. 651–9

Sheringham, J. G. T. 'Les machtierns', *MSHAB* 58 (1981), 61–72

Smith, J. M. H. 'The "Archbishopric" of Dol and the Ecclesiastical Politics of Ninth-Century Brittany', *Studies in Church History* 18 (1982), 59–70

Smith, J. M. H. 'Carolingian Brittany', Oxford D. Phil. thesis 1985 [to be published shortly by Cambridge University Press]

Smith, J. M. H. 'Celtic Asceticism and Carolingian Authority in Early Medieval Brittany', *Studies in Church History* 22 (1985), 53–63

Smith, J. M. H. 'The Sack of Vannes by Pippin III', *Cambridge Medieval Celtic Studies* 11 (Summer 1986), 17–27

Smith, J. M. H. 'Culte impérial et politique frontalière dans la vallée de la Vilaine: le témoignage des diplômes carolingiens dans le Cartulaire de Redon', in Simon, M. ed. *Landévennec et le monachisme breton*, pp. 129–39

Tonnerre, N-Y. 'Contribution à l'étude de la forêt bretonne: la forêt dans la région de Redon à l'époque carolingienne', *Enquêtes et Documents du Centre de Recherches sur l'Histoire de la France Atlantique, Nantes* 3 (1975), 57–75

Tonnerre, N-Y. 'Le diocèse de Vannes au IXe siècle d'après le Cartulaire de Redon', Paris X, thèse de troisième cycle 1977

Tonnerre, N-Y. 'L'esclavage dans la Bretagne du haut moyen âge', *Questions*, pp. 105–15

Wallace-Hadrill, J. M. *The Vikings in Francia* (Reading, Stenton Lecture, 1975)

Wormald, F. (with Alexander, J. J. G.) *An Early Breton Gospel Book from the collection of H. L. Bradfer-Lawrence* (Roxburghe Club, 1977)

Wright, N. 'Knowledge of Christian Latin poets and historians in early medieval Brittany', *Etudes celtiques* 23 (1986), 163–86

Chapter 8

Allenou, J. *Histoire féodale des marais, territoires et église de Dol. Enquête par tourbe ordonnée par Henri II, roi d'Angleterre* (Paris, 1917)

Bienvenu, J-M. 'Aux origines d'un ordre religieux: Robert d'Arbrissel et la fondation de Fontevraud (1101)', *Cahiers d'histoire* 20 (1975), 227–51

Blanchard, R. *Airard et Quiriac, évêques de Nantes (1050–1079)* (Vannes, 1895)

Brunterc'h, J-P. 'Puissance temporelle et pouvoir diocésain des évêques de Nantes entre 936 et 1049', *MSHAB* 61 (1984), 29–82

Cassard, J-C. 'Eon de l'Etoile, ermite et hérésiarque breton du XIIe siècle', *MSHAB* 57 (1980), 171–98

Chédeville, A. 'L'immigration bretonne dans le royaume de France du XIe au début du XIVe siècle', *AB* 81 (1974), 301–43

Clay, C. T. *The Honour of Richmond* (Early Yorkshire Charters, extra series, 2 vols 1935–6)

Devailly, G. 'Une enquête en cours: l'application de la réforme gregorienne en Bretagne', *AB* 75 (1968), 293–316

Duby, G. *The Chivalrous Society*, trans. Cynthia Postan (London, 1977)

Dunbabin, J. *France in the Making 843–1180* (Oxford, 1985)

Fossier, R. *Enfance de l'Europe. Aspects économiques et sociaux* (Paris, 2 vols 1982)

Fuchs, Rüdiger, *Das Domesday Book und sein Umfeld* (Stuttgart, 1987)

Guillotel, H. 'Les vicomtes de Léon aux XIe et XIIe siècles', *MSHAB* 51 (1971), 29–51

Guillotel, H. 'Une famille au service du Conquérant: les Baderon', *Droit privé et institutions régionales. Etudes historiques offertes à Jean Yver* (Paris, 1976), pp. 361–7

Guillotel, H. 'Les origines du bourg de Donges', *AB* 84 (1977), 541–52

Guillotel, H. 'Les évêques d'Alet du IXe au milieu du XIIe siècle', *Société d'histoire et d'archéologie de l'arrondissement de Saint-Malo*, année 1979, 251–66

Guillotel, H. 'Le premier siècle du pouvoir ducal breton (936–1040)', *Actes du 103e Congrès national des sociétés savantes, Nancy-Metz, 1977, Section de philologie et d'histoire jusqu'à 1610* (Paris, 1979), 63–84

Guillotel, H. 'Des vicomtes d'Alet aux vicomtes de Poudouvre', *Société d'histoire et d'archéologie de l'arrondissement de Saint-Malo*, année 1988, 201–15

Guillotel, H. 'La place de Châteaubriant dans l'essor des châtellenies bretonnes (XIe–XIIe siècles)', *MSHAB* 66 (1989), 5–46

Irien, J. 'Le site médiéval de Lezkelen en Plabennec: le castel Saint-Ténéran', *BSAF* 109 (1981), 103–19

Jones, M. 'Notes sur quelques familles bretonnes en Angleterre après la conquête normande', *MSHAB* 58 (1981), 73–97 [*The Creation of Brittany*, pp. 69–93]

Jones, M. *The Family of Dinan in England in the Middle Ages* (Dinan, 1987)

Lebigre, A. 'Les débuts de l'abbaye cistercienne de Buzay en pays de Rais, 1144–1250', *RHDFE* 4ème sér. 45 (1967), 451–82

Leyser, H. *Hermits and the New Monasticism. A Study of Religious Communities in Western Europe, 1000–1150* (London, 1984)

Minois, G. 'Bretagne insulaire et Bretagne armoricaine dans l'oeuvre de Geoffroy de Monmouth', *MSHAB* 58 (1981), 35–60

Niderst, R. and Raison, L. 'Le mouvement érémetique dans l'Ouest de la France à la fin du XIe et au début du XIIe siècle', *AB* 55 (1948), 1–46

Pocquet du Haut-Jussé, B-A. 'Les prodromes de la réforme grégorienne en Bretagne', *Bulletin philologique et historique année 1960*, 871–91

Poly, J-P. and Bournazel, E. *La mutation féodale Xe–XIIe siècles* (Paris, 1980)

Sanquer, R. 'Les mottes féodales du Finistère', *BSAF* 105 (1977), 99–126

Smith, J. 'Robert of Arbrissel: *procurator mulierum*', *Medieval Women*, ed. Baker, D. (Studies in Church History, Subsidia 1, 1978), pp. 175–84

Chapter 9

Bachrach, B. S. 'Geoffrey Greymantle, count of the Angevins, 960–987: a study in French Politics', *Studies in Medieval and Renaissance History* vii (Old series xvii) (1985), 1–67

Baldwin, J. W. *The Government of Philip Augustus* (London, 1986)

Boussard, J. *Le gouvernement d'Henri II Plantagenêt* (Paris, 1956)

Cassard, J-C. 'Arthur est vivant! Jalons pour une enquête sur le messianisme royal au moyen âge', *CCM* 33 (1989), 135–46

Douglas, D. C. *William the Conqueror* (London, 1964)

Dumas, F. 'La monnaie dans les domaines Plantagenêt', *CCM* 29 (1986), 53–9

Guillot, O. *Le comte d'Anjou et son entourage au XIe siècle* (Paris, 2 vols 1972)

Halphen, L. *Le comté d'Anjou au XIe siècle* (Paris, 1906)

Hillion, Y. 'La Bretagne et la rivalité Capétiens-Plantagenêt. Un exemple: la duchesse Constance (1186–1202)', *AB* 92 (1985), 111–44

Jolliffe, J. E. A. *Angevin Kingship* (London, 2nd edn 1963)

Jones, M. 'The Capetians and Brittany', *Historical Research* 63 (1990), 1–16

Jones, M. 'La vie familiale de la duchesse Constance: le témoignage des chartes', *Bretagne et pays celtiques. Langues, histoire, civilisation. Mélanges dédiés à la mémoire de Léon Fleuriot* (forthcoming, Rennes, 1991).

Lemarignier, J. F. *Recherches sur l'hommage en marche et les frontières féodales* (Lille, 1945)

Lemarignier, J. F. 'Les fidèles du roi de France (936–987)', *Recueil de travaux offert à M. Clovis Brunel* (Paris, 2 vols 1955), ii. 138–62

Le Patourel, J. 'Henry II Plantagenêt et la Bretagne', *MSHAB* 58 (1981), 99–116

Martindale, J. 'Succession and Politics in the Romance-speaking World, *c.* 1000–1140', in Jones, M. and Vale, M. eds *England and her neighbours, 1066–1453. Essays in Honour of Pierre Chaplais* (London, 1989), pp. 19–41

Planiol, M. 'L'Assise au Comte Geffroi. Etude sur les successions féodales en Bretagne', *Nouvelle revue de droit français et étranger* xi (1887), 117–62, 652–708

Warren, W. L. *King John* (London, 1961)

Warren, W. L. *Henry II* (London, 1973)

Chapter 10

Allan, J. P. *Medieval and Post-Medieval Finds from Exeter, 1971–1980* (Exeter, 1984)

André, P. 'Un village médiéval breton du XIe siècle: Lann-Gouh, Melrand (Morbihan)', *Archéologie médiévale* 12 (1982), 155–74

Bautier, R. H. ed. *La France de Philippe Auguste: le temps de mutation* (Paris, 1982)

Bertrand, R. and Lucas, M. 'Un village côtier du XIIe siècle en Bretagne: Pen-er-Malo en Guidel (Morbihan)', *Archéologie médiévale* 5 (1975), 73–101

Brejon de Lavergnée, J. 'La très ancienne coutume de Bretagne', in Balcou and Le Gallo, *Histoire littéraire et culturelle de la Bretagne* i. 44–60

Cassard, J-C. 'Les marins bretons à Bordeaux au début du XIVe siècle', *AB* 86 (1979), 378–97

Cazelles, R. 'La réglementation royale de la guerre privée de Saint Louis à Charles V et la précarité des ordonnances', *RHDFE*, 4ème sér., 38 (1960), 530–48

Chapelot, J. and Fossier, R. *The Village and House in the Middle Ages*, trans. H. Cleere (London, 1985)

Dieudonné, A. 'L'ordonnance ou règlement de 1315 sur le monnayage des barons', *BEC* 93 (1932), 5–54

Hoffmann, H. 'Französische Fürstenweihen des Hochmittelalters', *Deutsches Archiv* 18 (1962), 92–119

Jones, M. 'La vie quotidienne de trois nobles bretons au XIIIe siècle d'après leurs testaments', *MSHAB* 60 (1983), 19–33 [*The Creation of Brittany*, pp. 95–109]

Jones, M., Meirion-Jones, G. I., Guibal, F. and Pilcher, J. R. 'The Seigneurial Domestic Buildings of Brittany: a provisional assessment', *The Antiquaries Journal* 69 pt ii (1989), 73–109

Kaeuper, R. W. *War, Justice and Public Order: England and France in the Later Middle Ages* (Oxford, 1988)

Le Roy, N. 'L'influence française en Bretagne (1213–1341) et les institutions privées bretonnes', Ecole nationale des Chartes, *Positions des thèses*, 1965, pp. 51–6

Levron, J. 'Catalogue des actes de Pierre de Dreux, duc de Bretagne', *MSHAB* 11 (1930), 173–261

Oheix, A. *Essai sur les sénéchaux de Bretagne des origines au XIVe siècle* (Paris, 1913)

Olivier-Martin, F. 'Le finport', *MSHAB* 2 (1921), 35–96

Painter, S. *The Scourge of the Clergy. Peter of Dreux, duke of Brittany* (Baltimore, 1937)

Sarrazin, J. L. 'Les cisterciens de Buzay et l'aménagement des marais de l'estuaire de la Loire au moyen âge (XIIème–XVème siècles)', *MSHAB* 65 (1988), 57–79

Strayer, J. R. *The Reign of Philip the Fair* (Princeton, 1980)

Touchard, H. 'Les brefs de Bretagne', *Revue d'histoire économique et sociale* 34 (1956), 116–40

Chapter 11

Bock, F. 'Some new documents illustrating the early years of the Hundred Years War, 1353–6', *Bulletin of the John Rylands Library* 15 (1931), 60–91

Cazelles, R. *La société politique et la crise de la royauté sous Philippe de Valois* (Paris, 1958)

Déprez, E. 'La querelle de Bretagne', *MSHAB* 7 (1926), 25–60

Fowler, K. *The King's Lieutenant. Henry of Grosmont, First Duke of Lancaster, 1310–1361* (London, 1969)

Jones, M. 'Sir Thomas Dagworth et la guerre civile en Bretagne au XIVe siècle: quelques documents inédits', *AB* 87 (1980), 621–39

Jones, M. 'The Breton Civil War', in Palmer, J. J. N. ed. *Froissart:*

Historian (Woodbridge, 1981), pp. 64–81, 169–72 [*The Creation of Brittany*, pp. 197–218]

Jones, M. 'Edward III's Captains in Brittany', in Ormrod, M. W. ed. *England in the Fourteenth Century* (Woodbridge, 1986), pp. 99–117

Jones, M. 'Sir John Hardreshull, King's lieutenant in Brittany, 1343–1345', *Nottingham Medieval Studies* 31 (1987), 76–97

Jones, M. 'Les capitaines anglo-bretons et les marches entre la Bretagne et le Poitou, 1342–1373', *Actes du 111e Congrès national des sociétés savantes, Poitiers 1986, La France 'Anglaise'* (Paris, 1988), pp. 357–75

Jones, M. 'Relations with France, 1337–1399', in Jones and Vale eds *England and her neighbours, 1066–1453* (London, 1989), pp. 239–58

Jones, M. 'Nantes au début de la guerre civile en Bretagne', *Villes, bonnes villes, cités et capitales. Mélanges offerts à Bernard Chevalier*, ed. Bourin, M. (Tours, 1989), pp. 105–20

Spinosi, C. 'Un règlement pacifique dans la succession de Jean III, duc de Bretagne, à la vicomté de Limoges', *RHDFE* 4ème sér. 39 (1961), 453–67

Chapter 12

André, P. 'Le château de Suscinio, XIIIe–XVe siècles', *Congrès archéologique de France, 141e session, 1983, Morbihan* (Paris, 1986), pp. 254–66

Bossard, E. *Gilles de Rais, maréchal de France, dit Barbe-bleue (1404–1440)* (Paris, 2nd edn 1886)

Boulton, D'A. J. D. *The Knights of the Crown. The Monarchical Orders of Knighthood in Later Medieval Europe 1325–1520* (Woodbridge, 1987)

Bourdeaut, Abbé A. 'Jean V et Marguerite de Clisson. La ruine de Châteauceaux', *Bulletin de la société archéologique de Nantes et de la Loire-Inférieure* 54 (1913), 331–417

Bourdeaut, Abbé A. 'Gilles de Bretagne. Entre la France et l'Angleterre, les causes et les auteurs du drame', *MSHAB* 1 (1920), 53–145

Brejon de Lavergnée, J. 'La confiscation du duché de Bretagne par Charles V (1378)', *MSHAB* 59 (1982), 329–43

Cassard, J-C. 'Un historien au travail: Pierre le Baud', *MSHAB* 62 (1985), 67–95

Contamine, P. 'L'artillerie royale française à la veille des guerres d'Italie', *AB* 71 (1964), 221–61

Contamine, P. 'The Contents of a French Diplomatic Bag in the Fifteenth Century: Louis XI, regalian rights and Breton bishoprics', *Nottingham Medieval Studies* 25 (1981), 52–72

Copy, J-Y. 'Du nouveau sur la couronne ducale bretonne: le témoignage des tombeaux', *MSHAB* 59 (1982), 171–94

Cosneau, E. *Le connétable de Richemont (Artur de Bretagne) 1393–1458* (Paris, 1886)

Fery-Hue, F. 'Le cérémonial du couronnement des ducs de Bretagne au XVe siècle: édition', *Questions,* pp. 247–63

Guiomar, J-Y. *Le Bretonisme. Les historiens bretons au XIXe siècle* (Mayenne, 1987)

Jeulin, P. 'L'hommage de la Bretagne', *AB* 41 (1934), 380–473

Jones, M. ' "Mon pais et ma nation": Breton Identity in the Fourteenth Century', in Allmand, C. T. ed. *War, Literature and Politics in the Late Middle Ages* (Liverpool, 1976), pp. 144–68 [*The Creation of Brittany*, pp. 283–307]

Jones, M. 'Education in Brittany in the later Middle Ages: a survey', *Nottingham Medieval Studies* 22 (1978), 58–77 [*The Creation of Brittany*, pp. 309–28]

Jones, M. ' "Bons Bretons et bons Francoys": the Language and Meaning of Treason in Later Medieval France', *Transactions of the Royal Historical Society*, 5th ser. 32 (1982), 91–112 [*The Creation of Brittany*, pp. 329–50]

Jones, M. 'The Chancery of Brittany from Peter Mauclerc to Duchess Anne, 1213–1514', *Landesherrliche Kanzleien im Spätmittelalter* (Munich, 1985), pp. 681–728 [*The Creation of Brittany*, pp. 111–58]

Jones, M. 'L'armée bretonne, 1449–1491: structures et carrières', in Chevalier, B. and Contamine, P. eds *La France de la fin du XVe siècle: renouveau et apogée* (Paris, 1985), pp. 147–65 [*The Creation of Brittany*, pp. 351–69]

Jones, M. 'The Finances of John IV, duke of Brittany, 1364–1399', *The Creation of Brittany*, pp. 239–62

Jones, M. 'Aristocratie, faction et état dans la Bretagne du XVe siècle', in Contamine, P. ed. *L'Etat et les aristocraties (France, Angleterre, Ecosse) XIIe–XVIIe siècle* (Paris, 1989), pp. 129–60

Keen, M. and Daniel, M. J. 'English Diplomacy and the sack of Fougères in 1449', *History* 59 (1974), 375–91

Kerhervé, J. 'Aux origines d'un sentiment national. Les chroniqueurs bretons de la fin du moyen âge', *BSAF* 108 (1980), 165–206

Knowlson, G. A. *Jean V, duc de Bretagne et l'Angleterre 1399–1442* (Rennes and Cambridge, 1964)

Labande-Mailfert, Y. *Charles VIII et son milieu (1470–1498). La jeunesse au pouvoir* (Paris, 1975)

Labande-Mailfert, Y. 'Le mariage d'Anne et de Charles VIII vu par Erasme Brasca', *MSHAB* 55 (1978), 17–42

La Borderie, A. de 'Jean Meschinot. Sa vie et ses oeuvres. Ses satires contre Louis XI', *BEC* 56 (1895) and separately (Nogent-le-Rotrou, 1896)

La Borderie, A. de *Etude sur les neuf barons de Bretagne* (Rennes, 1895)

Laigue, R. de *La noblesse bretonne aux XVe et XVIe siècles, Réformations et montres* (Vannes, 2 vols 1902)

Leguay, J-P. *La ville de Rennes au XVème siècle à travers les comptes des miseurs* (Paris, 1969)

Leguay, J-P. 'Un aspect du travail du métal dans les villes armoricaines au moyen âge: la fabrication des canons et des armes blanches', in Benoit, P. and Cailleaux, D. eds *Hommes et travail du métal dans les villes médiévales* (Paris, 1988), pp. 185–226

Lewis, P. S. 'Breton Estates', in his *Essays in Later Medieval French History* (London, 1985), pp. 127–38

Manning, A. *The Argentaye Tract, edited from Paris, BN, fonds français 11,464* (Toronto, 1983)

Mussat, A. 'Le château de Vitré et l'architecture des châteaux bretons du XIVe au XVIe siècle', *Bulletin monumental* 131 (1975), 131–64

Pocquet du Haut-Jussé, B-A. 'Les faux états de Bretagne de 1315 et les premiers états de Bretagne', *BEC* 86 (1925), 388–406

Pocquet du Haut-Jussé, B-A. 'Les séjours de Philippe le Hardi en Bretagne, 1372, 1394, 1402', *MSHAB* 16 (1935), 11–62

Pocquet du Haut-Jussé, B-A. *Deux féodaux, Bourgogne et Bretagne, 1363–1491* (Paris, 1935)

Pocquet du Haut-Jussé, B-A. 'Couronne fermée et cercle ducale en Bretagne', *Bulletin philologique et historique jusqu'à 1715 du Comité des travaux historiques et scientifiques, années 1951–1952* (Paris, 1953), 103–12

Pocquet du Haut-Jussé, B-A. 'Le grand fief breton', in Lot, F. and Fawtier, R. *Les institutions françaises au moyen âge* (Paris, 3 vols 1957–62), i. 267–88

Pocquet du Haut-Jussé, B-A. 'Le conseil du duc de Bretagne d'après ses procès-verbaux', *BEC* 116 (1958), 136–69

Pocquet du Haut-Jussé, B-A. 'Une idée politique de Louis XI. La sujétion éclipse la vassalité', *Revue historique* ccxxvi (1961), 383–98

Pocquet du Haut-Jussé, B-A. 'La genèse du législatif dans le duché de Bretagne', *RHDFE* 4ème sér. 40 (1962), 351–72

Pocquet du Haut-Jussé, B-A. 'De la vassalité à la noblesse dans le duché de Bretagne', *Bulletin philologique et historique (jusqu'à 1610) du Comité des travaux historiques et scientifiques, année 1963* (Paris, 1966), ii. 785–800

Pocquet du Haut-Jussé, B-A. 'La dernière phase de la vie de Du Guesclin; l'affaire de Bretagne', *BEC* 125 (1967), 142–89

Spilsbury, S. V. 'On the date and authorship of *Artus de Bretaigne*', *Romania* xciv (1973), 505–22

Thomas-Lacroix, P. 'Jean de Malestroit, chancelier de Jean V, et l'indépendance de la Bretagne', *Bulletin de la société archéologique de Nantes et de la Loire-Atlantique* (1979), 135–93

Vale, M. *Charles VII* (London, 1974)

Chapter 13

Auzias, P-M. 'Le trésor de Saint-Jean du Doigt', *MSHAB* 59 (1982), 227–50

Badone, E. *The Appointed Hour. Death, Worldview and Social Change in Brittany* (London, 1989)

Bouguin, E. 'La navigation commerciale sur la basse Loire au milieu du XIVe siècle d'après un compte de péage inédit', *Revue historique* clxxv (1935), 482–96

Castel, Y-P. *Atlas des croix et calvaires du Finistère* (Brest, 1980)

Chauvin, M. *Les comptes de la châtellenie de Lamballe, 1387–1482* (Paris, 1977)

Chauvin, Y. 'Livre de miracles de Sainte-Catherine-de-Fierbois (1375–1470)', *Archives historiques du Poitou* 60 (1976)

Cintré, R. 'Les Marches de Bretagne au XVe siècle', Rennes, Mémoire de maîtrise d'histoire, 1972

Contamine, P. 'The French Nobility and the War', in Fowler, K. *The Hundred Years War* (London, 1971), pp. 135–62

Croix, A. *La Bretagne aux 16e et 17e siècles. La vie, la mort, la foi* (Paris, 2 vols 1981)

De Bourdellès, I. 'Etat de misère de la paroisse de Marcillé-Robert en 1479', *Bulletin de la société archéologique d'Ille-et-Vilaine* 46 (1919), 139–44

Du Halgouët, H. *Le duché de Rohan et ses seigneurs* (Saint-Brieuc, 2 vols 1925)

Fichet de Clairefontaine, F. 'La Poterie (Côtes-du-Nord), le centre potier dans les comptes de la châtellenie de Lamballe au XVe siècle', *MSHAB* 65 (1988), 81–91

Gallet, J. 'Une société rurale bretonne: Carnac en 1475', *Bulletin de la société polymathique du Morbihan* 108 (1981), 15–36

Guillotel, H. 'Du rôle des cimetières en Bretagne dans le renouveau du XIe et de la première moitié du XIIe siècle', *MSHAB* 52 (1972–4), 5–26

Herbaut, C. 'Exploitation et législation minière en forêt de Quintin aux XVe et XVIe siècles', *MSHAB* 65 (1988), 93–104

Jones, M. 'Les manuscrits d'Anne de Bretagne, reine de France, duchesse de Bretagne', *MSHAB* 55 (1978), 43–81 [*The Creation of Brittany*, pp. 371–409]

Jones, M. 'The Breton Nobility and their Masters from the Civil War of 1341–64 to the late Fifteenth Century', in Highfield, J. R. L. and Jeffs, R. eds *The Crown and Local Communities in England and France in the Fifteenth Century* (Gloucester, 1981), pp. 51–71 [*The Creation of Brittany*, pp. 219–37]

Kerhervé, J. 'Une famille d'officiers de finances bretons au XVe siècle. Les Thomas de Nantes', *AB* 83 (1976), 7–33

Kerhervé, J. 'Jean Mauléon, trésorier de l'Epargne. Une carrière au service de l'état breton', *Questions*, pp. 161–84

Kessedjian, M. 'Une seigneurie rurale des marches de Bretagne au XVème siècle. Saint-Brice-en-Coglès sous la famille de Scepeaux (Etude des comptes)', Rennes, Mémoire de maîtrise d'histoire, 1972

König, E. 'Un atelier d'enluminure à Nantes et l'art du temps de Fouquet', *Revue de l'Art* 35 (1977), 64–75

König, E. 'L'enluminure à Rennes à la fin de la Guerre de Cent Ans', in Barral i Altet, X. ed. *Artistes, artisans et production artistique* (Rennes, 1983), pp. 121–6

Leguay, J-P. 'La confrérie des merciers de Rennes au XVe siècle', *Francia* 3 (1975), 147–220

Leguay, J-P. 'Le Léon, ses villes et Morlaix au Moyen Age', *BSAF* 106 (1978), 103–60; 107 (1979), 181–236

Leguay, J–P. 'La criminalité en Bretagne au XVe siècle. Délits et répression', *Actes du 107e Congrès national des sociétés savantes, Brest 1982, Philologie et histoire jusqu'à 1610 i. La Faute, la répression et le pardon* (Paris, 1984), 53–79

Le Mappian, J. 'Etat actuel des recherches sur Yves de Tréguier', *MSHAB* 48 (1968), 15–30

Le Mené, M. 'La construction à Nantes au XVe siècle', *AB* 68 (1961), 361–402

Le Mené, M. 'La population nantaise à la fin du XVe siècle', *AB* 71 (1964), 189–220

Le Mené, M. *Les campagnes angevines à la fin du moyen âge* (Nantes, 1982)

Le Menn, G. 'La littérature en moyen-breton de 1350 à 1650', *Questions*, pp. 89–104

Le Menn, G. 'Les Bretons bretonnants d'après quelques textes et récits de voyages (XIVe-XVIIe siècles)', *MSHAB* 61 (1984), 105–34

Mackay, A. 'The Lesser Nobility in the kingdom of Castile', in Jones, M. ed. *Gentry and Lesser Nobility in Late Medieval Europe* (Gloucester, 1986), pp. 159–80

Martin, H. 'Religieux mendiants et classes sociales en Bretagne au XIVe et XVe siècles', *AB* 82 (1975), 19–46

Martin, H. 'La fonction polyvalente des croix à la fin du moyen âge', *AB* 90 (1983), 295–310

Martin, H. *Le métier de prédicateur à la fin du moyen âge 1350–1520* (Paris, 1988)

Martin, H. and Martin, L. 'Croix rurales et sacralisation de l'espace. Le cas de la Bretagne au Moyen Age', *Archives de sciences sociales des Religions* 43 (1977), 23–38

Meuret, J-Cl. 'La métallurgie ancienne au sud-est de l'Ille-et-Vilaine', *MSHAB* 66 (1989), 355–75

Minois, G. 'La démographie du Trégor au XVe siècle', *AB* 83 (1976), 407–24

Pocquet du Haut-Jussé, B-A. 'La règle d'idiome en Bretagne au XVe siècle', *Mélanges bretons et celtiques offerts à M. Joseph Loth* (Paris-Rennes, 1927), pp. 236–52

Pocquet du Haut-Jussé, B-A. 'Les emprunts de la duchesse Anne à Julien Thierry (1488–1491)', *AB* 69 (1962), 269–93

Sournia, J. C. with Trevien M. 'Essai d'inventaire des léproseries en Bretagne', *AB* 75 (1968), 317–43

Touchard, H. 'La consommation et l'approvisionnement en vin de la Bretagne médiévale', *MSHAB* 40 (1960), 29–76

Chapter 14

Argentré, Bertrand d' *Histoire de Bretagne* (Paris, 1588; 3rd edn 1618)

Du Fail, Noël *Les Baliverneries d'Eutrapel*, ed. Milin, G. (Paris, 1970)

Hélias, P-J. *Le Cheval d'orgueil* (Paris, 1975) [trans. J. Guicharnaud, as *The Horse of Pride. Life in a Breton Village*, New York and London, 1978].

Jones, I. E. *D'Argentré's History of Brittany and its Maps* (University of Birmingham, Department of Geography, Occasional Publication no. 23, 1987)

Le Goff, T. J. A. *Vannes and its region. A study of Town and Country in Eighteenth-century France* (Oxford, 1981)

McDonald, M. 'Celtic Ethnic Kinship and the Problem of Being English', *Current Anthropology* 27 (1986), 333–47

Meyer, J. *La noblesse bretonne au XVIIIe siècle* (Paris, 2 vols 1966)

Morin, E. *Commune en France. La métamorphose de Plodémet* (Paris, 1967) [trans. A. M. Sheridan-Smith, as *Plodémet. Report from a French Village*, New York, 1970 and London, 1971]

Reece, J. E. *Bretons against France. Ethnic minority nationalism in Twentieth-century Brittany* (Chapel Hill, 1977)

Sévigné, Marie de Rabutin-Chantal, madame de *Correspondance*, ed. Duchêne, R. (Paris, 3 vols 1972–8)

Index

Armorica, Brittany, France and Gaul have not been indexed because of frequent usage; personal names, including those of kings and princes, are generally indexed by fore-name and most archaeological sites by commune.